Timothy H. Ball

Lake County, Indiana, from 1834 to 1872

Timothy H. Ball

Lake County, Indiana, from 1834 to 1872

ISBN/EAN: 9783337304065

Printed in Europe, USA, Canada, Australia, Japan

Cover: Foto ©ninafisch / pixelio.de

More available books at **www.hansebooks.com**

AUTHORITIES.

THINKING it desirable that the early and rapidly perishing history of the settlement of Lake County should be preserved, and believing myself to possess some peculiar facilities and motives for such a work, and feeling sure that the time will come when there will be many to appreciate its value, I have, amid severe pressures and hindrances, endeavored, as faithfully as the circumstances would allow, to accomplish this object. The authorities are:

1. THE CLAIM REGISTER.—This is a document of 1836, twelve inches by seventeen in size, containing eighty pages, which I accidentally found in Kankakee City.

2. ROBINSON'S RECORDS.—This document is in the form of a lecture which was given in the Old Log Court House not long before its author left this State to enter on life in New York.

3. DIARY OF JUDGE BALL, of Cedar Lake.

4. MY OWN DIARY, commenced when thirteen years of age.

5. DIARY OR WEATHER RECORD OF REV. H. WASON.

6. PERSONAL RECOLLECTIONS, from August, 1837.

7. CONVERSATIONS WITH OLD SETTLERS AND THEIR DESCENDANTS.

8. PUBLIC RECORDS AND DOCUMENTS.

To the many who have kindly aided me in furnishing items of information I here return my sincere thanks.

Crown Point, Indiana, 1872.

T. H. BALL.

CORRECTIONS.

A FEW typographical errors, from which a first edition is rarely altogether free, will be found on these pages. On page 68, ninth line, for the word *opened* read *speared*. In the last quotation, on page 107, the words *received* and *recovered* are transposed. On pages 155, 156, and 157, Liverpool is mentioned as having been on the Calumet. This is of course a mistake. Please read Deep River. A few other errors the reader will easily correct.

By an oversight of my own two burial places are omitted; one in Hanover, connected with the German Evangelical Church; the other at Crown Point belonging to the Church of the Blessed Virgin Mary. Both are well kept.

CONTENTS.

CHAPTER I.

	PAGES.
Locality, Water Shed, Water Courses, Cedar Lake, Congressional Townships and Ranges, and Ridges,	5–17

CHAPTER II.

Purchases from the Indians, Early Settlements, Squatters' Union, Land Sale,	18–66

CHAPTER III.

The Pottawatomies,	67–84

CHAPTER IV.

Growth, 1840–1849,	85–95

CHAPTER V.

New Growth, 1850–1859, Rail Roads, Swamp Lands,	96–110

CHAPTER VI.

Our War Record, The Crown Point Institute, Teachers' Institutes,	110–136

CHAPTER VII.

Burial Places,	137–144

CHAPTER VIII.

Towns and Villages,	145–165

CHAPTER IX.

Temperance Societies, Agricultural Society, Sabbath School Convention, College Graduates and Students, Literary Societies, Church Organizations, Physicians, Lawyers, Contrasts, - - - - - - - - 166-198

CHAPTER X.

The Nail, Commissioners' Records, Center of Lake, Ten Mile Line, Indian Floats, Mounds, Views, Granges, Weather Record, Timber Stealers, Indian Incident, Long Lanes, North Township, First Things, Schools, Wolves, Wild Cat, White Owl, Bald Eagle, Swan, Periodicals, Records of Ministers, Kankakee Detectives, Wells and Springs, South East Grove, Orchard, Plum, Lost on the Prairie, Native Wild Animals, Specimen Poems, - - - - - - - - - 199-275

CHAPTER XI.

Sketches of Early Settlers, - - - - - - 276-347

CHAPTER XII.

Sun Dogs, Ice Cutting, K. V. D. Company, Cumberland Lodge, The Burglar, Concluding Reflections, - 348-364

LAKE COUNTY, INDIANA,

1834—1872.

CHAPTER I.

LOCALITY, GEOGRAPHICAL AND PHYSICAL FEATURES.

I.

LAKE COUNTY is situated in the northwest corner of the State of Indiana. It is bounded on the north by Lake Michigan, and on the south by the Kankakee River. On the east an air line running north and south separates it from the county of Porter. On the west lies the State of Illinois. Its east and west sides are parallel, and its width is sixteen miles. Its northern limit, the beach line of one of the world's most magnificent lakes, is a quite regular curve. Its southern limit is a very irregular line, as marked out by the windings of one of the small but remarkable rivers of our country. The length of this region on the east side is about twenty-seven miles. On the west side it is thirty-six miles. Its area is, in round numbers, five hundred square miles. Although not large, yet one of the largest among the ninety-two counties of Indiana, it is twice as large as the ancient Attica, that division of Greece which was "in many respects one of the most interesting regions of the earth," and which once contained 300,000 inhabitants. It is twice as large as the celebrated island of Malta, which, "anciently little else than a baren rock" has been made, by the exportation of soil from Africa, so fertile as to support a population of 90,000.

It has about the same area as that division of the German Empire called Saxe Altenburg, which contains more than 140,000 inhabitants. It is larger than the Friendly Islands, which sustain a population of 25,000.

If possessing no natural features to render it of more than ordinary interest, if not ". beautiful for situation," as was one ancient spot of earth, it is nevertheless peculiarly situated. Its northwest corner is within twelve miles of the court house in Chicago, and, occupying that space south of the head of Lake Michigan, across its territory every railroad must pass which from the east or southeast enters that growing city, evidently destined to become the mighty metropolis of the northwest and one of the world's great cities.

Five hundred square miles of surface lying where Lake county does cannot be unimportant.

II.

Across its borders runs the water shed which separates the Mississippi Valley from the St. Lawrence Basin.

This line enters the county from the west in St. John's Township, in Section 36, a mile and a half north of the line due west from Crown Point, passing north of the head waters of West Creek in this section; it runs near the village of St. John's, and passes in a winding southeasterly direction across Hanover Township to a point half a mile north of the head of Cedar Lake. From thence it winds along the ridges of that strip of woodland in Centre Township, its main direction eastward, passes south of Fancher's Lake, between that and the Mill Pond, comes out upon the prairie about one mile south of Crown Point and enters School Grove. It runs along a ridge in the grove south of the Sherman marsh, and passes in a southerly direction across the prairie to a point not far from Cassville. It then turns northward around the head of that arm of Deep River, and bearing a little toward the east passes on north between Deep River and Eagle Creek, south of Deer Creek, and still bearing eastward leaves Lake county on a line almost due east from Crown Point, passing north of that little lake which is the source of Eagle Creek. The continuation of this water shed eastward is in a northerly direction, north of all tributaries of the Kankakee, and comes up to the portage between this and the St. Joseph River. The distance between these two rivers at this point, across which portage La Salle and Hennepin carried their canoes in their famous exploring expedition of 1679, is only five or six miles. The western continuation of this water shed is yet more singular. From that Section 36, crossing the Illinois line it runs southwest, passing west of Eagle Lake and around the head waters of Thorn Creek, having made of southing some seven miles. It then turns northward and runs up to the head waters of the Des Plaines River, between that and the Chicago River, running within some eight miles of the shore of Lake Michigan. This Des Plaines River, running past Joliet, meeting with the Kankakee which has turned its course toward the northwest, as though in haste to meet its sister river, forms there, in conjunction with the Kankakee, the Illinois River. The head waters of Thorn Creek, which runs into Lake at Dyer, and the south head of Deep River near Cassville, are the two most southern points in the Lake Michigan Basin; and on both the east side and the west, the Mississippi sends up its tributaries to obtain water with which to swell its mighty current very near to Michigan Lake. And from the center of Lake county, all along this winding line, drops of water start but a few feet apart, one of which will plunge down the cataract of Niagara and flowing through the St. Lawrence Gulf, will enter the Atlantic Ocean in latitude 46 deg.; while the other, flowing along the great, muddy, Father of Waters and the Gulf of Mexico, enters the same Atlantic in latitude 24 deg., in the warm region of the Tropic of Cancer. Perchance, after traveling thousands of miles these drops will meet and mingle on the shores of Greenland or of Iceland. The height of the Lake county water shed above the ocean level has never been ascertained? but how singular, that almost from within sound of Michigan's dashing waves water should flow down into the Gulf of Mexico.

III.

The principal streams of Lake county are, the Calumet, Deep River, and Turkey Creek, flowing into Lake Michigan; and West Creek, Cedar Creek and Eagle Creek, flowing into the Kankakee. The main direction of the first three streams is eastward and westward. The main direction of the last three is southward. Turkey Creek is a small stream which, starting northwest of Centreville, passing near this village, running a little north of east, empties its waters into Deep River a little south and west of Hobart. Deep River has two small sources; the one near Brown's Point, northwest of Crown Point, which flows eastward, and the other commencing in the marshy ground some six miles southeast of Crown Point which flows northward. These two unite east of Crown Point, three and a half miles and north about two miles, and flow eastward, cutting the edge of Porter county. The river then flows northward returning into Lake county, and bears northwest to the mouth of Turkey Creek, having made some three and a half miles westing. It then flows northeasterly to Hobart; and passes from thence northward into the Calumet. The Calumet enters the county from Porter, two miles south of Lake Michigan, and flows westward bearing a little south along a marshy valley across the county. It continues on in the State of Illinois, running northwesterly till it reaches the Blue Island bluff, having made about seven and a half miles westing from the Indiana line. Meeting this bluff it turns back and flows but little south of east, in a line nearly parallel with its westward flow, until it has again almost crossed the county of Lake, and enters Lake Michigan two miles

west and two north of its entrance from Porter into Lake.
This was its original channel. I am told that the Indians, some eighty years ago, opened, with the paddles of their canoes, a new channel for this singular river in the marshy ground between Calumet Lake in Illinois, and Wolf Lake in Indiana and Illinois, both near Lake Michigan, and thus turned a portion of its waters into this lake by a northern course of a few miles, beginning two miles west of the state line. The Calumet has therefore now two mouths, some twenty miles apart, one in Indiana and one in Illinois. The eastward and westward flow of these northern streams is produced, evidently, by the peculiar ridges crossing the northern portion of the county from east to west. These are, north of the Calumet, ridges of sand, the first ones covered with pines and some cedar trees, also producing huckleberry bushes, wintergreens, and other plants natural to a very sandy soil. Further south a growth of oak comes in, the smaller plants remaining the same. These ridges of pure sand are comparatively narrow, their elevation being from ten to thirty or forty feet above the level of Lake Michigan. The water of this lake has an elevation of about six hundred feet above the Atlantic Ocean. Between the ridges are marshes, or narrow, sandy valleys, and north of the Calumet these ridges are numerous. They extend also between the Calumet and Turkey Creek, and between this and Deep River, but there is little sand south of Turkey Creek on the eastern side of the county. The last ridge on the western side of the county commences just south of Dyer on the Illinois line, passing northward into Illinois in a low, broad ridge of sandy prairie soil, and east-

ward, containing some grand sand banks exactly, in appearance, like those now along the beach of Lake Michigan, until it gives way to a prairie ridge east of the village of Schererville. The appearance near Dyer is as though the water of Lake Michigan, a number of years ago, washed this ridge and dashed its waves upon this sand, finding here its southwestern limit, then retiring northward, ridge by ridge, reached its present bounds, leaving its old beach to show where once its free waves dashed their spray. The eastward continuation of this apparently lake beach is a broad prairie ridge between Turkey Creek and Deep River.

South of Deep River, and especially south of the water shed, the ridges and slopes of the woodland and the prairies cause the streams to flow northward or southward. West Creek, commencing at the water shed on that section 36, before named, about half a mile from the Illinois line, flows south, bearing a little east, and runs into the Kankakee, passing along a broad, marshy valley, forming, before bridges were built, an almost impassable barrier near the western border of the county. Its length, in a straight line, is nineteen miles.

Cedar Creek is the outlet of Cedar Lake, and winds along a narrow valley, at first eastward and then running southward, reaching the Kankakee at a distance, on a straight line, of about thirteen miles from its out-flow at Cedar Lake.

Eagle Creek starts in Porter county, being the outlet of a little lake lying due east of the north part of Crown Point, but soon crossing the line, as it bears westward; it reaches the Kankakee about 13 miles from that little lake.

One of its main tributaries flows from a marsh at the south end of School Grove.

Besides these six named, there are still smaller water courses, as Deer Creek, Duck Creek, Plum Creek, and Willow Creek. Springs will be hereafter mentioned.

IV.

The county is now divided into ten townships. These are, commencing at the north : North, which extends across the country from east to west, and is, therefore, sixteen miles long, and is two miles wide at its eastern limit and twelve on its western border; St. John's, Ross, and Hobart; Hanover, Center, and Winfield; West Creek; Cedar Creek, and Eagle Creek. North and Center are so named from their geographical position. The three southern townships are named from their creeks. These creeks received their names, the first from its position, the second from the lake of which it is the outlet, and the third from an eagle's nest on a tree near its banks, found by the early settlers. This nest was near the Gregg place, and was shown to Luman A. Fowler by Jacob Hurlburt in 1835. Ross was named after an early settler who was killed by the falling of a tree in 1836. St. John's was named from the Church of St. John the Evangelist; and Hanover, from the German Hanover, its inhabitants being mostly German, and several coming from that kingdom. Hobart was named after Frederick Hobart Earle, of Falmouth, England, brother of George Earle, an early settler of Lake; and Winfield, in honor of Gen. Winfield Scott.

V.

The principal lake in the county is Cedar Lake or Red Cedar Lake, five miles southwest of the geographical center. Its eastern shore is in Center Township and its western in Hanover. It was named from the red cedar trees growing on its bank. Its length is two and a half miles. Its greatest breadth is one mile. It has no inlet; is evidently fed by springs; its waters are clear, pure, and soft; and when first seen by the white settlers it abounded in fish, water-fowls, musk-rats, and minks. On its banks the Red Men reared their wigwams; on its waters they paddled their light canoes; and on its northern bank, in the pure sand, close by a high bluff, they buried their dead. As a sheet of water, comparing as it does well in size with some of the noted ones of England, it is called, by some good judges, very beautiful. Other small lakes are: Fancher's, Lake Seven, Lemon Lake, Sheehan's Lake, and Wolf Lake. Lake George is found on some maps, but, like the mountains of Northern Indiana, in Cummings' Atlas of 1815, it is more imaginary than real.

VI.

The surface and the soil in this region are quite varied. Darby's Universal Gazetteer, of 1827, says, article Indiana: " The country round the extreme S. bay of Lake Michigan has the appearance of the sea marshes of Louisiana. Low flooded prairies intersected by lakes and interlocking creeks. No eminences are seen, one unbroken horizon encircles the eye." There *is* some low, level, marshy land. There is low and level prairie.

There is rolling prairie with long ridges of woodland.
There is rolling prairie with long and graceful slopes and
broad valleys, and some prairie with deep and short valleys equal almost to the rolling prairie of Iowa. There
are long and broad ridges and table lands, and hills and
dales, and heavy woodland. There are beds of white
sand as clean and pure as sand can well be. There are
miles of yellowish sand where corn and potatoes will
grow quite successfully. There is a whitish clay soil,
producing oats, grass, and winter wheat, and rye. There
is the rich black soil of the prairie, and the still deeper
and richer soil of the high and dry marsh. The large
Cady Marsh, the Calumet and Kankakee marshes, and
other smaller ones, contain many thousands of acres of
land that must one day become very valuable. Some of
it, once called waste land and "swamp land," already
produces large crops of grass and oats.

VII.

Over Lake county and above the line of the Water
Shed, the warm vapor from the southern valleys and the
slopes, or from the rivers and waters of the South meets
with the cooler vapor of Lake Michigan, giving to this region, in ordinary seasons, an abundance of moisture, and
causing the atmosphere to be very seldom perfectly
cloudless. As, however, late in the season the water of
Lake Michigan becomes quite warm, and continues
during those golden days of October and sometimes
through November which we call Indian Summer, the
north wind bringing that vapor and warm air over the
ridge and down our southern slope to the Kankakee

keeps off the early autumnal frosts, and this county is sometimes protected for weeks after the frost appears further west and further south. If the springs, therefore, are wet and backward occasionally, the autumns are, quite usually, warm, late, and delightful.

VIII.

This region contains, as laid out by the United States surveyor, two entire ranges, Eight and Nine, three rows of sections in Range Seven on the east, and one row of sections in Range Ten on the west. The congressional townships are from Thirty-two to Thirty-seven in each range, some of which, on the north and south, are not full. Ten congressional townships are almost entire. The prairie region covers, probably, about two-thirds of the county. The first prairie, beginning at the northeast of the prairie portion, is just south of the town of Hobart, is level, rather low, and was formerly wet. It is now sufficiently dry for successful cultivation. It is small, not more than two miles in extent. The second, lying west of Deep River, which is here running northward, is much larger, quite level, and was formerly wet. As it spreads southward and westward it grows higher and slopes upward along a ridge, that broad prairie ridge south of Turkey Creek. This ridge, and for several miles, is high but not rolling prairie. Southward slopes the broad expanse, spreading also out for miles to the westward, of what was called, in early times, Robinson's Prairie. Its landmarks were the Hodgeman place, Wiggins, Point, Brown's Point, and Solon Robinson's, afterwards Lake C. H.—that is Court House,—and finally, Crown

Point. This large extent of prairie contained some that was low and wet, some high ridges, but very little that could be called rolling. South of the center of the county the prairie spreads out over nearly the whole width, and having passed the water shed becomes, in the south central part, truly rolling. It is not, to much extent, broken and hilly, but contains magnificent slopes, one succeeding another, gradually descending toward the Kankakee meadow lands, and between these slopes are broad but not deep valleys where armies of ten thousand men in each might form in line of battle. The landmarks here are, School Grove, South East Grove, Plum Grove, Orchard Grove, Hickory point, and Pleasant Grove. Between South East Grove and Hickory Point, and extending southward there is some low and level prairie. West of Pleasant Grove and of Cedar Lake, and extending south to the Belshaw Grove and west to the West Creek timber, lies the gem of the prairie region of Indiana, known as Lake Prairie. Robinson's Prairie has more size, Door Prairie more celebrity; but Lake Prairie possesses, according to my taste, more perfect beauty. Door Prairie is rich and beautiful. It has been called the Garden of the West. It lies on the route of travel. Lake Prairie is seldom seen by travelers' or tourists' eyes. South of the prairie proper, extending across the county, lies a belt of marsh or meadow land five or six miles in breadth, interspersed with islands of timber, and bordering the channel of the Kankakee River. A part is dry, a part is wet marsh. This marsh region makes that river remarkable. A river is known to be there. The blue line of trees marking its course can be discerned from the prairie heights; but only occasionally, in mid winter or in a time of great drouth, can one come near its water channel. So far as any ordinary access to it from this county is concerned it is like a fabulous river, or one the existence of which we take on trust. The fowlers, the trappers, and the woodmen have looked upon its sluggish waters.

CHAPTER II.

1834—1839. SQUATTER LIFE.

I.

In the year 1800 Indiana became an organized territory. Before that time it had formed a part of the almost unknown and trackless wilds of the North-West, slightly explored by some adventurous Frenchmen and penetrated for the purpose of traffic by fur traders. As early as 1679 and 1680 there is evidence that French explorers passed along the border, and perhaps across the very center of what is now Lake county. The first settlement in Indiana was made by the French in 1690, at Vin- *1733* cennes. In 1816 Indiana was admitted into the Union as a State. But the northern part was a wilderness. As late as 1820 it contained only fifty counties, and of these Wabash had 147 inhabitants, Owen 838, and Martin 1032. There was then no La Porte or St. Joseph; there was no Marshall, or Pulaski, or Steuben; no northern Indiana. Although for four years a State, and containing 147,178 inhabitants, this Lake Michigan region was still the home of the Red Men and the fur traders.

Chicago became Fort Dearborn in 1804, and was a trading post for corn raised by the Pottawatomies in their corn villages on the Des Plaines and in the Fox River

Valley, of which their adopted chief, Alexander Robinson, or Chee-chee-bing-way, shipped, in 1809, about 100 bushels; and also for fur, which the Calumet and Kankakee region furnished abundantly. In 1812 took place the Fort Dearborn Massacre. In 1816 the fort was restored. The fur trade was then vigorously carried on, and connection, of course, kept up between Fort Dearborn and Detroit.

By the treaty of the United States with the Pottawatomies in 1828, a strip of land ten miles in width was acquired along the northern border of Indiana, which extends in a narrow strip to the extreme southern limit of Lake Michigan. This was the first land purchased from the Indians in what is now Lake county. By the treaty of 1832 the remainder of this county was acquired and all which the Pottawatomies owned in the State.

Up to this time there were no whites in all this region except fur traders, perchance some hunters and trappers, and the soldiers at Fort Dearborn. In this year took place the Black Hawk War, and a few white settlers came into what is now La Porte county. A route for travel was immediately opened along the beach of Lake Michigan. Three men, Hart, Steel, and Sprague, started a stage line from Detroit to Fort Dearborn, or Chicago. probably in 1833, and four-horse coaches were placed upon the road. And now the stillness of nature and the repose of wild life was broken. White covered wagons came, with white men, and women, and children, *white* as to race but *brown* from exposure,—"boys in their sunny brown beauty and men in their rugged bronze,"—to start new echoes in the wilderness, to lay claim to the beautiful prairies, and plant all over, where savages had reared their wigwams and buried their dead, the seeds of a Christian civilization. In this same year of 1833 a man named Bennett settled with his family on this stage route, in the limits of our county, near the old mouth of the Calumet, then called Calumic, and opened a house of entertainment, a new country tavern. The Old Soc Trail, began also to be traveled about this same year, leading from La Porte to the Hickory Creek Settlement in Illinois, and past Cedar Lake to the Rapids of the Kankakee. It was but a trail, requiring a pioneer's eye, or an Indian's sagacity, to enable one to follow it safely. A family by the name of Farwell, afterwards becoming settlers on West Creek, a well-known family among us, then from the Green Mountain State, were endeavoring to follow this trail to Hickory, missed the way, and spent the 4th of July 1833, where Crown Point now stands, amid an unbroken solitude, while a messenger returned eastward for a guide. Mrs. Farwell, therefore, a decidedly superior woman, was the first white woman, so far as is known, ever on this spot of ground, where on festive occasions the crowds now gather. Indian with his pony could not now follow that Soc Trail; but a multitude of movers' teams annually pass along near its track, on the Joliet Road.

In the spring of 1834 another tavern was opened on the beach of Lake Michigan by a man named Berry. The accommodation at these log cabin taverns was sufficiently scanty to show the borders of civilization, sometimes as many as fifty sleeping at night in and around the mudded walls, and the food was flour and coffee, without meat, butter, milk, or sugar, and the price of grain and provisions sufficiently high to satisfy an ordinary landlord, oats for horse feed costing three dollars a bushel at one of these stage houses.

During the summer of 1834 United States surveyors laid out most of the land in Lake county into sections, the range or township lines having been previously run. This party of surveyors camped, for a week in June or July, in that part of the grove now owned by Dr. Pettibonea, in the town of Crown Point. One who accompanied this party, J. Hurlburt, an old settler of Porter, remembers no cabin and no settler at that time in any of our central groves. As yet the squatters were not here. He remembers some cabins along the stage road on the lake beach and thinks that Goodrich, in the place of Bennett, then kept the tavern at the mouth of the Calumet. Burnside had this job of surveying from the Government, but the work here was done by St. Clair.

After the surveyors came the claim seekers. There is evidence that either before or soon after that week of encampment just mentioned, one Wm. Butler was on this ground before Solon Robinson came, and made four claims, for himself, for his brother E. P. Butler, for George Wells, and for Theodore Wells. He also erected cabins and departed. I find the existence of three cabins recognized by those who are called Lake county's earliest settlers. I think they were the Butler cabins. I now reach more certain data.

In September 1834, Richard Fancher, Charles Wilson, Robert Wilkinson and two nephews, left Attica on the Wabash, three in a wagon and two mounted on good horses, to look for claims in the newly surveyed northwest corner of the State. They crossed the Kankakee at the head of the rapids, crossed West Creek at a place which was selected at once by Wilkinson for a home, and came up to Cedar Lake. They camped at its head near the old inlet. They found on that sand ridge an Indian burial ground. They kept their headquarters at the lake. R. Fancher and Charles Wilson, being well mounted, traveled considerably over the county. They were at the South East Grove and at all the central parts. The surveyors had just been over the region. They found no settlers. They saw no Indians, but found signs of late Indian occupancy. R. Fancher selected a part of section 17, and his claim gave the name to that little lake. Wilson and the other two made claims near Cedar Lake. Charles Wilson selected that quarter section afterwards bought by Jacob L. Brown and then by Hervey Ball. They saw a black bear in the woods west of Cedar Lake. They stayed about three weeks, broke up their encampment, returned to the Wabash and waited for the spring.

The October sunshine came, the large fields of maize at Indian Town had ripened, when a family from Jennings county, Indians, crossing the Kankakee south of La Porte, finding J. Hurlburt for a guide to show them that central grove where the surveying party had camped for a week, entered, as settlers seeking a home, on the borders of Lake. They passed Porter sand ridges, and the timber that skirted Deep River, they came out on a broad expanse of prairie and looked admiringly round. He who was to give that prairie name, who was to map out the county, count its sections, keep its first records, now stood upon its soil,—SOLON ROBINSON,—who was afterwards called "The Squatter-King of Lake." I will let him speak for himself here. I quote from "The Cultivator," published at Albany, New York, Vol. VIII, page 19: "It was the last day of October, 1834, when I first entered this 'arm of the Grand Prairie.' It was about noon, of a clear, delightful day, when we emerged from the wood, and, for miles around, stretched forth one broad expanse of clear, open land. At that time the whole of this county scarcely showed a sign that the white man had yet been here, except those of my own household. I stood alone, wrapt up in that peculiar sensation that man only feels when beholding a prairie for the first time—it is an indescribable, delightful feeling. Oh, what a rich mine of wealth lay outstretched before me. Some ten miles away to the southwest, the tops of a grove were visible. Toward that onward rolled the wagons, with nothing to impede them. * * * * Just before sundown we reached the grove and pitched our tent by the side of a spring. What could exceed the beauty of this spot! Why should we seek farther? Here is everything to indicate a healthy location which should always influence the new settler. * * * * After enjoying such a night of rest as can only be enjoyed after such a day, the morning helped to confirm us that here should be our resting place. In a few hours the grove resounded with the blows of the axe, and in four days we moved into our 'new house.'"

In that same October two, perhaps three, from the Wabash region, also coming by way of La Porte, passed

on horseback to the northwest bank of Cedar Lake
There were Dr. Brown, David Hornor, and probably, also,
Thomas Hornor.

On the first day of November, Henry Wells and Luman A. Fowler, having left their horses on Twenty
Mile Prairie, came to Solon Robinson's tent. They, too,
passed on to Cedar Lake and found the three just
mentioned there. Hungry and tired, they partook of
some roasted raccoon meat for supper, lodged "in a
leafy tree top," and returned the next day to the Robinson camp. The little party from the Wabash made
several claims, on the west side of the lake, and then returned to their homes, to be ready for removing in the
coming spring.

There is in my possession the original Claim Register,
containing not only a record of the claims, when made,
by whom, where the settlers were from, with date of settlement, but also the General Record and Constitution
of the Squatters' Union of Lake County. This document I have had occasion quite thoroughly to examine.

According to the Register, claims were made in the
year 1834 by the following persons:

E. L. Palmer, in April, for himself and for J. B. Cox,
L. Cox, and E. Cox; (The timber connected with these
was not claimed till December 8, 1836, and they are all
afterwards marked "forfeit." They lie in the western
tier of sections in Range 10. I conclude that none of
these settled in 1534, and in April the sections were not
laid off by the U. S. surveyors.) Wm. S. Thornburg,
Thomas Thornburg, Wm. Crooks, and Sam'l Miller, in
June; Robert Wilkinson, Noah A. Wilkinson, Noah B.

Clark, R. Fancher, Thomas Childers, Thomas Hornor, Solon Robinson, and Milo Robinson in October; T. S. Wilkison, Robert Wilkison, B. Wilkison, Thomas Brown, Jacob L. Brown, Thomas H. Brown, Wm. Clark, J. W Holton, H. Wells, David Hornor, L. A. Fowler, J. B. Curtis, Elyas Myrick, Wm. Myrick, Thomas Reed, in November; and W. A. W. Holton, Harriet Holton, widow, Jesse Pierce, David Pierce, John Russell, and Wm. Montgomery, in December.

I find none of these settling in 1834 except Childers, S. Robinson, Crooks and Miller, L. A. Fowler, Robert Wilkison, and Jesse and David Pierce. The fact of the settlement, in this year, of Crooks, Miller, and the two Pierces, rests only on the somewhat uncertain data given in the Register — uncertain, because intentions were there recorded as facts, and men then as now could not always accomplish their intentions. The date of the claim in the Register is certain; of time of settlement, slightly uncertain.

I have inserted two names as claimants of land in 1834 which I do not find thus registered, R. Fancher and Thomas Childers; but both these were on section 17, upon which was laid an "Indian float." The following is, according to Solon Robinson's Records, the order of settling of the first few families in Lake.

In October, 1834, Thomas Childers and family settled on the South-east Quarter of Section 17, in the edge of School Grove. His name and that of his wife must therefore stand on this record as the first known settlers in the central part of the county. On the last day of October Solon Robinson and family settled in that point of the timber which now forms such a well known part of the town of Crown Point.

To Solon Robinson must be awarded the honor of being first in Crown Point, and second only, as a resident, in the central part of the county. It is said, on good authority, that he once gave great offense to Thomas Childers by remarking that his wife, Mrs. Robinson, was the first *white* woman settling in Lake county. The word *white* was understood to be in contrast, not with *red*, denoting Indian women, but with *dark* or *swarthy*, thus casting a reflection on the complexion of Mrs. Childers.

The third family arriving was that of Robert Wilkinson, who settled on Deep River, where the only ford known in early times was situated.

This family settled late in November. In January, 1835, Lyman Wells, and with him an unmarried man, John Driscoll, settled a little south-east of what is now the town of Lowell. Lyman Wells had a wife and four or five children.

About the middle of February, coming from Jennings county, Indiana, William Clark and family, and with them W. A. W. Holton, and mother, and sister, reached the hospitable home of Solon Robinson, making the fifth and sixth families, and increasing to eight the number of men as settlers. I count here eight, as a young man was that winter domiciled with the Robinson family whose name was afterwards well known to the inhabitants of Lake. This was Luman A. Fowler. A few days afterwards the seventh family arrived, the fourth for the Robinson settlement, J. W. Holton with his wife and child. In the spring Richard Fancher with his family reached his claim on the bank of what has since been called Fancher's Lake. Ceasing now to name the families in their order, I insert some of the incidents connected with the winter trip of the Clark family.

The route by way of the rapids, of Sugar, and Bunkum, and Parrish Grove, to the Wabash, was dreary enough and desolate in the early fall of 1848, when I first tried that road to Indianapolis; but what must it have been in mid-winter in 1835! That February was a winter month unusually severe. The wagons drawn by ox teams, which most of the settlers then used instead of horses, had slowly wended their way, bearing one family with several children, the father and mother then in the full prime of life, the other family a widowed mother with a son who had entered manhood and a daughter also grown up, and having crossed the bleak open prairie north of Sugar they came to the Kankakee marsh. This was " covered with ice upon which night overtook them endeavoring to force their ox teams across. There was no house, and they were unprepared for camping out, and one of the most severe cold nights about closing in upon them surrounded by a wide field of ice upon which the already frightened and tired oxen refused to go further, and not a tree or stick of firewood near them. These families upon this night might have perished had they not providentially discovered a set of logs that some one had hauled out upon a little knoll near by to build a cabin with, and with which they were enabled to build a fire, to warm a tent made out of the covering of their wagons, and which enabled them to shelter themselves from the blast that swept over the wide prairie almost as unimpeded as over the mountain waves of the ocean. The next day, by diverging ten miles out of their course, they reached a little miserable hut of an old Frenchman, who lived with his half Indian family on the Kankakee; here they stayed two days and nights. Such was the severity of the weather that they dared not leave their uncomfortable quarters, and when they did so they had to make a road for the oxen across the river by spreading hay upon the ice and freezing it down by pouring on water." The name of this French trader who so kindly gave them shelter was pronounced Shobar. He lived where now is Kankakee City, forty miles from their destination. They found at Yellow Head one family. Stayed there over night. Came to West Creek, following a blind Indian trail. The oxen broke through the ice of this stream, and were extricated with difficulty. At length the wagons were brought over, and the trail leading across Lake Prairie was followed up. On different trails Solon Robinson had erected guide-boards, and these voyagers just before dark found one which they gladly hailed: "To Solon Robinson's, 5 miles North." Soon after night-fall they reached his lone but hospitable cabin. There are those yet among us, Thomas Clark and Alexander Clark, who remember well the severities of that winter trip. The pioneers in every part of this country, whether they came amid the snows and ice of winter or the flowers of summer, or, as the family of which I was a member came, amid the deep mud, and crossing the bridgeless streams of December, knew the meaning of privations and of hardships. But all seem to have borne them with great cheerfulness. The hardy came, the intelligent came, men and women mostly young or in the prime of life, and happy, light hearted children. Years afterwards the Pierian Society at Crown Point, some of them descendants of these early pioneers, adopted for their motto, *Per aspera ad astra;* that is, Through difficulties to success. *Then* were some *difficulties*, in the squatter period of our history; and *now*, as our respected citizen, A. CLARK, looks at the young, growing city two miles from his home, hears the whistle of the cars, looks over his well cultivated farm, and at his spring in the meadow that will furnish water daily for a thousand cattle, enjoys the facilities that have come into being since those days of his boyhood, he enjoys with others the *success*.

I return to the winter of 1834. Four families were on sections 8 and 5, at its close, one was in School Grove, one near Lowell, one probably on Deep River, one on Turkey Creek, and three or four, it is probable, were scattered among the sand ridges of North Township. Gladly would I record all their names on this page of history could I only rescue them from the oblivion which has already come. Some incidents of the first winter are pressing forward for a record.

The oxen lived on browse and a little corn, and that was more than the deer had. But the oxen grew hungry and became lean. Food for the children became scarce. Corn bins and mills were forty miles away. Provisions gave out in L. Wells' family and they made a supper of a big owl, and were on the point of roasting a wolf when a different supply arrived. At a later period this same Wells, returning from a mill in La Porte county, "coming from Wilkinson's crossing of Deep River after dark, missed his course, for there was no path, and got on to Deep River somewhere about south of the Hodgman place, broke through the ice, and with great difficulty succeeded in getting his horses loose; and in undertaking to get back to a house on Twenty Mile Prairie, riding one horse and leading the other, he came unexpectedly to a steep bank of the river in the dark and pitched headlong down a dozen feet into the water and floating ice. He clung to one horse and succeeded in reaching the other shore and getting near enough to the house to make himself heard by the loud cries he gave as the only means of saving his life. About noon next day he found his other horse on a little island near where they made the fearful plunge, but it was near night when he found his wagon."

Solon Robinson's account of "the first trip to mill" from his cabin, published in the Cultivator in 1841, Vol. VIII, page 67, was one of those sketches which gave to him his earlier celebrity as a writer.

It is too lengthy to be reproduced here. I give, however, a few sentences. December had arrived. It was found that the supply of food would last five or six days only, when "a trusty and persevering messenger was dispatched" to obtain a new supply. "Never were such appetites seen before as those which daily diminished the fast failing stock of provisions of our little family in the wilderness." The meal was exhausted, "the knife had scraped the last bone for breakfast," on the sixth day after the messenger's departure. A small bag of wheat bran was found. No lard, no butter, no meat, no milk.

"Bran cakes and cranberries sweetened with honey then were sweet diet. Although the owner of a gun that rarely failed to perform good service, it seemed that every living thing in the shape of game had hid up in winter quarters." "On the sixth, seventh, eighth and ninth days, anxious and watchful eyes scanned the prairie by day, and tended beacon fires by night, for this precaution was necessary, as there was nothing to guide the expected teamster home, should he undertake the perilous passage of the prairie just at night fall. It was about midnight of the last day, and I had tired of watching and had laid down, but not to sleep." A sound was heard as of steps on the frozen ground. Soon a voice was heard. "What joyful sounds! But the joy was soon damped, as it became manifest that he drove a team without a wagon. Where is that? was the first question. 'Fast in the river a few miles back on the prairie.' 'Do you know we have nothing in the house for your supper?' 'I expected so, and so I brought along a bag-full; here is both flour and meat.'" Then the hickory logs began to blaze, and soon there was a supper. 'Such scenes of excitement, of pain and pleasure, often occur to the western emigrant." "And it is because the emigrant's life is full of such exciting scenes, and because the days of pleasure are long remembered, when those of pain are buried in oblivion, that induces thousands annually to add themselves to that irresistible wave of emigration that is rolling onward to the Pacific ocean." Many other families had their mill trips in the few next succeeding years, some of which may find their place in this record. If some were hungry, none starved, and no one died during the first winter spent by squatters in Lake.

In the spring of 1835 settlers began to come in more rapidly. In March, Richard Fancher again entered the county, with two assistants, and erected a cabin on his claim. He brought up a load of provisions and goods, drawn by two yoke of oxen, deposited them at Solon Robinson's, and returned for his family. He arrived with them and settled in April. In the same month Wayne Bryant, Simeon and Samuel D. Bryant, a brother-in-law named Agnew, and David Bryant, commenced what was known for years as "the Bryant Settlement." Elias Bryant also joining them in the Fall. To E. W. generally called Wayne Bryant, is attributed the naming of the grove where they settled. His wagon reached a grove in the afternoon. They camped there for the night. In the morning the bright spring sunshine of April shone over the broad prairie lying eastward, and gilded the trees westward, then putting on their green foliage. The little birds, which had been accustomed to sing only for the Indian children and the deer, were no doubt flitting amid the green boughs, and as the white family looked around that morning and listened, they said, "How pleasant. We will stop here." And they gave it the name which it has ever since borne, of "Pleasant Grove." But a trial came upon them in that early springtime. On the fourth of April there came "a most terrible snow storm, the weather previous having been mild as summer," and the brother-in-law, Agnew, overtaken by night on the prairie east of Pleasant Grove, perished with the cold. This was the first death among the settlers; no places had been selected for burial; and these remains were deposited in a cemetery on Morgan Prairie, in Porter county.

The Agnew family, nevertheless, took possession of the claim and the settlement went on.

In May the Myricks came, Elias and William, and Thomas Reed, and commenced the "Myrick Settlement." Robert Wilkinson took possession of his claim on West Creek; and in the month of May S. P. Stringham and J. Foley settled on Centre Prairie.

Cedar Lake was not forgotten. A party of seven, Dr. Thomas Brown, Jacob L. Brown, David Hornor and four sons, Thomas, George, Amos, and Levi, came from the Wabash region, in the month of September, and camped near the bank on the west side of Cedar Lake. They took up more claims, erected cabins, put up hay, staid about two weeks. During this stay they found a bee tree in the grove a little north of their camp, which tree they cut down. They filled a three gallon jar with strained honey, they filled a wash tub full, and made an ash trough and filled that, all from the contents of this tree, which was estimated to yield at least five hundred pounds of good honey. The honey-bee is known to precede the white man. The early settlers cut a good many bee trees; Solon Robinson speaks of "a dozen honey trees to be cut and taken care of" during his first winter; but few probably yield as much honey as this one on the Brown claim.

This party was fortunate in securing food. Passing out of the county, returning home, they saw on the Illinois prairie seven wild turkeys. They unharnessed the four horses from their wagon, and four of them mounting, gave chase, taking care to keep the turkeys from entering the wood. They captured five out of the seven without firing a shot. They paid two for their meal at the next stopping place. Lacy, the landlord here, was the only settler on the route between Parrish Grove and Butterfield's. His hotel was about twelve feet square. On a rainy night the floor and the very hearth-stone would be covered all over with men seeking repose.

In October, this party returned with their families, and the Hornor settlement was now made. On the west bank of Cedar Lake was Jacob L. Brown, and next north of him was Aaron Cox. In the edge of the grove west was Thomas Hornor, and in the West Creek woods the cabin was situated containing the large family of David Hornor. About half way between the cabin of Thomas Hornor and that of Robert Wilkinson, Jesse Bond settled during this summer, and south of him, Thomas Wiles. There also came in this year Robert Hamilton; John Wood, from Massachusetts, came and made a claim; Milo Robinson from New York city joined his brother Solon in November; and in December, Henry Wells, of Massachusetts, became a resident of Lake.

I cannot find sufficient data for tracing out all the settlers of the summer of 1835; yet, the claim register being authority, they were not very numerous; although Robinson's record says, "In the fall of 1835 we had grown into so much importance that the tax collector from La Porte came up to pay us a visit, which was about as welcome as such visits generally are."

I return to the Robinson settlement, the spring of 1835.

Four families, it will be remembered, from Jennings county, were settled near together.

The prairie sod was not favorable for an early garden, but an old Indian corn field furnished a garden spot which the four families divided out and cultivated, and on which they raised their first vegetables. A breaking plow was started May 12th, and the first furrow turned was across the quarter section where now Main street runs, beginning at the present line of North street and ending on South street, or at the Eddy place. Twelve acres of oats were raised, and some corn and buckwheat. Some of this buckwheat sent to mill by the Clark family, was probably the first grist sent from Lake county. The mill was forty miles distant. The first speculation made was in oats. Wm. Clark and Wm. Holton had bought oats in the spring of '35, in La Porte county, intending them for seed, for fifty cents a bushel. Thinking it too late to sow when they reached their claims, they hauled the oats back and sold them for one dollar and fifty cents a bushel. The price had gone immediately up. Oats, corn, and wheat, then, all sold for the same price.

Warner Holton dug a well. He dug four feet and found water which supplied two families. This well was near the present railroad depot. As the water receded the well was made deeper until in after years it reached the depth of twelve feet.

Not forgetful of their national history in their isolation, this little colony celebrated the Fourth of July, 1835, by going to Cedar Lake and taking a boat ride on its crystal waters. In the fall these settlers saw their first prairie fire, and some of them were quite alarmed at its threatening aspect. A true prairie fire is a magnificent and sometimes an alarming sight. Many a time were the first settlers called out to fight for hours by day and by night against this raging element, endeavoring, sometimes vainly, to protect their fences, to protect their hay stacks, and even obliged to protect their log cabins. There was then little to obstruct and, with a favorable wind, the fire would sweep along the surface, consuming the tall dry grass, with fearful rapidity. The great hope of protection lay in setting back fires and controlling them before they gained much headway.

The winter of 1835–36 was one of some hardships and privations. As an illustration I go to a family west of Cedar Lake. Six hundred Pottawatomie Indians are camped within half a mile of their little home. The Indians bring venison to exchange for salt pork. They give a large amount of venison sometimes for a few pounds of pork. Venison is plenty; pork is scarce. The winter is nearly gone, the Indians leave their camping ground, the pork is low in the barrel, and two teams start for the Wabash—the great place of supply—to obtain more provisions. The winter breaks up. The water rises, as the spring flood comes. The streams are bridgeless. Return is impossible. Weeks pass, and eatables are very scarce. One-half bushel of buckwheat, brought up for seed, is in the house. This is ground in a coffee mill, and made into cakes. The mother eats very little. A son says to her, "Mother, we shall not starve. We can kill a cow if it becomes absolutely necessary." Spring has come. Two of the sons go out with the oxen to break some prairie. Presently Levi says to his brother, "I am so faint and weak, I can go no further." It seems like the time for giving up. They look off on the prairie far to the south, and lo! the white covered wagons are coming. Two settlers some miles northward, Bea and Chase, who had seen them too, and were living on venison, hastened down and obtained a half bushel of corn meal before the wagons were unloaded. This was, for that family, a happy day. About two months had passed since the wagons left home to get more food, and no tidings from them came. The joy of that return, and of again partaking of abundant food, one yet living remembers well, Amos Hornor of Ross, the only one left of all the earliest settlers west of Cedar Lake.

Other families had their privations; and other families experienced the great joy of a father returning and bringing plenty.

At the session of the Legislature of Indiana of 1835–36, the territory north of the Kankakee and east of La Porte county was divided into Porter and Lake. Porter was organized and Lake attached to it. Both had been previously attached to La Porte for judicial purposes.

In the spring of 1836 the commissioners appointed to make this division divided the territory of Lake into three townships, North, Centre, and South, and ordered an election for justice of the peace in each township. This was the first election held in Lake County. Amsi L. Ball was elected in North, Solon Robinson in Centre, and Robert Wilkinson in South Township. These justices held office till the county organization took place. According to my authority here, the justice in North had two or three cases, in Centre one, in South none.

Settlers came in this year rapidly. On the east side of Cedar Lake Adonijah Taylor and Horace Edgerton, Horace Taylor and Dr. Calvin Lilley established themselves. At the head of the lake the Nordyke family, Hiram Nordyke, sen., and sons, and sons-in-law, H. Bones and J. C. Batten, made claims; and also Solomon Russell. On the southwest shore of the lake the two fishermen families settled, Jonathan Gray and Lyman Mann. The Church family, Richard Church and sons, Darling, John, and Charles, and son-in-law, Leonard Cutler, from the state of New York, settled on Prairie West. James Farwell and sons, Major, Abel, and Carlos, took up claims over West Creek, and a number of others soon joined them. Of these others Charles Marvin yet remains. I name a few others among the many whose names are given as claimants in 1836. John McClean, in the Belshaw Grove; Jacob Mendenhall and Wm. A. Purdy, near Lowell; Moffard, Orrin Smith, and Joseph Morris, in South East Grove; William Merrill and Dudley Merrill near Centreville; three brothers by the name of Greene, Sylvester T., Edward, and Elisha, north of Cedar Lake; and three families of Van Volkenburgs, also Cassidy, Prentice, and David Fowler, north of the Robinson settlement. In September George Earle settled at Liverpool.

Squatter life was busy during the summer of this year, erecting cabins in the groves and making little patches of breaking on the prairies. Here and there also fences appeared; yet over the larger prairies few were the signs of civilization when this season closed.

A Methodist Episcopal missionary preacher named

Jones, sent by the Presiding Elder of the Northern Indiana Conference, who was then residing at South Bend, found his way, during this summer, into the county, and preached at the house of Thomas Reed and probably at Pleasant Grove.

The town of Liverpool was laid out, probably, in the spring of this year; and in July lots were sold there amounting to $16,000. Payment was made partly in cash, partly in notes. Bonds were given for the execution of deeds upon the payment of the notes. One of these bonds is now in my possession, binding John B. Chapman, Henry Fredrickson, and Nathaniel Davis, "in the penal sum of one hundred and sixty dollars, good and lawful money of the United States,"—there was "wild cat money" in those days—to execute a deed to S. Edwards of lot number 107, on the payment of notes amounting to sixty dollars, twenty dollars having been paid in cash. The bond bears date July 12th, 1836, and was signed in presence of George H. Phillips.

On the fourth day of July, in this year, the "Squatters' Union of Lake County" was organized. The following is a copy from the original record:

"At a meeting of a majority of the citizens of Lake County, held at the house of Solon Robinson on the 4th of July, 1836, for the purpose of adopting measures and forming a constitution for the better security of the settlers upon the public lands, Wm. Clark was unanimously elected to preside over the meeting, and Solon Robinson for secretary. After hearing the object stated for which the meeting was called it was moved that a committee of five be appointed to report a constitution and rules for the government of the members of this Union. Whereupon, Henry Wells, David Hornor, Solon Robinson, Thomas Brown, Thomas Wiles were elected. After due deliberation they reported to the meeting the Constitution hereto annexed, recorded on pages 4, 5, and 6 of this book, which, after being read by the secretary, was afterwards discussed, examined and finally adopted article by article, being fully approved by a majority of the meeting.

"On motion, the meeting then proceeded to elect a Register and a board of three County Arbitrators, Solon Robinson being nominated Register, and Wm. Clark, Henry Wells, and S. P. Stringham being nominated Arbitrators, were all unanimously elected.

"After some further discussion the meeting informally adjourned."

The record says this meeting was held "at the house;" it does not say "in;" and evidently not very many could have found comfortable standing room inside of that small cabin. I am told by an eye witness, that the meeting really was held in the grove, and that over the officers' stand a knife and a tomahawk were suspended, as the emblems of squatter sovereignty, the significant warning of what speculators might expect.

The following is the Constitution then adopted:

"CONSTITUTION OF THE SQUATTERS' UNION, IN LAKE COUNTY, INDIANA.

"PREAMBLE. *Whereas,* The settlers upon the public lands in this county, not having any certain prospect of having their rights and claims secured to them by a preëmption law of Congress, and feeling the strong present necessity of their becoming *united* in such a manner as to guard against speculation upon our rights, have met and united together to maintain and support each other, on the 4th of July, 1836; and now firmly convinced of the justness of our cause, do most solemnly pledge ourselves to each other, by the strong ties of interest and brotherly feeling, that we will abide by the several resolutions hereto attached (and to which we will sign our names), in the most faithful manner.

"ARTICLE 1st. *Resolved*, That every person who bears all the dangers and difficulties of settling a new and unimproved country is justly entitled to the privilege heretofore extended to settlers by Congress, to purchase their lands at a dollar and a quarter an acre.

"ARTICLE 2d. *Resolved*, That if Congress should neglect or refuse to pass a law before the land on which we live is offered for sale, which shall secure to us our rights, we will hereafter adopt *such measures as may be necessary* effectually to secure each other in our just claims.

"ARTICLE 3d. *Resolved*, That we will not aid any person to purchase his claim at the land sale, according to this constitution unless he is at the time an actual settler upon government lands, and has complied with all of the requisitions of this Constitution.

"ARTICLE 4th. *Resolved*, That all the settlers in this county, and also in the adjoining unsold lands in Porter county (if they are disposed to join us), shall be considered members of this Union as soon as they sign this Constitution, and entitled to all its advantages, whether present at this meeting or not.

"Article 5th. *Resolved,* That for the permanent and quiet adjustment of all differences that may arise among the settlers in regard to their claims, that there shall be elected by this meeting, a County Board of three Arbitrators, and also a Register of claims, who also shall perform the duties of clerk to the County Board, Arbitrators, and also the duties of a general corresponding secretary. In all elections, the person having the highest number of votes shall be elected.

"Article 6th. *Resolved,* That the person who may be elected Register (if he accept the office) shall take an oath or affirmation, that he will faithfully perform all the duties enjoined upon him. He shall forthwith provide himself with a map of the county (which shall be subject to the inspection of every person desiring it), on which he shall mark all claims registered, so that it can be seen what land is claimed and what is not; and also a book in which he shall register every claimant's name, and the number of the land which he claims, when it was first claimed, and when the claimant settled upon it, and the date when registered, where the occupant was from, and any other matter deemed necessary for public information, or that the County Board may order.

"He shall give persons applying all information in his power in regard to claims or vacant land, that shall be calculated to promote the settlement of the county. He shall also reply in the same manner to letters addressed him on the subject (provided the applicant pays his own postage.) He shall attend all the meetings of the County Board, record their proceedings, and perform their orders. When required by a member, stating the object, he shall issue notice to the County or District Board, when, where, and for what purpose they are to meet.

"Fees: For every claim he registers, twenty-five cents; and he shall, if required, give the claimant a certificate stating the number of the land, and when registered. For issuing notice to Arbitrators to meet, 12 cents. For attending their meeting the same fees that are allowed them. For duties of corresponding secretary no fees shall be required.

"ARTICLE 7. *Resolved*, That its hall be the duty of every person, when they sign this Constitution, or as soon thereafter as may be, to apply to the Register to have the land he claims, registered (paying the Register his fees at the same time). Where the claimant now resides upon the land which he claims, his claim shall be considered and held good as soon as registered. Every sale or transfer of titles shall be registered the same as new claims. Any person desirous of claiming any land now unoccupied, shall apply to have the same registered, and if he is a resident of the county at the time he applies, residing with, or upon any claim belonging to any other person, or upon any land that has been floated upon by Indian or preëmption claims, he shall be entitled to hold the claim he registers, while he remains a citizen of the county, provided, he shall within thirty days after registering it, make or cause to be made some prominent improvement upon it, and continue to improve the same to the satisfaction of the County or District Board of Arbitrators. Any non-resident who may hereafter be desirous to join this Union shall first sign the Constitution, and after registering his claim, shall proceed, within thirty days, to occupy it with his family, or else make a durable and permanent improvement, either by building a good cabin for his residence, or by plowing at least four acres, and then if he is not able to continue the occupancy of his claim either personally or by a substitute, he shall apply to the Arbitrators, stating his reasons for necessary absence, whether to move on his family, or whether for other purposes; and they shall certify to him what amount of labor he shall perform or cause to be performed within a given length of time to entitle him to hold his claim while he is absent, or for a certain time, which when done and proved to the Register and entered on record, shall as fully entitle the claimant to his claim as though he resided on it. *Provided*, the Board shall never grant a certificate to extend his absence one year from the date, unless the claimant has performed at least one hundred dollars worth of labor on his claim, and satisfied the Board fully that he will within that time become an *actual settler* upon it.

"Any member of this Union may also register and improve claims for his absent friends, as above provided, if he can and will satisfy the Board (of the county or district), that the identical person for whom he makes the claim will actually become a settler and reside upon it within the specified time.

"Any person found guilty by the Board of making fraudulent claims for speculating purposes, shall, if a member, forfeit his membership in this Union, and forfeit all right and title to hold the same, and it shall be declared confiscated and shall be sold as provided for all forfeited claims, in Article 9th.

"Every person requiring the services of the Arbitrators shall, if required, secure to them before they are bound to act, one dollar and fifty cents for each day's services, of each and all other necessary expense of magistrate, witnesses, Register, or other unavoidable expense.

"ARTICLE 8th. *Resolved*, that each congressional township, or any settlement confined in two or more townships containing twenty members, may unite and elect a Board of three Arbitrators, who shall possess the same power to settle disputes (when applied to) within their district that the County Board have. And any member of that district may either submit his case to the District or County Board. The opposite party may object to one or two of the District Board, and call one or two of the County Board, or some disinterested member, to sit in their places, provided he pays the extra expense so occasioned. All decisions of County or District Board shall be final.

"Either of the parties, or the District Board, may require the Register to attend their meetings and record their proceedings. But if he is not present they shall certify their judgment to him immediately, and he shall register it as any other claim.

"Any member may also object to one of the County Board, upon the same terms, and require one of a District Board, or some disinterested member, to sit in his place. The same proceedings shall also take place where one of the Board are interested in the dispute. The District Board may order district meetings, and the County Board county meetings.

"ARTICLE 9th. *Resolved*, That the Board of Arbitrators shall, as soon as may be, take an oath or affirmation before some magistrate, faithfully and impartially to perform all the duties enjoined upon them, not inconsistent with law, and that they will do all acts in their power for the benefit of members of this Union.

"On being duly notified, they shall convene, and if they see proper, they shall make their acts a rule of court before some magistrate, according to the statute provided for arbitrated cases.

"They may require the parties in the case to be tried, to be sworn, or affirmed, and hear arguments of parties or counsel, and finally decide which party is justly entitled to hold the claim, and which party shall pay costs or damages.

It shall be the duty of the County or District Board where the claim is situated, to take possession of any claim confiscated under the provisions of article seven, or any unoccupied non-resident claim, the claimant of which has neglected to occupy or improve the same, according to the terms and within the time specified in the certificate, and sell the same to some other person who will become a settler on it, keeping the money obtained for it in their hands (unless hereafter a treasurer shall be appointed) for a fund to defray any expense that may be deemed necessary to maintain our just rights or advance the interest of the Union. And if a fund so accumulated shall not be required for such purpose, the Board shall use it toward purchasing land for any needy widows, or orphan children, or needy members of this Union.

" Provided that the Board having jurisdiction may extend the time to any claimant holding a certificate from them, or application through the corresponding secretary, if the claimant can give them satisfactory reasons therefor, and they may also, when they have sold a forfeited claim, if they deem it just and reasonable, for good cause thereon, refund to the certificate claimant the amount he had actually expended upon it, and retain in the fund only the overplus that the same sold for.

"Any officer of this Union, or any member, shall be discarded if convicted of gross neglect of duty, or immoral conduct tending to injure the character of the Union.

"ARTICLE 10th. *Resolved*, That every white person capable of transacting business, and making or causing to be made, an improvement on a claim, *with the evident design of becoming a settler thereon*, shall be entitled to be protected in holding a claim on one quarter section, and no more—except, where persons holding claims on the prairie or open barrens, where the Board may decide they have not sufficient timber to support their farm, shall be allowed to divide one quarter section of timber between four such prairie claims.

The Board of Arbitrators may require any person making a claim to take an oath or affirmation that he intends the same for actual settlement, or (if timber) use of his farm. No person settling in thick timber shall be allowed to hold more than eighty acres of timber, but shall be protected in a claim of eighty acres on the prairie.

"ARTICLE 11th. *Resolved*, That before land is offered for sale, that each district shall select a bidder to attend and bid off all claims, in the claimant's name, and that, if necessary, every settler will constantly attend the sale, prepared to aid each other to the full extent of our ability in obtaining every claimant's land at government price.

"ARTICLE 12th. *Resolved*, That after the board of Arbitrators have decided that any individual has obtruded upon another claim, and he refuses to give the legal owner peaceable possession, that we will not deal with, or countenance him as a settler until he makes the proper restitution.

"ARTICLE 13th. *Resolved*, That we will each use our endeavors to advance the rapid settlement of the county, by inviting our friends and acquaintance to join us, under the full assurance that we shall now obtain our rights, and that it is now perfectly as safe to go on improving the public land as though we already had our titles from government.

"ARTICLE 14th. *Resolved*, That a meeting duly called by the County Board may alter and amend this Constitution.

"Lake County, Indiana, July 6, 1836.

" I do certify that the foregoing Constitution, as here recorded, is a true copy from the original draft reported by the committee, and adopted by the meeting, except slight grammatical alterations not varying the true sense of any article.

"Attest. SOLON ROBINSON, Register."

Attached to it are 476 signatures.

A few cases of arbitration occurred in regard to disputed claims. To enter upon land which another had claimed was called "jumping" it; and there were, it seems, a few accidental or intentional "jumpers."

The following extracts from the records will surely be of interest as showing the customs of squatter rule:

"Aug. 12. Notified County Board of Arbitrators to meet August 13, at G. W. Turner's, to decide disputed claim between Sam'l Haviland and John Harrison, on Sec. 13, sw. ½ T. 36, R. 8. Aug. 13. * * They decided that Haviland hold the claim on paying Harrison five dollars for his labor, and that Harrison pay the costs, amounting to four dollars and fifty cents."

Harrison, it is to be supposed, had "jumped" this claim and so was the aggressor.

"1837, March 16. This day an arbitration was held between Denton and Henry Miller and John Reed, who had gone on to Millers' claim and built a cabin, and the Arbitrators decide that Reed shall give up the cabin to Millers, and pay the costs of this arbitration, but that Millers shall pay Reed seventeen dollars for the cabin which he has built."

In some cases the costs were divided equally between the parties.

From the decisions of the arbitrators there seems to have been no appeal, in the nature of the case there could be none; and with the decisions the parties appear to have been satisfied. Ten cases of arbitration are on the records.

While improvements were going on during this busy summer every family needed food. The settlers of 1835 had raised provisions sufficient for themselves; but not even in La Porte county had a supply been raised sufficient to meet the wants of new settlers. And on this account "most of the Lake county settlers had to draw their provisions from the Wabash during the summer of 1836."

In the fall the first regular physician, Dr. Palmer, was numbered among the settlers. The nearest physician up to this time resided at Michigan City, where was also the nearest postoffice until the spring of this year.

In March, Solon Robinson, having made application for a post office, was appointed postmaster, authorized to bring the mail from Michigan City for the proceeds of the office. These proceeds were, up to October 1, $15. This would hardly pay for bringing it often. The office was named Lake Court House, usually written Lake C. H. The next offices west then were Joliet and Chicago.

The first settlers' store also dates its opening in 1836, established by Solon and Milo Robinson, who sold, during the winter of 1836–37, about $3,000 worth of goods out of a little log hut that used to stand beside the "old log court house." Their best customers were the Pottawatomies, from whom they "obtained great quantities of furs and cranberries" in exchange for goods.

A saw mill was commenced in the fall of this year, on the outlet of Cedar Lake, by Calvin Lilley and David Reed; but the one first in operation was built by Wilson S. Harrison, which, in the spring of '37, furnished oak lumber for $15 per thousand.

III.

In 1837 Lake county was organized. The mail was slow, and a special messenger, John Russell, was sent to Indianapolis to obtain the appointment of a sheriff, and authority to hold an election. He made the trip on foot and outstripped the mail. Henry Wells was appointed sheriff. An election was ordered and held. Officers elected: Wm. Clark and Wm. B. Crooks, associate judges; Amsi L. Ball, Stephen P. Stringham, and Thos. Wiles, county commissioners; W. A. W. Holton, recorder; Solon Robinson, clerk. First assessor, John Russell. Justices of the peace elected: in North township, Peyton Russell; in Center, Horace Taylor; at Cedar Lake, Milo Robinson, and in South, E. W. Bryant. In August Luman A. Fowler was elected sheriff, and Robert Wilkinson, probate judge.

The log building used for several years as a court house and place of worship, connected with which are many interesting associations, was erected this summer by Solon and Milo Robinson, who also erected a frame building, one of the first in the county, which was used as a hotel for several years. It became a part of the home of H. S. Pelton. Other frame buildings were, during this summer, erected.

The first Methodist class was probably organized this year at Pleasant Grove; and there was preaching several times at Solon Robinson's and in the court house. Lake county being this year a part of the Porter County Mission, Rev. — Beers minister in charge. Claims were taken up during this year very rapidly, and the year 1837 closes up the entries in the Claim Register.

Of the many settlers this season I name here especially Bartlett Woods and Charles Woods, natives of Winchelsea, England; Hervey Ball and Lewis Warriner, of Agawam, Massachusetts; George Flint, Benjamin Farley, Henry Torrey, and Joseph Jackson; Henry Sanger, Ephraim Cleveland, William Sherman, A. D. Foster; and, first of the German settlers on Prairie West, John Hack, with his large family and, according to current report, a chest well filled with five-franc pieces.

Among so many it is difficult to select any out, as most of the permanent early settlers became well known over the county. I therefore insert here the names, in the order of the years, of those whose early citizenship can be established by documentary evidence.

SETTLERS IN 1834.

According to Robinson's Records there was a settler, probably, by the name of Ross this summer on Sec. 6, Township 35, Range 7, and on the same section one was seen by S. Robinson, in October, "in a little shed cabin," whose name he was unable to record, his claim afterwards becoming "Miller's Mill." From the Claim Register I extract the following: "Wm. Crooks and Samuel Miller in Co. Timber and Mill Seat." Claim made June, 1835. Settled Nov., 1834. Sec. 6, Township 35, Range 7. Crooks, from Montgomery county. It is probable that this W. Crooks was the settler there seen in October.

Also, those Records state, that an old man named Winchell, from La Porte county, settled, in the summer of this year, and commenced a mill near the mouth of Turkey Creek, which claim and mill he afterwards abandoned.

Naming those, I now record as settlers in fact:

October.

    Thomas Childers.

November.

Solon Robinson.
Luman A. Fowler,   Robert Wilkinson,

SQUATTER LIFE. 53

December.

Jesse Pierce, David Pierce.

The last two settlers, according to the Claim Register, on Deep River and Turkey Creek.

SETTLERS IN 1835.

January.

Lyman Wells, John Driscoll.

February.

J. W. Holton, W. A. W. Holton,
Wm. Clark, from Jennings County.

March.

R. Fancher, Robert Wilkinson, Attica.

Spring.

Elias Bryant, Nancy Agnew, widow,
J. Wiggins, E. W. Bryant.

May.

Elias Myrick, Thomas Reed,
Wm. Myrick, Aaron Cox,
S. P. Stringham, Vermillion, Ill.

June.

Peter Stainbrook.

November.

David Hornor, Jesse Bond,
Thomas Wiles, Jacob L. Brown,
Thomas Hornor, Milo Robinson.

December.

Henry Wells, John G. Forbes,
Wm. S. Thornburg, R. Hamilton,
R. Dunham, John Wood.

SETTLERS IN 1836.

William A. Purdy, New York.
Elisha Chapman, Michigan City,
S. Havilance, Canada,　　　William N. Sykes,
David Campbell,　　　　　　W. Williams, La Porte,
Benj. Joslen,　　　　　　　　John Ball.
Richard Church, Michigan, Darling Church, Michigan.
Leonard Cutler,　　　　"　　Charles Cutler,　　　"
B. Rhodes, La Porte,　　　　J. Rhodes, La Porte,
Jacob Van Valkenburg, New York.
Jas. S. Castle, Michigan City,
Hiram Nordyke, sen., Tippecanoe.
Charles H. Paine, Ohio.
Hiram Nordyke, jr., Tippecanoe County,
Joseph C. Batton, Boone County,
James Knickerbocker, New York,
John T. Knickerbocker,　　G. C. Woodbridge,
H. Bones,　　　　　　　　　John J. Van Valkenburg,
Horace Taylor,　　　　　　　S. D. Bryant,
Daniel E. Bryant,　　　　　　Peter Barnard,
Jonathan Brown,　　　　　　E. J. Robinson,
David Fowler,　　　　　　　Cyrus Danforth,
M. Pierce, State of New York,
Sprague Lee, Pennsylvania,
John A. Bothwell, Vermont,
Peleg S. Mason,
Adonijah Taylor, "Timber and Outlet."

The last according to Claim Register, "May 15th."

John Cole, New York,　　　F. A. Halbrook, New York,
Stephen Mix, New York,　　Silas Clough, New York.

Rufus Norton, Canada,   Elijah Morton, Vermont,
Francis Barney,   Hiram Holmes,
Samuel Halsted "Timber and Millseat."

"Nov. 29th transferred to James M. Whitney and Mark Burroughs for $212."

Calvin Lilley, South Bend,
Samuel Hutchins, La Porte,
Jacob Nordyke, Tippecanoe.
Hiram S. Pelton, New York,
Ithamar Cobb,
J. P. Smith, New York,—settled July 5th.
G. Zuver, Bartholomew County,
H. McGee,
Henry Farmer, Bartholomew County.
William S. Hunt, "blacksmith," Wayne County.
George Parkinson,

S. Wilson,   James Farwell,
Abel Farwell,   Carlos Farwell,
M. C. Farwell,   Henry Horner,
Ruth Barney, widow,   J. V. Johns.
James Anderson,   E. W. Centre,
Simeon Beedle,   Isaac M. Beedle,
William Wells,   S. D. Wells,
W. W. Centre,   T. M. Dustin,
E. Dustin, jun.,   C. L. Greenman,
Charles Marvin,   Mercy Perry, widow,
Peter Selpry,   Jacob Mendenhall,
H. M. Beedle,   B. Rich,
D. Y. Bond,   S. L. Hodgman,
John Kitchel,   Henry A. Palmer,

Paul Palmer,
D. Barney,
George Earle,
A. Hitchcock,
O. Hitchcock,
Russell Eddy,
Wm. Brown,
Charles Walton,
Jonathan Gray,
Edward Greene,
Elisha Greene,
R. Wilder,
Solomon Russell,
A. Albee.

H. Edgarton,
Wm. Hodson,
Jackson Cady,
E. H. Hitchcock,
J. V. Johns,
C. Carpenter,
R. S. Witherel,
Wm. Farmer,
Nathan D. Hall,
S. T. Greene,
W. Page,
John McLean,
Daniel May,

Settlers in 1837.

James Westbrook,
John Bothwell,
Henry Torrey,
Joseph Batton,
N. Hayden,
N. Cochrane,
Lewis Warriner,
E. T. Fish,
John Fish,
George Flint,
Benjamin Farley,
D. R. Stewart,
H. Galespie,
J. H. Martin.
T. Sprague,
J. Hutchinson,

Samuel Sigler,
John Brown,
S. Hodgman,
John Kitchel,
H. R. Nichols,
A. Baldwin,
Josiah Chase,
Charles R. Ball,
Hervey Ball,
Lewis Manning,
Ephraim Cleveland,
Wm. Sherman,
T. Sprague,
John Hack,
G. L. Zabriska,
John Hutchinson,

E. L. Palmer,
N. Reynolds,
B. Demon,
Joel Benton,
John L. Ennis,
Dennis Donovan,
Patrick Donovan,
Thomas Donovan,
Daniel Donovan,
Oliver Fuller,
Thomas Tindal,
Orrin Dorwin,
H. Severns,
Hiram Barnes,
Bartlett Woods,
Charles Woods,
Dudley Merrill,
J. F. Follett,
A. D. Foster,
Adam Sanford,
Charles Mathews,
James Carpenter,
Jacob Ross,
Patrick Doyle,
W. J. Richards.

Lewis Swaney,
Francis Swaney,
O. V. Servis,
Thomas O'Brien,
Orrin Smith,
D. B. Collings,
Z. Collings,
Timothy Rockwell,
Jesse Cross,
E. Cross,
R. Cross,
A. L. Ball,
Daniel Bryant,
Wid. Elizabeth Owens,
E. D. Owens,
N. Pierce,
Wm. Vangorder,
G. W. Hammond,
J. Rhodes,
Joseph Jackson,
O. Higbee,
Z. Woodford,
Wm. Hobson,
P. Anson.

The register is not entire, and the names of all the settlers of 1837 cannot now be ascertained by any means at my command.

In the winter of 1837–38 Congress established some mail routes through this county, which had been crossed till now by only the Detroit and Fort Dearborn mail, carried in coaches along the Michigan beach, then by way of Liverpool, and again removed to the Bradley route. The new ones of 1838 were: first, from La Porte to Joliet, taken by H. S. Pelton, and the principal mail line of the county for a number of years, probably till the railroad era commenced; and the second, from Michigan City to Peoria, let to be carried in four-horse coaches, but the coaches did not run, and a remnant of that route, from City West to West Creek, gave us a mail carried on horseback, which continued for several years, its western terminus being Bourbonnois Grove, near Kankakee City; and the third, from Lake Court House to Monticello, in White county. This last was also taken by H. S. Pelton, "but was afterwards found to be through such an interminable wilderness that it was discontinued." Congress had not at that time studied the geography and history of the Kankakee Marsh, and of the counties of Iroquois and Newton and Jasper.

This year marked the beginning of bridge-building in our borders. The two northeast of Crown Point were built by Daniel May and Hiram Nordyke, at an expense of $500. The bridge across West Creek, near Judge Wilkinson's, built by N. Hayden, cost $400. The one across Cedar Creek, near L. Warriner's, by S. P. Stringham and R. Wilkinson, cost $200. The Deep River bridge, at B. Wilkinson's, cost $400, built by A. L. Ball. Several smaller ones were also built. Our streams were no longer "bridgeless," like the modern Euphrates. The money for building came from "the three per cent. fund."

It was also a year of saw-mill building. Accredited to this year are Walton's, Wood's, Dustin's, and Taylor's.

Only one of these, Wood's, furnished much lumber. Of one of them it was expressly said, it was "about half the time without water, and the other half without a dam." The first mill-builders found great difficulty in making their earth dams secure against the freshets. The beavers of this region, in the days before the fur-traders came, seem to have been more successful. The remains of their earthen works may still be traced west and south of Crown Point.

In October of this year was held the first term of Circuit Court, Judge Sample presiding, Judge Clark associate. The session was very quiet and peaceable. There were then no drinking places. Men were not cross, nor quarrelsome, nor drunk. Nine lawyers were present. Of the members of the first grand jury, only John Wood and Henry Wells remain among us. Of the first petit jury, Richard Fancher alone remains. On the docket of that term were thirty cases.

The first marriage license here issued seems to belong to this year. It was for John Russell and Harriet Holton. The first citizen married in the county was David Bryant (the bride's name is not given), the license having been obtained in Porter county. The ceremony was performed December 2, by S. Robinson, who says, "Another of my official acts, as a Justice of the Peace. Done on a most excessive cold day."

The second marriage was that of Solomon Russell.

The fourth, that of John Russell, has just been mentioned; and the second and fourth parties married became the first and second to obtain divorce, an example which has been followed by far too many ever since.

The year 1838 marks the commencement of Baptist meetings in Lake. A church was constituted in the Cedar Lake school-house, June 17th, nine Baptist members from Massachusetts and New York entering then and there into self-constituted church relationship. Elder French, of Porter county, was present and acted as moderator of the meeting.

"Meetings on Sabbath appointed to be held at Prairie West, Centre Prairie, and H. Balls, alternately." The Church and Cutler families lived on Prairie West and Norman Warriner on Centre Prairie. According to the church records meetings were held according to appointments for five Sabbaths, after which sickness for a season prevented attendance. Says the next record: "From continued distressing sickness no meetings were held until the latter part of winter." The church was not, therefore, publicly recognized until May 19th, 1839, but its constitution dates June 17, 1838. On the record book of that first Baptist church are the names of ninety-five members, forty-two of them baptized in Cedar Lake.

The sickness of the summer of 1838 was long remembered. It is probable that more died during that season, in proportion to the inhabitants, than during any other season in our history. Among them were, the wife of Lewis Warriner, who died Aug. 24th, and also his youngest daughter, Sabra.

This was a summer also of excessive drouth.

Many improvements were made in the county this year, notwithstanding the sickness. An addition was made to the German settlement on Prairie West. The town house at Liverpool was completed, a line of daily stages running then through that city.

Russell Eddy completed his frame house and moved his family up from Michigan City. In that house, which is now standing just north of the new residence of E. C. Field, was, without much doubt, the first piano of the county, brought with the household goods from Michigan City, and over its keys presided the graceful Eliza, fresh from the schools of Troy, N. Y., the most polished and accomplished, at that time, of the young ladies of Lake. She soon married and left us, and her place was filled by the less accomplished but lovely and beautiful Ruth Ann.

She grew up, married D. K. Pettibone, soon after died, and by most is probably forgotten, or I should not have named her here in mentioning her father's first home.

An addition was made this year to the settlement over West Creek. Solomon Burns and family, with his brother, Harry Burns, a brother-in-law named Hazelton, and George Willey and family, came together, with four wagons drawn by horses, from the State of New York. They were on the road four weeks. They crossed on the Torrey bridge, then went northward and bought claims of the Farwell family. The Hazelton family afterward removed westward. The Burns family settled where Abel Farwell, who married a daughter of S. Burns, now resides. For the claim a pair of valuable young horses had been transferred to James Farwell. These the lightning, not long afterward, struck and killed. George Willey was then commencing life, when he settled on a claim just east of the present village of Klaasville. He remained there many years, accummulated property, sold his farm, purchased land near Crown Point, and built one of the five best country residences in the county in which he now lives, surrounding himself and family with those conveniences and elegances which wealth procures. His is more properly a surburban than a country residence.

Another daughter of S. Burns married H. P. Robbins, who some years ago, having lost both his sons in the war of the Rebellion, removed to Lowell and became one of its business men, and now also marshal of the town. Solomon Burns died in 1847, at the age of 47. As a somewhat singular coincidence it may be noted here, that a cousin of his, Clark Rice, who came out to make a visit in 1846, died there, at the home of George Willey, at the age of 46. The remains of the two cousins lie side by side in that neglected West Creek burial-place, both born in 1800. This little West Creek settlement, consisting of the families, Rankin, Hitchcock, Gordinier, Marvin, Burns, Farwell, Willey, Fuller, remained quite isolated until the building of the Hanover bridge.

Among the German settlers of this summer on Prairie West were Joseph Schmal and Peter Orte, Michael Adler and Matthias Reder. These four families came over together.

Another settlement was commenced this year in Hanover. The pioneer of the Lutheran Germans was Henry Sasse, sen., who bought the claim of A. Cox, and also one made by Chase and Taylor, paying for the improvements on the latter $150. In the same year came H. Van Hollen, and other families soon followed these until a large settlement occupied the northern part of Lake

Prairie, and along the West Creek woods made farms of the choice hunting grounds.

The privilege had been granted to the State of selecting a certain amount of government lands for the benefit of the Wabash Canal. This selection in Lake was made in the month of June, this year, and Col. John Vawter, one of the commissioners, while here, preached in the log court house "to a very respectable congregation."

"The Methodist Episcopal Church," says an old manuscript, "may be considered as regularly organized in the county from this time;" that is, from the summer of 1838, "forming with Porter county a circuit, and supplied with preaching at stated times." I find no early documents or records in the hands of any of this denomination, and am obliged to glean my information from other sources. It seems strange that such a large and growing body have preserved so little of their early history.

A number of the settlers, late in the fall of this year, proved up their preëmption rights and entered their land before the public sale.

The first of these, probably, were S. Robinson and Judge Clark.

As the first of January, 1839, opened, death for the first time visited the little settlement at Lake Court House. It came in the form of consumption and laid low one of the active business men, Milo Robinson. After his death Luman A. Fowler kept the tavern house until the next fall, when he removed to Lockport, Illinois, where canal building was going on. After his removal H. S. Pelton married, took the house, afterwards purchased it, and occupied it until his own death.

In March of this year that event of so much interest to those early settlers, the sale of United States Lands, took place at La Porte. The sales commenced on the 19th. The squatters of Lake were in large force gathered there. The hardy pioneers, accustomed to frontier life and to depend on their strong arms and trusty rifles; the New Englanders and the Yorkers, almost direct from those centers of culture, and possessing their share of the intelligence and energy of those regions; and the firm, sturdy, solid Germans, like those that of late broke the power of the third Napoleon,—Germans who had just left the despotisms of the Old World and had received their lessons of freedom in the New, amid the wildness of untrodden Western prairies; all were there, determined that no speculator should bid upon their lands. Some trouble had been anticipated. The principle upon which the squatters insisted was of importance to them. They were probably prepared,—from what I heard in those days of my youth, I am satisfied they were prepared—armed men were among them—to use force, if it should be necessary, to secure the right which each squatter claimed of buying his own quarter section at one dollar and a quarter an acre. They knew that in the wilds of Lake, in the retreats of the Kankakee marsh, no officers of justice would search for them if their mode of enforcing their claim should be called lawless. But there arose no necessity. The impression was strongly made that it would not be safe for a speculator to overbid a squatter, about five hundred of whom had solemnly pledged themselves to each other to abide, in the most faithful manner, by their own assertion of squatters' rights. The moral force employed was sufficient. Solon Robinson was bidder for one township, William Kinnison for another, and A. McDonald for the third. The sale passed off quietly, and the sons of Lake returned peacefully to their homes. But unfortunately for some of them, they had expended their silver and gold in making improvements and amid the sickness, and suffering, and death of 1838, "the wild cat" money was not current at the land office, and now what the speculators could not effect in one way they easily accomplished in another. They offered to loan these men money for entering their claims, on the security of their lands, and charged them twenty, thirty, or more, per cent. And thus, after all their care, considerable tracts of Lake county land came into the hands of non-residents.

Another event of some importance took place this year, the location of the county seat at the town of Liverpool by commissioners appointed by the Indiana Legislature. Cedar Lake and Lake C. H. had both sought the location; and the actions of these commissioners produced much dissatisfaction. Before a petition for a relocation could be granted, before this summer closed, the proprietor on the east of Cedar Lake, Dr. Calvin Lilley died, and his place passed into the hands of another.

During these years, from 1834 to 1839, while there were the quiet of peace among us and friendliness on the part of the Pottawatomies, and the activity of new settler life,—the Black Hawk War having terminated in 1832, after which nearly all of Iowa and Wisconsin was ceded to the United States—in Florida the Seminole War was raging, commenced in '35, and not actually ended till '42.

In one of these years, 1836, Arkansas was admitted into the Union, and in 1837 Michigan was admitted, and in 1837 took place the Canadian Rebellion. The short war with the Creek Indians took place in 1836.

Amid such events of national interest the squatters of Lake formed a community by themselves; feeling most of all, probably, the great financial crash of 1837, when the banks suspended payment, when in two months in the city of New York were failures amounting to more than a hundred millions of dollars, the effects of which " were felt to the remotest borders of the Union."

In that crash our two youthful cities, Liverpool and Indiana City, also died.

CHAPTER III.

THE POTTAWATOMIES.

Venable, in his History of the United States, a new and an excellent work, divides the Indians into eleven large families. These families were divided into tribes or nations. The Indians known as the Miami Confederacy held most of the territory of Indiana. The northwestern part was occupied by a tribe called Pottawatomies. For many "thousands of moons," for centuries, so far as any history can record, the Red men had held undisputed possession of the whole Northwest. Two hundred years ago the French penetrated these wilds and came in contact with the scattered tribes, both as fur traders and as religious teachers. The Indians, therefore, of 1834 were not altogether those, as Sprague expresses it, "of falcon glance and lion bearing," but those who acknowledged the white man as a conqueror.

By the treaty of 1832 the Pottawatomies had disposed of their lands to the Government; but they were still on their hunting and trapping grounds in considerable numbers, when the first settlers came in. They were friendly and inoffensive, yet Indians still. Their favorite resorts seem to have been along the streams, around Cedar Lake, and at Wiggins' Point. The Calumet river was especially attractive. As to facilities for fishing, and as to abodes for wild fowls and fur bearing animals, this region could not well be surpassed. The Calumet and Deep rivers furnished some hundred miles of canoe navigation, abounding in fish, fowls, and fur; the Kankakee Marsh is even yet a grand resort for trappers and fowlers, and in earlier years its islands were a favorite retreat for deer; and Cedar Lake and the West Creek woods were haunts that it would scarcely seem Indians could peacefully leave. Having seen Cedar Lake myself in 1837, when its waters and the large marsh south of it literally swarmed with fish,—A. Cox opened a pike that is said to have weighed twenty six pounds, and I have seen a quite large boat loaded down with fish at a single draw of the net,—when its shore was sentineled all round with muskrats in the water's brink; having seen its surface so many times since black with ducks and geese, or white with gulls and other water fowls; I can believe almost any story about the abundance of such game. The old and sacred Lake of Gennesaret, noted as it now is in this respect, amid its modern solitudes, can scarcely have a more abundant supply of fish and fowls in and on the same square miles of depth and surface.

At Wiggins' Point, on the place now owned by E. Saxton, the Indians had, in 1834, a village, a dancing-floor, and a burial-place. From this dancing-floor sixteen trails diverged, leading off in every direction. These trails were well trodden foot-paths. In the grove are now a number of black-walnut trees, whether native there or set out by the Indians is uncertain. The dancing-floor was very smooth and well worn, and the well trodden pathways leading to it indicated that it was a place of general resort. Not many rods distant, the situation well chosen and beautiful, was the village burying ground.

In the center of this was a pole, perhaps twenty feet in height, surmounted constantly by a white flag. Here the Indian dead of this neighborhood were decently buried, according to the custom of this tribe. Sometimes they buried in a sitting attitude, in their more retired cemeteries, leaving the head uncovered; and at other times in a supine position. From the French they had received some religious ideas, and seem to have had some belief in a future resurrection of the body. It is related of one of these French-taught men, who was about to die near Miller's Mill, that he gave instructions not to have his body buried, as he expected it to be restored to life at some day, when the Indians would be the head race of the world. The bodies of those who expressed such a wish were placed in solitude upon the boughs of living trees. An Indian child's body in a basket, with bells attached, was found, suspended in a tree, by some of the early settlers. At the burial ground above mentioned a body was exhumed, probably in 1835, supposed to be the body of one of the head men of the tribe, about which were a blanket, a deer skin, a belt of wampum, and outside of the feet a fur hat; and with the body were found a rifle and a kettle full of hickory nuts. Dr. Burleigh, supposed to be from Michigan City, has the credit of removing this body, acting on the principle attributed to the students of a certain medical institution, who are said to have adopted as their motto, *De mortuis nil nisi bonum*, thus translated: There is nothing good about the dead except their bones. So, the conclusion is, take these when you can get them. It is said that one day, after the robbing of the grave, two Indians, armed with rifles, came into the field where Wiggins was at work alone. They went to the grave, and sat down their rifles, and talked. Wiggins was alarmed. He conjectured that avengers were near, and he was in their power. The Indians were evidently much displeased, but finally withdrew without offering any violence. Wiggins, who had claimed this part of the Indian village, allowed his breaking-plow to pass over the burial ground.

This desecration did not pass unnoticed by the Red men. When, in 1840, General Brady, with eleven hundred Indians from Michigan, five hundred in one division and six hundred in the other, passed through this county, some of both divisions visited these graves, and some of the squaws groaned, it is said, and even wept, as they saw the fate of their ancient cemetery. Thoroughly have the American Indians learned the power and the progress of the Anglo-Saxon civilization, but not much have they experienced of its justice towards them and theirs.

Leaving, for the present, the village at Wiggins' Point, some camping grounds near the Kankakee are worthy of record. On an island in the marsh, known as Red Oak Island, which is nearly south of the residence of Mrs. Pearce, was one of these camps or Indian gardens. About two hundred camped at that garden during the winter of 1837–38. South of Orchard Grove was another garden, on Big White Oak Island. Here during this same winter camped, perhaps, one hundred and fifty. These camping grounds were called gardens because the Indians there cultivated grapes and some corn. Just across the river they had quite a vineyard. It does not appear that they made wine, but used the grapes as delicious food. There are now in this county some small productive vineyards, and many orchards of excellent fruit; but we should not forget that those who here first gave attention to the culture of the grape were our predecessors, the Pottawatomies.

On Red Oak Island they had two stores, kept by French traders, who had Indian wives. The names of these traders were Bertrand and Lavoire. At Big White Oak was one store, kept by Laslie, who was also French, with an Indian wife. Here a beautiful incident occurred on new year's morning, 1839. Charles Kenny and son had been in the marsh looking up some horses. They staid all night, December 31st, with Laslie. His Indian wife, neat and thoughtful, like any true woman, gave them clean blankets out of the store, treated them well, and would receive no pay. The morning dawned. The children of the encampment gathered, some thirty in number, and the oldest Indian, an aged, venerable man, gave to each of the children a silver half-dollar as a new year's present. As the children received the shining silver each one returned to the old Indian a kiss. It was their common custom, on such mornings, for the oldest Indian present to bestow upon the children the gifts.

A beautiful picture, surely, could be made by a painter of this island scene; the marsh lying round, the line of timber skirting the unseen river, the encampment, the two white strangers, the joyous children, and the venerable Pottawatomie who, long years before, had been active in the chase and resolute as a warrior in his tribe, bestowing the half-dollars and bending gracefully down to receive the gentle kisses of the children. Such a picture on canvas, by an artist, would be of great value among our historic scenes.

Leaving these gardens, the loaded grape vines,—some excellent *wild* grapes are found on some of the Kankakee islands now—the corn patches, and domestic scenes of the Red children, we may look upon the Pottawatomies in other haunts and amid other scenes.

They had quite a camp south of the present Lowell, on Cedar Creek, at the same time that parties were camping on the gardens; also one near what is now the Jones school-house. During this same winter, or the preceding one, some thirty Indian lodges were in one camp north of Cedar Lake, on a ridge near a cranberry marsh. Along the Calumet there were many wigwams, and at Indian Town, just east of the county line, there was a large village. As already mentioned, an encampment of six hundred was in the West Creek woods, in the winter of 1835-36; and a less number camped there in the winter of 1836-37. This camp was on section 20, town 34, range 9, about two miles west of the head of Cedar Lake. Around this lake they hunted; the burial ground at its head proved that they formerly resided near it. One of their canoes was left there, and was used by Job Worthington, staying on the claim bought by Hervey Ball; but the first settlers mention no large encampment on its banks. That canoe was a well made dug-out. It became the property of the Ball family. It would upset very easily, as Mrs. Mann and Loretta Cox ascertained one day, when it left them both in the water, the former losing her gold ring, but both reaching the shore in safety. I find no evidence that the Indians left more than two canoes in the hands of the whites at Cedar Lake.

There were probably Indians on the islands west of Cedar Creek, but I have not succeeded in tracing them there. One other camping place remains to be noticed. This was near the present village of Deep River. After the Wood family settled there the Indians had a small camp about a mile from the mill. They were sometimes seen by the white children going up and down the river in their canoes, but were not around there much after 1836. This part of the river has a swift current and some quite high banks, and must have been attractive to the native fisherman. There is evidence of its having been a place of much resort. Near the river bank, on one of the intervals or bottoms, is a singular mound. It is shaped like a common flatiron, except that the sides are not curved. The height of this mound is about twenty feet, and it slopes regularly down on each side to the meadow land. The two long sides are in length about ten rods each. There was not a tree or shrub upon this in 1836. Against the sharp angle where the long sides met was a round opening in the ground, about twenty or twenty-five feet in diameter, and of unknown depth. Into it have been thrown the grubs from eight or ten acres of land; but, like the gulf at Rome into which, it is said, Quintus Curtius plunged,—noble Roman on noble steed,—it is difficult to fill it up. As yet, after thirty-six years, it is still an opening in the ground. The object of this artificial mound and opening is not known.

There are also, in this locality, as many as eight places where the Indians are supposed to have "steamed" themselves when sick. In fact, it appears to have been a kind of water-cure establishment. The holes in the rocks where the water was heated are still to be seen. About the use of these collected rocks, it is true, there is some conjecture. But it being known that Indians employed such treatment for some diseases, it is easy to fancy the sick and enfeebled gathering there. Again, on some of the flats near by are many arrow-heads. Ever busy conjecture has therefore located here a savage battle, of which no tradition has reached us, and how many red warriors fell no history records. On the other hand, as indicating the arts of peace, a stone pestle found in this same locality, in the possession of Nathan Wood, shows careful workmanship. It is smooth, regularly rounded, and stained or curiously stamped. It must have been used for pounding corn in a mortar.

On this quarter section of land, which includes the mill-seat, a "float" was laid in the name of a Pottawatomie, Quash-ma, after it had been claimed by John Wood; and to obtain the title, after the U. S. patent was issued to Quash-ma, cost the claimant one thousand dollars. While, therefore, the Indians had at this place little intercourse with the early settlers, there are evidences that it was one of their homes of ancient occupancy.

Some incidents of life at Indian-town belong to our history, although the village itself was in Porter county. Simeon Bryant selected that section for a farm, and leaving Pleasant Grove, built his cabin near the village. The Indians at first were not well pleased with the idea of a white neighbor; but the resolute squatter treated them kindly, would gather up land tortoises and take to their wigwams, for which, when he threw them on the ground, the women and children would eagerly scramble; and after he had fenced around some of their cornfields he still allowed them to cultivate the land. This kindness and consideration secured their regard. A father and son from La Porte county were stopping with this Bryant family while improving their claims, and the daughter and sister, a girl of eighteen or twenty, came out to assist in the housekeeping. She was necessarily brought in contact with the villagers. Among these were two young Indians about her own age, sons of a head man, who were quite inclined to annoy the white girl and play pranks. They would lurk around and watch her motions, and sometimes when she would enter the little outdoor meat-house, would fasten her in. One day, when she was coming out with a pail of buttermilk, one of these young Pottawatomies stood in the doorway, with his arms stretched across, and refused to allow her to pass out. Reasoning and entreaty were unavailing, and as a last resort she took up her pail and, to the great surprise of the impolite young savage, dashed the buttermilk all over him. He then beat a retreat, and left her mistress of the field, with only the loss of one bucket of milk. Sometime afterward an errand took her among the wigwams, and at a time, it appeared, when the occupants had obtained some "fire-water." Raising the curtain of their doorway, according to custom, to make an inquiry, the young savages sprang up and threatened her with their tomahawks. She stood and laughed at them, and at length, ashamed perhaps to injure the bold, defenceless girl, they let her pass on and accomplish her errand.

This she succeeded in doing, and then returned in safety to the Bryant cabin, glad to have escaped the peril through which she had passed. The heroine of these incidents soon afterward married, and became an inhabitant of Lake, having now several grown up daughters, and being the head of one of our well known and highly respected families.

A still greater peril was experienced by Mrs. Saxton, who became a resident on the Wiggins place. Her husband was away, and she was at home with small children. The evening was cold and stormy, and, as it advanced, an Indian called at the door requesting shelter. At first his request was refused, but one of the children pleaded for him; the storm was pelting without, and he was admitted. He was a young man, and unfortunately had with him a bottle of whisky. He wanted some corn bread. It was made, but did not suit him. He drank whisky and was cross. An intoxicated man, whether white or red, is an unpleasant guest. A second trial in the bread line was made, using only meal, and salt, and water, which succeeded better. The Indian talked some, sat by the fire, drank. He went to the door and looked out. Something to this effect he muttered. " Pottawatomies lived all round here; white man drove them away. Ugh!" Then he went back to the fire. A little child was lying in the cradle, and he threatened its life. The alarmed mother and children could offer little effectual resistance. But the Indian delayed to strike the fatal blow. At length he slept. Then the startled mother poured out what was left in the bottle, and waited for the morning. The savage and drunken guest awoke, examined his bottle, and finding it empty, said, "Bad Shemokiman woman! Drink up all of Indian's whisky." He then went off to Miller's Mill, replenished his bottle and returned. Sometime in the day Dr. Palmer came along and succeeded in relieving this family of their troublesome guest. The next night this Indian's father came; apologized as best he could; said that was bad Indian and should trouble them no more.

One pleasant Cedar Lake incident may be here recorded. A party of nine, eight men and one squaw, called one morning at the residence of H. Ball, and desired breakfast. It was soon prepared for them, and all took places at the table and ate heartily. At first only the men took seats for eating, but their entertainer insisted that the squaw also should sit down with them. This caused among the Indians no little merriment. They had brought with them considerable many packages of fur, and as they passed out each one took two muskrat skins and laid them down as the pay for his breakfast. They then went into a little store on the place and traded out quite a quantity of fur. After some hours trading they quietly departed.

The following has been kindly prepared for this record by an early settler of Pleasant Grove. It contains some recollections of his boyhood:

"At the time referred to, as late perhaps as 1840, bands of Indians would frequently come into the settlements, erect their tents, and remain as long as the hunting was good. They would then go to some other hunting ground and remain for a time. These companies consisted frequently of from twenty to fifty, including men, women, and children; dogs and Indian ponies not included. The Indians were generally peaceful and it is not remembered that they committed any acts of depredation, when they were properly treated, during the time they remained in that section of the country. They visited Wayne Bryant and family often; were said to be uniformly kind, were anxious to exchange such commodities as they had for provisions. They inquired the name of Mr. Bryant, and on being told that his name was 'Wayne' they exhibited surprise and indications of fear, and by their language and deportment Mr. Bryant was led to believe that they had some knowledge of the manner in which some of their race had been treated by Mad Anthony Wayne of historic reputation.

"An instance may be given of the result of an attempt to trifle with the Indians. Two of the early settlers concluded to amuse themselves with them, and one evening they went to their camp near where Lowell now stands and proposed to sell them a gallon of whisky. The Indians said they would trade fur, and brought out a respectable quantity which they offered for the gallon of whisky. The men said, ' It is not enough.' So the Indians brought more fur, and, on being refused, continued to pile up the fur, and gathered around the men, until they were told that they were only joking, and they had no whisky. But the Indians declared they would have it, and proceeded to enforce their demand, when the whites broke and ran, being closely followed by the Indians in a race, until the whites took shelter in their own log cabin, an Indian following one of the men into his door-yard."

The Indians evidently had not learned the ways of *civilized* grain dealers " on 'Change,"to be able to buy and sell what one did not possess.

It is a pity to spoil a good story, but justice requires that another version of this occurrence should be recorded. I have conversed with one of the actors in this scene and he relates that, on going to the Indian camp at a certain time, he found them quite merry and animated, and he remarked, "I guess you have had some whisky." They eagerly caught up the word *whisky* and offered to give fur, professing to understand that he had some whisky for sale. In vain he explained to them that he had none, but supposed they had been drinking some. They piled up the fur and crowded around. As his only alternative he *did run*, and ran well; but a swift-footed savage came up abreast of him in the race, although he had a pathway and the Indian was in deep snow, and presented his knife to stop his flight. The white man seized the Indian by the arm, threw him into the snow, and reached in safety the shelter of a cabin. He probably concluded that it was not very prudent even to name whisky in the presence of the Indians. The French traders on the gardens did not sell whisky to the Indians, but some few settlers and other traders had the name of doing it.

As still further illustrative of the mode of living and customs of these French-taught Pottawatomies, let us look again upon the village and white family at Indian Town.

A head man resides there called a chief. J. W. Dinwiddie, his father, and sister, are staying with the Bryant family until their own claim is ready for occupancy. The chief keeps a cow, and so do the whites. The chief's wife would bring up their cow, and also would drive along sometimes the other cow, saying as she passed the settler's cabin, "Here, John, I have brought up Margaret's cow." This squaw had a quite fair complexion; was between thirty and forty years of age, in appearance; could talk some English, and was very kind to the whites. The chief's name was called Shaw-no-quak. Here also was a dancing-floor. The Indians would form in a line for a dance according to age, the oldest always first, the little children last. They danced in lines back and forth. The old chief, a young chief, and an old Indian sat together and furnished the music. This was made by shaking corn in a gourd. The song repeated over and over the name of their chief. After the dance they feasted on venison soup, with green corn, made in iron kettles, served in wooden trenchers with wooden ladles. The white neighbors present at one of these entertainments were invited to partake. This the women declined doing, which the chief did not like. And thus he expressed his displeasure: "No good Shemokiman! no good! no eat! no good Shemokiman woman!" Then he would pat S. Bryant and say, "Good Shemokiman! Good Shemokiman! Eat with Indian!"

This Indian Town belongs to Porter county; but the Dinwiddie family make this history our own, and it gives us a more full view of Pottawatomie life.

The camping-ground at Wiggins' Point was called McGwinn's Village, being named after one of their head men.

The Indians here, on the gardens, and elsewhere, lived in lodges or wigwams. These were made of poles driven into the ground, the tops converging, and around the circle formed by the poles was wound a species of matting made of flags or rushes. This woven flag resembled a variety of green window shades seen in some of our stores and houses. The Indian men wore a calico shirt, leggins, moccasins, and a blanket. The squaws wore a broadcloth skirt and blanket. "They "toted" or "packed" burdens. The Indians along the marsh kept a good many ponies. These they loaded heavily with furs and tent-matting when migrating. They also used canoes for migrating up and down the Kankakee. The village Indians lost some eighty ponies one winter for want of sufficient food. Those at Orchard Grove wintered very well. During the winter the men were busy trapping. Three Indians caught, in one season, thirteen hundred raccoons. They sold the skins for one dollar and a quarter each, thus making on raccoon fur alone $1625. Other fur was very abundant and brought a high price in market. They trapped economically until they were about to leave forever the hunting-grounds of their forefathers. They then seemed to care little for the fur interests of those who had purchased their lands, and were destroying as well as trapping, when some of the settlers interfered.

One of these was H. Sanger. He, in company with some others, went on to the marsh to stay the destruction it was said was there going on. He went in advance of the others after reaching the trapping ground, and told the Indians they must cease to destroy the homes of the fur-bearers. He is himself a tall, and was then an athletic man, and said he, "Look yonder. Don't you see my men?"

They did see men coming, and were alarmed, and mentioned to others the threatening aspect of the "tall Shemokiman." One Indian burial-place has been mentioned, the one at the McGwinn village. This contained about one hundred graves. Another has also been referred to at the head of Cedar Lake. This one has not been specially disturbed. At Big White Oak Island was a third. Here were a good many graves; and among them six or seven with crosses. There were probably others over which the plowshare has passed and no memorial of them remains. At Crown Point was a small garden, and on the height Indians seem to have camped, but no burial-place is known to have been found here. It has been claimed that sick Indians were brought here to be restored to health. As there were no springs of water close by, and no unfailing stream, it would not have been desirable for a permanent camping place. A few tomahawks have been found near the present town.

Besides the mound already mentioned, there is one quite large and circular on the west side of Cedar Lake; growing upon it were, thirty years ago, some large oak trees; one at the south end of the lake also circular; one a short distance north of Lowell; and some other evidences of human existence. Whether the mounds were the work of the Pottawatomies, or of those Old Mound Builders who long ago disappeared, is quite uncertain. Some chiefs have been mentioned. The principal chief of all the Pottawatomies, becoming such by adoption in

1825, was Alexander Robinson, a man part Indian, part French, and part English, who died but a few months ago at his home on the Des Plaines, at the supposed age of one hundred and four years. As early as 1809, having become connected with Joe Baies, the founder of Baileytown, in the fur trade in the service of John Jacob Astor, he was engaged in taking corn around the head of Lake Michigan. This corn was raised by Pottawatomies and brought to that young trading post, now Chicago, "in bark woven sacks on the backs of ponies." In August, 1812, as he was on a canoe voyage to Chicago to buy corn, friendly Miamis hailed him from the shore with the warning "*not to go to Chicago, as it would storm tomorrow.*" He therefore left his canoe at the mouth of the Big Calumet, and passed in safety through the August Massacre. The next winter he was living in Indian style as a hunter on the Calumet. In 1829 he took a three-quarter Indian wife from the Calumet. His headquarters were Chicago, and he made fur-trading journeys extending, it is said, as far as the Wabash.

This is the man whom our Pottawatomies, as well as others, recognized as head Chief, who during the Black Hawk War "convened one of the last Indian councils ever held in Chicago." In 1836 the great body of this tribe, then five thousand strong, met for the last time in Chicago,—one of our citizens, J. Hurlburt, was in Chicago at that time, and he says that there were then gathered ten thousand Indians,—"received their presents and assurance of the distinguished esteem of the Great White Father," and then, led by this chief, called Chee-chee-bing-way, or Blinking Eyes, left these hunting grounds for their Kansas reserve. But, according to the reliable authorities for the statements in this chapter, many still lingered within the bounds of our county. Few of these, if any, remained after 1839. To us the Pottawatomies have left many of their bones in their known and unknown burial-places, the name of one of our rivers, and their own perishing memorials and remembrances as treasured up by those with whom they had intercourse. Some of us who are now living enjoyed for a few years their rich hunting grounds and trapping region; but the deer that remained around their wigwams will not tarry long around the White man's home, and the fur-bearing animals decrease as civilization advances; and soon there will be only now and then a bone, an arrow head, a tomahawk, or a mound, to bear witness to the existence of Aborigines. Already it is said that the tribe who once occupied this soil has dwindled to less than half its numbers in 1836, and like the other tribes of North American Indians, a strange and an injured people, it is passing into western wilds, crowded on by the whites, and rapidly becoming extinct. It is surely but just that the citizens of Lake County should treasure up and transmit to posterity among their own records some memories and incidents of the once powerful Pottawatomies.

CHATER IV.
GROWTH. 1840—1849.

Squatter sovereignty ceased after the land sale of the last year. Many of the settlers were now the legal owners of the soil, holding their patents from the United States. Others were hoping to become such owners.

The leading event of this year, 1840, which opened a new career and a hopeful prospect before the newly made lords of the soil, was the relocation of the county seat. An act was passed by the State Legislature in the winter of 1839–40, ordering such relocation. The commissioners appointed were, Jesse Tomlinson and Edward Moore of Marion county, Henry Barclay of Pulaski, Joshua Lindsey of White, and Daniel Doale of Carroll county.

Benjamin McCarty, who, with his brother-in-law, had laid out the town of Valparaiso, which became the county seat of Porter county, was desirous of also giving a county seat to Lake. He had purchased the Lilley place, on the northeast side of Cedar Lake, had laid out a town called West Point, and was now a competitor with Solon Robinson for the honor and privilege of the location. The commissioners came into Lake in June. Offers of comparatively large donations were made by the friends of each locality. The commissioners rode around, looked over the ground, canvassed the claims and offers of the competitors, and finally selected Lake Court House as the proper place for the county seat.

7

Town Lots, in number seventy-five, were soon afterwards laid out upon sixty acres of land in Section 8, twenty acres belonging to Judge Clark and forty to Solon Robinson.

A large public square was laid out and donated, upon which no buildings are ever to be erected, and an acre of ground was set apart exclusively for a court house and public offices. Another acre was given for school purposes. If I understand the old record correctly, the two proprietors also donated one-half of the lots laid out, and Judge Clark gave, in addition, thirty-five acres adjoining on the east; Solon Robinson also gave twenty acres on the west. Also Russel Eddy gave ten acres and J. W. Holton fifteen acres. Other donations were also made in money and labor. These donations, of course, went to the public or the county; and George Earle of Liverpool was appointed County Agent. He and the two proprietors met to name the new town.

"I have a name to propose," said the County Agent.

"So have I," said Solon Robinson.

"What is your name?"

"*Crown Point.*"

"And that also is mine."

So, although Judge Clark did not at first quite fancy the name, it was soon adopted, having been suggested, perhaps, as in contrast with the West Point at Cedar Lake, and containing, it may be, a concealed allusion to Solon Robinson's well known title of Squatter-king. As such, his place should have the crown. Thus, although certainly named *after* the Crown Point in New York, whether named in *honor* of it is not so certain. The Agent and the proprietors sold the first lots at auction Nov. 19th, 1840. The prices ranged from $11.00 to $127.50 a lot, on two, three, and four years credit, the first year without interest.

The United States census, taken this year by Lewis Warriner, showed the population of the county to be 1468.

During this summer occurred "the great wheat blight." The whole crop, it was said, was entirely lost. Not a favorable beginning for growth.

This summer also, S. Robinson and Dr. Palmer obtained from the East some Berkshire pigs, the first in the county. E. S. McCarty, at Cedar Lake, put up and burnt the first kiln of brick.

Political excitement was running quite high this summer, as a presidential election was coming on. Says Lossing, "The contest was very exciting, and was characterized by demoralizing proceedings hitherto unknown in the United States." It was the "log cabin" and "hard cider" campaign. A large political gathering took place at the Tippecanoe battle-ground. To this S. Robinson, Leonard Cutler, and some other zealous Whigs of that day, went down, across the country, with, I think, a four horse team and flying colors. They had the credit of going and returning without becoming demoralized. They at least claimed that credit. The majority of our citizens of that day were Democrats and in favor of Martin Van Buren.

In the spring of 1843, the scarlet fever, in a very malignant form, visited Crown Point. In six weeks there were eight deaths. Until this time, from 1834 to 1843, the inhabitants here had felt no necessity for selecting a public burial ground. In March the old cemetery was opened. Eight burials soon took place. Solon Robinson makes this record: "And while our feelings were yet tender we promised that the ground should be fenced and improved. Perhaps our children, when they lay us there, will make the same promise and keep it as well." Not quite correct as a prediction, but too true in its spirit. None fenced, none improved that spot. A second location was selected for burial purposes. That proved unsatisfactory, and the "children" propose to transfer the remains of their dead to a third location, the Crown Point New Cemetery, already becoming a village of the dead. I have no record to make in this volume in regard to my fellow-citizens of Lake that is to me so saddening as that which I place here, which is, that many of them are so negligent in respect to protecting and keeping sacred the resting-places once set apart for the repose of the dead. I return to the events of the year.

A few sheep had been kept in the county for some years, but this season considerable numbers were brought in from Ohio, and this commenced to be quite a woolgrowing region. The wheat crop of this year was poor. In November the sale of "Canal Lands" lying in this county took place at Delphi.

Two church buildings were erected, the Methodist Church at West Creek, near the Torrey bridge, and the Catholic chapel on Prairie West. Rev. N. Warriner, the resident Baptist pastor, moved to Illinois, and Rev. M. Allman, a local preacher of the Methodist Episcopal church, settled, during the summer, in Crown Point.

The Presbyterian church at Crown Point was this year organized. Elias Bryant and Cyrus M. Mason were elected elders, Rev. Mr. Brown of Valparaiso the acting pastor.

From a diary the following extracts are taken: "September 16th. This morning Mr. Sherman was found dead, killed by a fall from a wagon." Also, same day, "James Farwell died."

"22nd. To-day have attended the funeral of Mr. Adonijah Taylor, who died yesterday."

July 8th is recorded. "Camp meeting commenced."

This meeting was doubtless held on Cedar Point, where, in a beautiful spot on the east side of Cedar Lake, a commodious camp-ground had been arranged. Interesting meetings were here held for a few seasons; and then such meetings, except among the German Methodists west of Cedar Lake, ceased to be, in our borders.

Of the events of 1844 I find little to record on this page. The wheat crop was much injured by rust, many fields were not "worth cutting." The average price of wheat for a period of years, now, did not exceed sixty cents a bushel. The average distance for hauling it was not less than forty miles, the market place being Chicago. The price of other productions was proportionately low. It is, therefore, no wonder that many settlers, who had borrowed money at the land sale at exorbitant rates of interest, failed to make payments, and that so many acres of Lake county lands went into the hands of small capitalists at La Porte. The wonder rather is, that during this period the county improved at all. Many settlers, who had toiled resolutely on their claims, who had stood firmly with their fellow-squatters in asserting a preëmption right, feeling how fully the speculators' grasp was upon them, abandoned their places and sought other homes in the more distant West. There is evidence from the assessment records, and from the lists of grand and petit jurors, and from the records of plaintiffs and defendants in the circuit court, that one half or more of the early settlers passed out of the county during the decade which is included in this chapter.

In the summer of 1845 the wheat crop was very good, the corn crop was good; large quantities of butter were now made for sale, and considerable cheese. The grist mill of Wilson & Saunders, on Deep River, was this year put in operation, and a large mill was erected outside of the county, at Momence.

Two church buildings were commenced at Crown Point, the old Methodist church and the present Presbyterian, neither one being complete until the following year.

On the fourth of May of this year was opened the Cedar Lake Sunday School, a school held continuously for a number of years, back to which may he traced many influences for good, connected with which was the first mission school of the county, held at Mrs. Farwell's over West Creek, and the associations around which scattered groups of the dead and the living will never forget.

Another diary record: July 25th, "Lewis F. Warriner died to-day, at 6.00 p. m., at Dr. Wood's, after an illness of about twelve days." He was a son of Lewis Warriner, who, as representative of the county at Indianapolis, was so fully and favorably known, and was one of the noblest young men in the community or the county. His death was, by those who knew him, deeply deplored. Sometime before the same neighborhood had lost a very promising young man, Franklin Edgerton; and near where the remains of these are resting was buried, May 19th, 1839, the body of a youth, George Taylor; but so sadly has that little mound on the east side of Cedar Lake been neglected that none can now point out these graves. The first settlers on that east side found enclosures or pens of logs marking the Pottawatomie graves in the sand ridge above the northeastern beach. To those some of their boys set fire, and now Indian's burial-place and White man's burial-place there are about alike neglected and forgotten.

In the spring of 1846 Rev. Wm. Townley settled at Crown Point as the first resident pastor of the Presbyterian Church.

The summer of 1846 was one of uncommon calamities. It was very dry and very hot. Sickness was almost universal. There were few to relieve the wants of the sick or to administer medicine. Fields of grain wasted, uncut or unstacked. Much of the wheat raised was badly shrunk; and half the potato crop was destroyed by a disease called the rot. The fall that followed was very favorable for cutting wild grass, and the succeeding winter was mild, so that cattle did not suffer for want of food. Thus often are calamities followed by mercies. The wind is tempered to the shorn lamb.

In 1847 there were in the county seven post-offices. A mail carried twice a week from LaPorte to Joliet supplied Crown Point office. A mail was carried once a week from

West Creek to Valparaiso and from West Creek to City West.

In connection with the mail from LaPorte to Joliet occurred the incident of Solon Robinson's killing the bear. The mail carrier then was John Church, of Prairie West. He came in with the mail one day and reported that a black bear was on the Soc Trail in advance of himself, and that he had, with his horse, actually driven him into the suburbs of the village. Solon Robinson, the post master, in the words of my informant, "hooted at it." Like the Indian on first hearing about railroads and telegraphs, he " poohed " it. Nevertheless, soon after—distributing that mail was not a lengthy task —he took up his trusty rifle and went out. Sure enough, he soon encountered bruin, fired away at him, and soon the villagers learned of the death of their new visitant, the tired black bear.

In this same year, of seven post offices, there were five saw mills in operation, Earle's, Dustin's, and Woods, on Deep River; McCarty's on Cedar Creek, and Foley's where it is now. There were three of earlier date, then dilapidated: Miller's, Dustin's old one, and Walton's, on Turkey Creek. Two others had been commenced, one on Plum, the other on Cedar Creek.

There were then two grist mills, Wood's, which for a time supplied both Lake and Porter counties, and Wilson and Saunders'. George Earle was then erecting the third, the mill at Hobart. There were in the county about fifty frame houses; five church buildings, four of which have been mentioned, and the fifth a Methodist church at Hickory Point; two brick dwelling-houses, the first one erected in 1844; and four or five stores. Two of these were at Crown Point, kept by H. S. Pelton and Wm. Alton ; one at Pleasant Grove, one at Wood's mill, one at St. Johns. There were five resident local Methodist preachers, one circuit preacher, and one Presbyterian minister. A Catholic missionary visited the church on Prairie West. There were two attorneys, six or seven physicians, and fifteen justices of the peace.

There were two, only, open drinking shops in our borders. Crown Point then contained about thirty families, two churches, two stores, one hotel, one small schoolhouse, four physicians, three ministers, the two lawyers, of course, and several mechanics. Its population was about one hundred and fifty. There was then no other place that could well be called a village. In this the log cabins were still standing. I have given the first county officers, those of 1837.

The officers ten years afterwards, or in 1847, were the following:

Henry Wells, Sheriff; H. D. Palmer, Associate Judge; Hervey Ball, Probate Judge; D. K. Pettibone, Clerk; Joseph Jackson, Auditor; Major Allman, Recorder; Wm. C. Farrington, Treasurer; Alex. McDonald, Assessor; S. T. Green, H. S. Pelton, and Robert Wilkinson, Commissioners.

I have passed over, in the order of events, the part taken by our citizens in the Mexican War, and insert it here, as a fitting close for this chapter.

This war, it may be remembered, was declared May 11th, 1846, and the President was authorized to raise fifty thousand volunteers. After the victories of the Rio

Grande, "everywhere the young men of America were now ready," says Mrs. Willard, to push for the "Halls of the Montezumas."

The military spirit of Capt. Joseph P. Smith was at once aroused. The drum and the fife were heard in Crown Point. Volunteers were soon enlisted, and in four counties a company was raised. Some twenty-five or thirty of these were from Lake. The Independent Military Company, which had been organized at Crown Point in 1840–41, under Capt. Smith, which had done military duty on celebration days and acted on other occasions, furnished most of these volunteers.

Their chief officer, Joseph P. Smith, an excellent man of business, had been captain of the Monroe Blues, called, in their day, one of the finest companies in the city of New York. Before the volunteers left, one of the company, Cornelius Cook, died suddenly at Crown Point, in 1846, and was buried with military honors. The gathering of people was very large, as this was the first military funeral in the county. In 1847 these volunteers joined the army in Mexico. They were not in battle. They served as guards. They were six months at Monterey. They returned in the fall of 1848, "all there were left of them." Forty-seven out of the one company died by sickness on the fatal route and amid the burning heats. One who experienced the sufferings of that march and the exposures of that guard duty, our well-known townsman, Capt. Alfred Fry, returned to meet the yet sterner conflict of the War of the Rebellion, and to endure and survive the suffering of the Libby prison. He knows what it means to sustain the honor of his country's flag.

Peace had again spread over a rapidly growing country. The telegraph had been invented, and a few thousand miles of railroad, mostly in Ohio, had been built since 1840. 1849 came and closed over Lake county, slowly and surely growing, her people cultivating the arts of peace, but waiting, as it were, for a new impulse and new facilities to rouse up her sons and to develop more rapidly her resources.

CHAPTER V.

NEW GROWTH. 1850—1859.

As this decade opened, and the year advanced which closed the first half of the Nineteenth Century, a new element of growth, of expansion, and of progress was found among the northern sand hills of Lake. This was the Michigan Central Railroad track, making its way from Detroit, having crossed the peninsula of Michigan, over marsh and sand bank and morass; at length leaving the land and laid on piles in the edge of Lake Michigan; and entering at last the young, growing city, known by the Indian name Chicago. This railroad was completed in 1850.

A station was located on Deep River, south of the Calumet, and named LAKE; the steam whistle was heard for the first time where had been the scream of the eagle and the sharp notes of water fowl; and the people of the county soon ascertained that they were in close connection, by rail and wire communication, with the Atlantic seaboard.

It was the beginning of a new era, the era of western railroads. One track had entered Chicago, if it was by water; and others were soon to follow. Up to this time every bushel of grain, every pound of butter, and cheese, and pork, all the produce of every kind not consumed at home, must reach the Chicago market by the slow transportation of ox and horse teams, and along a road, if road it should be called, where the water would often be, upon the Blue Island Sag, two or three feet in depth, and where it was needful sometimes to "double teams" when each team consisted of two or three yoke of stout oxen. And along the same road and by the same method of conveyance was until then transported every foot of lumber, and pound of nails, and every article of merchandise purchased in the city.

What profitable business farming was in those days may be readily learned by a little calculation. At the least, three days' time would be required for man and team, worth three dollars a day, or nine dollars. Two nights' expenses, on the road, worth or costing some two dollars. A single team might take thirty bushels of wheat. This would bring fifteen dollars; thus leaving four dollars to pay for the raising. Here is an actual and not a supposed case: J. W. Dinwiddie, a better calculator and manager than whom few farmers that knew him would claim to be, undertook farming before the days of steam power in the West. He hauled wheat to Chicago, paid the expenses, and had when he reached home, five dollars less than when he started for the market. He gave up farming, sold out, and went to Illinois to work upon the canal. But in 1852 he was again to be found among the farmers of the county, and the operations he conducted afterwards until the time of his death, show that a new era, even in farming, had commenced.

After the opening of business at Lake Station, a daily hack line was started, running between Crown Point and Lake Station, and passing through Centerville. This soon carried a daily mail. By means of this first railroad some facilities were afforded for sending off produce and bringing in merchandise. A second was soon after constructed—the Michigan Southern.

The Joliet Cut Off was built in 1854, giving us the stations of Ross and Dyer. The latter at once became the most important shipping point in our bounds.

The Fort Wayne railroad was completed in 1858. Hobart began to grow, and Crown Point was within twelve miles of a station, which then became its shipping point. A hack line was established and continued for a short time between Ross and Crown Point; but Hobart remained until 1865 the principal railroad station for the county seat and for the inhabitants of the eastern part of the county. Dyer continued to be an excellent shipping point for produce, and for lumber, and goods, until the same period; and up to the present time ships largely for the inhabitants of St. Johns and Hanover Townships.

Increased facilities for transportation enabled the farming community to realize more for their produce and obtain building materials more easily than in former years, and improved buildings, and fences, and barns, and stables, were the result.

The population of the county during these years continually increased.

In 1850 two brothers, Thomas and William Fisher, becoming residents, started, at South East Grove, a broom factory. This was about the commencement of industrial interests aside from farming. Something in the wagon making business had previously been done at the shop of Major Farwell, in Crown Point. At this broom factory one thousand a week were sometimes made, or fifty thousand a year during the more busy years. The proprietors both raised and bought the broom corn brush which they worked up. In harvest time they sometimes had as many as thirty-two hands at dinner. The brooms sold in Chicago at seventy-five cents a dozen. Work was carried on in the Grove till 1859, when they removed the factory on to the farm now known as the Hews place. Here in one year one hundred and eight acres of broom corn were raised, and then worked up into brooms. This, if not a large business for the East, was something in the new West.

In 1852 Joseph Hack bought out the shop of Major Farwell and commenced, with blacksmithing and wagon-making, which has now become quite an important item in our productive mechanical toil.

In 1850 or '51, James Hunt came into the county from La Porte; in 1852 Marshall M. Barber, and in 1853 Peter Burhans and Samuel Burhans. These all settled near together, south and a little west of Lowell, near the marsh, and being intelligent and enterprising men, were a great addition to the farming interests in that neighborhood.

In 1855 the "New Hampshire Settlement" on Lake Prairie, was commenced. Ten families, natives of New England, soon established themselves south of the center of that beautiful prairie, bringing their Eastern habits with them, organizing, in 1856, an Independent Presbyterian Church, erecting a school-house and sustaining an excellent school, and making that prairie wild, which for long years had blossomed abundantly, bring forth the rich fruits of a Christian civilization. The labors of the first spiritual husbandman among them, Rev. H. Wason, becoming pastor in 1857, were richly rewarded by a spiritual growth and increase; and a new Sabbath School and church-going center was recognized as having sprung vigorously up. Most of the early improvements connected with the founding and growth of Lowell belong to these ten years.

M. A. Halsted, one of the most enterprising men among all our citizens, laid out the town of Lowell, built a saw mill, a grist mill, and with some help from others, a brick meeting house; and was to a great extent the center of all the business life that during these years was growing at that place. The town plat, as recorded, bears date May 13, 1853, and bears the signature Melvin A. Halsted. A brick school-house was soon erected, in which for a time religious meetings were held; and the old religious centers of Pleasant Grove and West Creek were, as to their interests, soon transferred to Lowell, where a Baptist, a Methodist, and a Christian church, began to hold regular meetings.

A tavern, stores, and various shops came along in their natural order, as the supply for a demand created; and a steady town growth commenced. While the northern villages were built up by railroads, Lowell, the only business center in the southern townships, grew up by means of its water power and its men. Among these were Wm. Sigler, a son of an old settler, who engaged in merchandising, and carried on a large trade, and J. Thorn. The two brothers, Henry and Harvey Austin, came during this period, settling on a farm just out of Lowell, and added a new force in intelligence, and social, business, and moral enterprise, to those who were laying the foundation of business and social life. One of them was for many years the energetic and successful superintendent of the Lowell Union Sabbath School. The other returned, after a short residence here, to the State of Michigan. South and West of these two brothers, and near Henry and William Belshaw, and not far from the two Burhans families, Amos Brannon and James Brannon purchased Canal Lands and began farming; the date of entry of the former being 1847, of the latter 1851. These, like the others just named, proved to be solid, prosperous, reliable men, of sterling worth in a community.

In Hobart Township a number of new families found homes; but the growth of the village of Hobart, for some years after the opening of the Fort Wayne Road, was slow. It seemed to lack that class of men who finally came in and helped to make it what it now is.

In North Township Joseph Hess settled in 1850, and built up the village of Hessville, of which he is the principal man and the money maker.

In 1856 A. N. Hart, from Philadelphia, entering a large amount of swamp land, made his home at Dyer. In the second city of the Union he had been a book publisher and business man, and bringing with him capital and business talent, he became to the interests at Dyer a great acquisition. To his capital and energy that place owes no little of its celebrity and growth.

Over West Creek the Klaas family settled in 1850, the pioneer of a number of German families. In 1856 H. C. Beckman, a thorough business man, a successful merchant, late county commissioner, settled in Hanover. The Krinbill's, George and Andrew, with other families from Chicago, settled southwest of Cedar Lake, in the neighborhood of the large Beckley family, in 1850 and 1851. This Beckley family were the founders of the large and prosperous community of German Methodists in Hanover and West Creek Townships. Andrew Krinbill sold goods, sent East and obtained a shoemaker, sent to Chicago for a blacksmith, and commenced a flourishing village. The blacksmith and shoemaker made money and went to farming; and in 1858 Andrew Krinbill came up to the county seat. The village did not grow; but the farming interests flourished and the settlement increased.

In Eagle Creek Township, J. W. Dinwiddie, retiring from business at Crown Point, became again a farmer, and was soon recognized as one of the best calculating, most energetic, and prominent men, not only of the township but of the county. Under his administration as township trustee the three large and well constructed school houses were erected known as Plum Grove, Eagle Creek, and Bryant's. He commenced and carried on actively large farming operations.

At Southeast Grove were other energetic farmers and money makers, some of whom were residents of an earlier date, now making steady improvements and laying foundations for more rapid accumulations in the coming years. Their names will be found recorded in another connection. During these years the range for stock was abundantly large. Thousands of acres of excellent pasture lands invited the herds of cattle. The limit for stock raising was the amount of provender that could be provided for the winter.

In 1853, David Bryant returned again into the county, bought a large farm, and brought in from Ohio a flock of one thousand and sixty sheep in 1854. He now settled in Eagle Creek Township. The two Mitchells, David and Robert, at this time made business visits to the county, buying cattle and preparing the way for the location here of the Mitchell families. These afterwards went into the sheep business extensively. M. A. Halsted, also, and others, now commenced sheep keeping and wool raising. Parts of this region were found to be well adapted to this new pursuit.

In Winfield Township, also, additions were made to the inhabitants. The large Patten family came July 4, 1853; the Tarr families about the same year. The Wise, Hixon, and Sanders families came a few years earlier. James Cooper came in 1852, when soldier land warrants could be bought in the State of New York at the rate of fifty dollars for an eighty-acre warrant. Government land in this township could be found until about 1854.

New men appear also, entering into business and professional life, at Crown Point. James H. Luther, who came in 1849, was occupied during these years in hotel-keeping, merchandising, and farming, until in 1860 he was elected county auditor.

Zerah F. Summers became a resident in 1854, was elected county clerk in 1859, and has since become a grain buyer and leading business man.

Dr. A. J. Pratt, from Michigan, went into partnership with Dr. Farrington in 1854, and after the death of the latter, entered upon an extensive practice, rapidly gaining property and position. Dr. John Higgins, who graduated at a medical college in 1846, and had already located in Crown Point, was now pressing onward along the road to success. Dr. Brownell, from the state of New York, located in town in 1854. In 1856, still continuing to practice medicine, he removed to a farm not far from Plum Grove.

In 1852 was formed the firm of Turner & Cramer; David Turner being the son of an old resident in Porter and Lake, and E. M. Cramer being a new man in the county, having moved from the State of New York, and living for a short time on a farm at South East Grove. This firm did, for these years, a large business, but was dissolved before this decade closed, E. M. Cramer entering into public and political life and becoming one of the most popular men in the county, holding for two terms the office of county treasurer.

In 1854 Frederick Foster, with his large family of four sons and four daughters and a son-in-law, removing from Pennsylvania, became a resident on a part of what is now Railroad Addition, purchasing his farm for fifteen dollars an acre. In the same year came Wm. Blowers and family; and in February, 1855, the Sears family arrived at Crown Point.

Other improvements of this period and names of families becoming residents will be found in the more particular notice of Crown Point.

Into all parts of the county some new men came, Germans from the Old World and Americans from the East, mature men seeking fields for enterprise, and young families commencing life seeking for homes where they might grow up with the growth of the new region. This was the period of our most rapid increase in population, as will be shown by the figures from the census reports. I am not able to name even each prominent man that became during these ten years a citizen; much more will it be impossible for me to name them all.

The railroads, the business men, the capital, the new forms of industry, mark this as emphatically a period of NEW GROWTH.

There is a transaction belonging to the history of this county, in common with that of other counties in Indiana, which an impartial and faithful historian can hardly pass over in silence. It belongs to this decade and may be called the *Swamp Land Speculation*. The kind of notice which justice here demands has been a matter of grave consideration.

The United States donated to the State of Indiana certain portions of government lands within its borders, to be selected in a certain way, which took the name of Swamp Lands. The Legislature passed an act, in May, 1852, to regulate the sale of these lands and provide for draining and reclaiming them according to the condition of the grant.

Quite a quantity of land remained unentered ten years after the land sale at La Porte. This was taken out of market in the different counties until the lands had been selected which were to be drained, reclaimed, and sold. There were selected in this county as such swamp land some 180 sections. This, at the minimum price of one dollar and a quarter an acre, would amount to $144,000. Any portion of this amount not used in the necessary expenses connected with draining these wet lands was to become part of the common school fund of the State. The county auditors and treasurers were the authorized agents on the part of the State for selling these lands. A commissioner of swamp lands for each county was appointed by the governor, and the commissioner appointed and employed an engineer.

It became known to the Legislature of the State that the funds arising from the sale of these lands were supposed to be improperly used, and they appointed a swamp land committee of investigation. From the printed report of this committee, made to the governor of Indiana, two thousand copies of which were ordered to be printed, the following statements and extracts are taken. *Copies of this report are scarce in this county. Those sent here disappeared.*

This committee, after making several statements, say:

"The different laws in relation to the expenditure of the swamp land fund are very imperfect, giving many opportunities for dishonest men to prey upon the fund with impunity—these opportunities seem to have been well improved." After stating some of these imperfections they continue, "It seems that an opportunity to speculate thus opened was early discovered by a number of very prominent men, and large combinations formed to effect that object, and when a swamp land commissioner refused to be used as an instrument in their hands to carry out their views, they were potent in affecting his removal and in securing the appointment of one who would act in accordance with their wishes." Non-political readers might well exclaim, after hearing these statements, What sort of legislators were these to frame laws that offered such temptations! And what sort of an *executive* that thus allowed removals and made appointments! The committee continued, "By this process, the fund in many of the counties * * * was exhausted, and in some cases largely overdrawn, and very little good effected by ditching." The committee visited several counties to ascertain facts. In reference to one county, especially, they say: "These investigations show frauds to an extent that seems to preclude the idea that honesty had any part in these transactions." Under "Lake county," they say: "The operations in this county have been quite extensive. The first commissioner appointed was S. P. Smith. There is no evidence to raise a doubt as to the correctness of his administration." The S. here is evidently a misprint for J., as the proper name of the treasurer is evidently also a misprint. In regard to the third commissioner, Henry Wells, they say: "No evidence was obtained to implicate him in any improper transaction." In regard to the fourth they say: "Under his administration the committee think extensive frauds were perpetrated." In regard to one individual they say: "These two sums thus obtained, amounting to seven thousand three hundred and nine dollars and sixty-five cents can undoubtedly be recieved * * * if properly prosecuted. * * How many similar transactions were had with other parties, is not known. It is understood that all the money recovered for swamp lands was retained in the hands of the county treasurer, and not paid over to the State treasurer. * * *."

An example may be presented of the class of transactions referred to above, a few statements being given to make its features intelligible.

"The commissioner and engineer were required to locate and lay out ditches, to make contracts, &c. The engineer was not required by law to keep a record of his estimates, nor to make certificates of estimates from which the commissioner should issue ditching certificates. Hence there was no check kept by the engineer upon the arrears of those ditching certificates issued by the commissioner. Nor does the law require the commissioner to keep a record of the ditching certificates issued by him, and the committee were unable to find in any case a record of those certificates."

The example selected presents a case that may now be readily understood. A contractor assigned a blank ditching certificate to another person who filled it up, or had it filled, "in the sum of two thousand, six hundred and nine dollars and sixty-five cents," and obtained and retained the money, other certificates being issued to the contractor for all the work he had done; thus, in the language of the committee, "fraudently taking from the Swamp Land Fund the sum of two thousand, six hundred and nine dollars and sixty-five cents."

The committee even found certificates with forged signatures on which money was drawn. Also they found certificates issued and money paid when no work had been done. They say in regard to two individuals, whom they name, that they believe " from the written testimony and testimony not recorded * * * a judgment could now be obtained * * * * for a sum not less than twenty thousand dollars, * * *." The whole amount of money taken away from this fund, the committee had no means at hand, in this county, for summing up. The difference between the amount actually paid for work done and the whole amount for which these lands sold would probably be that sum.

I have given no names of those implicated by that committee in this transaction. Some, if not all of them, are still residents of this county, and I see no good to be accomplished by transmitting their names to posterity in this connection. The names of two commissioners, J. P. Smith and Henry Wells, two of the early settlers, it is a pleasure to me to be able to record as untarnished in respect to the Swamp Land speculations.

The lessons for the present and the future are obvious. Send both capable and honest men to the Legislature. Elect to office and secure for official appointments men of sterling integrity. And there is an old petition of which we might all do well to make more frequent use; "Lead us not into temptation." The citizens of the county in the present have doubtless the right, the official report of the Investigating Committee being authority, to hold some of their public men responsible for pocketing a large amount of money. And the citizens of the future will have the right to feel that incompetent or unfaithful legislators placed temptations before men in public life which resulted in defrauding the county of valuable drainage probably up to the amount of one hundred thousand dollars.

Those conversant with the facts will sustain the assertion that quite probably $100,000, during those few years of fraudulent or speculative management, passed into the pockets of a few of our public men. And the amount which beyond question passed into the hands of corrupt officials in high position at Indianapolis was by no means small. How large there is no data here on which to base a conjecture. Let it be repeated that, of this transaction, the lessons are obvious.

The grant of lands to the Wabash Canal has been already mentioned. The entries of the land seem to have extended from 1843 to 1856, the certificate of "lands sold in Lake county at the Canal Land Office," at Terre Haute, being dated February, 1857.

The amount certified to as having been thus sold is some sixty sections. It thus appears that about two hundred and fifty square miles or sections, one half the area of the county, were donated by the United States Government for the purpose of internal improvements in Indiana. If thus liberal in other counties and in other States, quite an amount of the public fund would be definitely appropriated. Whether it be wise in general to make such disposition of the public domain, is a question for political economists and statesmen.

CHAPTER VI.

OUR WAR RECORD AND PROGRESS. 1860—1869.

> " Higher, higher, let us climb,
> Up the mount of glory ;
> That our names may live through time,
> In our country's story :
> Happy, when her welware calls,
> He who conquers, he who falls."

Amid the political changes and excitements which marked in this land the sixth decade of the nineteenth century, this county, formerly Democratic, became strongly Republican, giving year by year those decided majorities which secured to Schuyler Colfax the representative of this district, his seat in Congress, and entering heartily, in 1860, into the campaign which resulted in the election of Abraham Lincoln. When, therefore, that shot was fired, at twenty minutes past four o'clock on the morning of April 12, 1861, against the granite wall of Fort Sumter, which inaugurated the great Civil War in America; and when the tidings was flashed along the wires that Fort Sumpter had actually surrendered to the rebels, and that, on the historic 19th of April, blood was shed in the streets of Baltimore ; and when the President's call for volunteers was heard ; it was to be expected that the loyal citizens of Lake would thrill in that intense wave of excitement that poured over the North, and press forward at once for marching orders, that they might hasten to the scene of conflict.

The entire population of the county in 1860 was 9,145. The number of families was about 1,800. So many of our young men went into Illinois regiments that the whole number of our citizens enlisting cannot be determined. So far as can be ascertained, as many as one thousand men from these eighteen hundred families entered the Union army.

They were thus distributed: In the Ninth Indiana regiment, called, from the severe battles through which it passed and its own war record, "the Bloody Ninth," were about seventy.

In the Twentieth Regiment were one hundred, Company B.

In the Seventy-third, one hundred, Company A.

In the Ninety-ninth, one hundred, Company A.

In the One Hundred and Twenty-eighth, twenty.

In the One Hundred and Fifty-first, eighty.

In the One Hundred and Fifty-fifth, about twenty.

In the Fifth Cavalry were about twenty-five.

In the Seventh, perhaps thirty.

In the Twelfth Cavalry, Edward Anderson, Colonel, we were represented by Company G.

There were also some thirty in one Indiana battery, and several in other batteries. Some of our young men enlisted in the regiments of other States, about three hundred enlisting in the State of Illinois.

The Indiana regiments acquired an honorable reputation on the field of battle, and their record belongs to the historic records of the State and of the Union.

The Ninth and the Twentieth gained special distinction on the various bloody fields where their flags waved in triumph. The Ninth was in battle at Shiloh, Perryville, Danville, Wild Cat Mountain, Chickamauga, Lookout Mountain, and Mission Ridge. It was also at Atlanta and in various connected engagements, and in the battles at Columbia and at Nashville.

The Twentieth went to Hatteras Inlet, to Fortress Monroe, aided in the capture of Norfolk, and joined the Army of the Potomac. Its various fortunes and conflicts as a part of this great army need not here be detailed. It finally reached Gettysburg, July 2, 1863, where, says Venable, "the greatest and most important battle of the whole war was fought." He adds, "The fury of the third day's engagement is indescribable. Whole brigades were almost utterly destroyed. The slope of Cemetery Hill, upon which the hardest struggle occurred, was literally heaped with the slain." Here the Twentieth, says our Adjutant General, "lost its commanding officer, Col. John Wheeler, and 152 men and officers killed and wounded." Among those killed were besides Col. Wheeler of Crown Point, two others of our soldier boys, George W. Edgerton and J. Richmond. The regiment was afterwards at New York City on guard duty, and then at the battle of the Wilderness, and at other noted engagements.

The Seventy-third Regiment was engaged in Kentucky, Tennessee and Alabama, in various battles, losing their commanding officer, Col. Gilbert Hathaway, formerly a lawyer at our bar, at Blount's farm, Alabama, and were on the next day, May 3, 1863, all captured at Cedar Bluffs.

The men were soon exchanged, but the officers were kept in a long imprisonment.

As an illustration of what our imprisoned officers experienced, I give the narrative of Captain Alfred Fry, of the Seventy-Third :*

NARRATIVE.

Alfred Fry enlisted as a private soldier July 26, 1862. and was mustered into the service of the U. S. at South Bend, August 16, as Orderly Sergeant of Company A, Seventy-third Regiment Indiana Volunteers. Proceeded to Lexington, via Louisville, Sept. 1st, was commissioned Second Lieutenant of Company A. The defeat of the Union forces at Richmond, Kentucky, obliged the regiment to leave Lexington and retire to Louisville, where he was ordered to report at the headquarters of Gen. Ward for duty as Brigade Commissary, which position he held until the reorganization of the army under Gen. Buell. On the first of October the regiment was assigned to the Twentieth Brigade, Sixth Division of Buell's Army, and commenced the pursuit of Bragg. Entered Nashville Nov. 26.

Dec. 2, 1862, he was commissioned as First Lieutenant, and engaged in the battle of Stone River. Was under fire for six days. Lost here Edward Welch, of Winfield Township, the first man killed in the regiment.

On the 19th of Jan., '63, Lieut. Fry was recommended by Col. Hathaway to Gov. Morton, and was commissioned as captain of Company A. April 10, '63, the regiment

---

*NOTE.—I have changed the form of the narrative furnished to me, from the first to the third person, and have made slight alterations in some expressions; but the substance remains the same. As the account of a well-known citizen who had a personal experience of the horrors of Libby Prison, I have felt it proper to place it on permanent record.

was assigned to Col. Streight's brigade. April 30 this brigade, only 1500 strong, was attacked by 4000 rebels under Gens. Forrest and Roddy, while on its march to perform duty. The enemy were repulsed and the brigade pushed on. Were attacked again in the evening at Crooked Creek. May 2d, again attacked at Blount's farm, Alabama. The 73d bore the brunt of this fight, and here the gallant Col. Hathaway fell, mortally wounded, while at the head of the troops and cheering on his men.

May 3d, being out of ammunition, exhausted by five days incessant marching and skirmishing, and surrounded by superior forces, the brigade surrendered on most honorable conditions, which were afterwards basely violated. The men were soon forwarded north and exchanged. The officers were kept in close confinement nearly two years. When they surrendered they were to be paroled and sent through our lines, but they were sent to Richmond, Virginia, and then on the 16th of May they entered the famous Libby Prison. Their paroles had been taken from them, and they had been told that they were not recognized as belonging to the army, but were highway robbers, bridge burners, negro stealers, and that they would be turned over to the civil authorities of Alabama, and be tried and *hung*. On their arrival at Libby they were searched, their greenbacks taken away and likewise their blankets, and up three flights of stairs they were placed in a room one hundred and twenty-five feet by fifty. Here Captain Fry found a rusty tin plate and a rheumatic knife and fork as instruments for house-keeping, and prepared little sacks for holding salt, sugar, pepper, and rice. These were not very well filled. The rations were three-fourths of a pound of coarse corn bread, one gill of rice, half a pound of beef, and a very little salt.

The vermin were the most revolting feature of the prison. No amount of personal cleanliness could guard against the insatiate lice, and only by examining their clothing and destroying them once or twice a day could these hideous creatures be kept from swarming on the persons of the prisoners. For other occupation during the long evenings the prisoners would sing the Star Spangled Banner, Old Hundaed, and Old John Brown. In this dreary abode Captain Fry remained a year, leaving Libby, in company with others, May 7, '64, for Danville. May 12th they left Danville. Arrived May 17th at Macon, Georgia, and were marched into the prison-pen, an area of some two acres, surrounded by a stockade fence fifteen feet high. July 27th were transferred to Charleston, South Carolina, and placed in the jail-yard under fire of the Union guns on Morris' Island. Here the ground was literally covered with vermin. The prisoners were without shelter. They were brought there to save the city from the shells of the Union batteries. October 5th they were sent to Columbia, and arrived in the midst of a terrific rain storm. The prisoners were compelled to leave the cars and to pass the night in an open field, without food, blankets, tents, at the mercy of the elements, and four pieces of artillery trained upon the ground they occupied. When the storm ceased they were removed two miles to another open field, and here, without even the shelter of a tree or bush, endured the scorching sunshine that followed the storm. The rations here, to last five days, were five quarts of very coarse corn meal, one quart of sorghum, two tablespoonfuls of coarse salt, two tablespoonfuls of rice.

A wild hog chanced to pass the guard line. As soon as he had fairly entered, a general advance was made, and he was captured. One seized a leg, another an ear, others twisted their bony fingers into the bristles and closed hands, eyes, and teeth, as if for a death struggle. Every man clung to the part he first seized until it was cut off and securely lodged in the kettle for supper. Between four and five hundred half-starved men were soon devouring him. This stray hog furnished the only meat tasted at Columbia, and for this no thanks were returned to the rebels.

February 14th, 1865, they were removed to Charlotte, were paroled, sent to Wilmington, and there, March 1st, entered once more the Union lines. Captain Fry returned to Crown Point and remained with his family from March 13th till April 14th, when he reported for duty at Columbus, Ohio, remained here a month, was exchanged, and returned to his company at Larkinsville, Alabama, and on the 4th of July, 1865, arrived at Indianapolis, where the regiment was finally discharged, officers and men returning to their homes.

The Twelfth Cavalry consisted of twelve companies, six only mounted, recruited in the fall and winter of 1863, eight being rendezvoused at Michigan City and four at Kendallville. The regimental organization was completed at Kendallville, and in May, 1864, the regiment left that place and proceded to Nashville. Remaining in a camp of instruction about three weeks, the regiment left for Huntsville May 29. Here, and over quite a territory, they performed guard duty, and were engaged in fighting guerrillas and " bushwackers," a large number of the regiment being killed or wounded in these engagements and skirmishes. After remaining about a month at Huntsville, the headquarters were removed to Brownsborough, where they remained until the 15th of September, when the regiment was ordered to Tallahassee. Here they watched the movements of the rebel General Forrest and had several skirmishes with bands of his men and with guerrillas. On the 26th of November they proceeded to Murfreesboro and took part in the battle of Wilkinson's Pike and Overall's Creek, and in December went into winter quarters at Nashville. February 11, 1865, the regiment started for New Orleans, stopped at Vicksburg, and reached New Orleans March 12. They proceeded to Mobile Bay, found occupation there and in Florida, and after the fall of Mobile, reporting to Major General Grierson, April 17th, they took part in a raid of over eight hundred miles into Georgia, and across Alabama to Columbus, Mississippi, arriving there May 20. Making some other changes, doing guard duty, protecting government cotton, and other property, the regiment was mustered out of the service at Vicksburg, November 10, 1865, and returned to Indiana. It was paid off and its members discharged November 22.

"The regiment was highly and specially complimented by Major General Grierson, in a letter to Governor

Morton, for its gallant conduct and military discipline."
Vol. III., page 268, Adjutant General's Report.

The following is an extract from a letter written by one of the officers of Company G, to his father, who then resided in Hanover township, and was taking an active interest in the events and issues of the war. It bears date June 11, 1865.

Camp near Columbus, Miss. " I see the *Register* thinks the Twelfth has not amounted to much in the service. I wont say how that may be, but we have certainly been on duty enough. Commanders of posts and brigades with which we have been connected have certainly called on us enough. Last summer the men were often on duty every other twenty-four hours for weeks at a time, and men have often been obliged to stand guard for three or four days at a time. People at a distance, or those who have to depend on *talk* for their information, seldom get it very correct. I suppose the Twelfth is as well disciplined as the average of cavalry regiments. Col. Karge, Second New Jersey, who has commanded different brigades ever since the war commenced, said that the Twelfth Indiana was the best regiment he ever commanded. So also said a steamboat captain, that the Twelfth had the finest, most gentlemanly officers and men of any regiment he ever saw. This is rather more praise than we deserve, but then the men are what their surroundings make them, and if we had been sent out on a campaign at first we might have won a different name. In short, I don't believe we are any better or worse than any one else."

That the Twelfth Cavalry gained no distinguished war

honors is doubtless true; but having no opportunity to engage in any noted battle, it is not just to infer that its arduous services were useless, or that its officers and men would not have borne themselves gallantly in fight.

Hanover township lost, out of Company G, two of its promising and energetic young men, sons and brothers whom their families knew not how to give up, CHARLES BALL, 2d Lieutenant, and STILLMAN A. ROBBINS; and Tinkonville lost one of its leading citizens, the son of an old settler, MILES F. MCCARTY.

The following extract from a letter, written by a member of the company to the author of this record, will be of interest to at least one circle of relatives and friends:

"I did not, in my former letter, say anything about FRANKLIN MCCARTY's death. He died the day after I got to Nashville"—May 27, 1864—"but I did not know he was dangerously ill till the night he died. Some one told Will Scrietchfield that he was not expected to live, about dark, and then he could not go. We were camped, by the way, some three miles from Nashville. Enlisted men are not entitled to receive the countersign which enables them to pass guards after dark, but, as it is generally known to me from my connection with the adjutant, I went down; but he was already dead. I think he never enjoyed himself very well in the company, and felt that he was not placed in a position that his age and talents warranted."

That he had reason thus to feel I doubt not; for, having known him well for many years, I am sure he had capabilities which favorable circumstances would have, rapidly developed. As he was one of a circle of boys living around Cedar Lake, in the early days, so many of whom are dead or scattered now, it is not strange that those pleasant associations of youth should make me linger here on this record. And, alas! he who wrote those lines quoted above, before the regiment returned to the West, permitting its members to enjoy the repose and comforts of their quiet homes, himself fell a victim to disease, and returned to Cedar Lake to die, where his hopes of life had so brightly budded.

While some fell, and some must ever fall—well has one said, "There is seldom a line of glory written upon earth's surface, but a line of suffering runs parallel with it; and he who reads the lustrous syllables of the one and stoops not to decipher the worn, and dimmed, and tear-stained inscriptions of the other, gets the least half of what even earth has to give;"—while some fell and were wept for in secret, others returned home with the scars of war, sharers in the glory of a just success, and are now filling positions of profit and honor. Three returned soldiers are this year candidates for three of our highest offices, John Brown, for Treasurer; John Donch, for Sheriff, and John M. Dwyer, for Recorder. Others are leading business men in our towns, and others still are the owners and the tillers of the soil. But let us return to the decade of the war.

The pulpits of Crown Point, as elsewhere in the West, patriotic but not political, were thoroughly on the side of the Union. Services were held from time to time appropriate to the several occasions of joy and sorrow, of hopes and of fears; fasts and thanksgivings were observed; and earnest words of religious teaching and patriotic feeling were uttered. After the fall of Vicksburg, and the capture of Fortress Monroe, in 1863, the President recommended the observance of a day of Thanksgiving. The following hymn, written by one of the pastors in town, was sung at Crown Point, during the services of that day, September 11, 1863:

THANKSGIVING HYMN.

God of our fathers, now to thee,
   Our grateful homage we would pay;
Thou leadest on the bond, the free;
   Help us to praise thy might to-day.

Thou lovest right, thou hatest wrong;
   By thee the bondmen's chains are riven;
Beleagured town and fortress strong,
   Into our hands by thee are given.

For this we praise thy matchless power,
   For this we lift our hearts to thee;
In each exultant, joyous hour,
   Do thou our God and Fortress be.

We recognize thy powerful hand;
   We bow before thy holy might;
Oh be thou gracious to our land,
   Oh bring us forth to noon-tide light.

When at length the war cloud passed, and in the spring of 1865 the rebel armies surrendered, the bronzed and war-worn veterans hastened back to their peaceful homes. But many a mother's eyes were dim with tears, the hearts of many a wife and maiden throbbed with anguish, as the "boys in blue" returned; for their own sons, and husbands, and brothers, had given their lives to maintain our national existence. Nobly did many of the families of Lake resign their loved ones to the grandness of the cause that had called them forth to dare, and do, and die; but they nevertheless felt that some of their choicest treasures had perished in the terrible conflict.

Of our one thousand men, how many fell on the red fields of blood, and died in camp and hospital, cannot now be ascertained. The names of some who perilled life for their country's welfare, and lost their lives on account of the Great Rebellion, are here recorded. There is an old saying: *Dulce et decorum est pro patria mori.* "It is pleasant and noble to die for one's country." In behalf of each one of these, his friends may say,—To perpetuate this Union of States he died.

From the Roll of Honor, of Indiana Volunteers, as found in Vol. VIII, of the Adjutant General's Report, the following list is made out:

TWELFTH CAVALRY—COMPANY G.

Names.	Where Dying.	When.
Charles Ball,	At home,	September 12, 1865
Henry Brockman,	New Orleans,	April 5, 1865
Charls Crothers,	Kendallville,	March 17, 1864
Sidney W. Chapman,	New Orleans,	April 18, 1865
Jacob Deeter,	Vicksburg,	January 4, 1865
R. L. Fuller,	At home,	October 27, 1864
Ephraim E. Goff,	Starkville,	August 16, 1865
Wm. Harland,	Nashville,	January 8, 1865
M. Hoopendall,	Huntsville,	June 22, 1864
Fred. Kahle,	Kendallville,	April 13, 1864
F. S. Miller,	At home,	———
Albert Moore,	Kendallville,	April 3, 1864
M. F. McCarty,	Nashville,	May 27, 1864
A. McMillen,	Michigan City,	February 3, 1864
Wm. M. Pringle,	Nashville,	November 4, 1864

S. A. Robbins,	Huntsville,	July 18, 1864
Wm. Stubby,	At home,	May 15, 1864
Wm. Stinkle,	Nashville,	February 1, 1865
Ezra Wedge,	At home,	February 3, 1864

TWENTIETH REGIMENT—COMPANY B.

Col. John Wheeler,	Gettysburg,	July 2, 1863
George W. Edgerton,	Gettysburg,	July 2, 1863
Horace Fuller,	Wilderness,	May 5, 1864
Lawrence Frantz,	Spootsylvania,	May 12, 1864
John Griesell,	David Island,	August 16, 1862
M. Hafey,	Pittsburg,	
C. Hazworth,		May 26, 1863
Wm. Johnson,	Petersburg,	June 18, 1864
Albert Kale,	Camp Hampton,	Dec. 17, 1861
Wm. Mutchler,	Camp Smith,	April 25, 1862
P. Mutchler,	Washington,	July 15, 1862
James Merrill,	Wilderness,	May 5, 1864
S. Pangburn,	Andersonville,	November 6, 1864
C. Potter,		
D. Pinckerton,		
J. Richmond,	Gettysburg,	July 2, 1863
John F. Torr,	Washington,	November 24, 1862
Isaac Williams,		July 5, 1863
Charles Winters,	City Point,	June 19, 1864

SEVENTY-THIRD REGIMENT—COMPANY A.

Lewis Atkins,	Nashville,	November 22, 1862
Eli Atwood,	Nashville,	November 29, 1862
John Childers,	Nashville,	December 3, 1862
John H. Earley,	Stone River,	December 31, 1862
R. W. Fuller,	Indianapolis,	August 2, 1863
Wm. Frazier,	Nashville,	December 15, 1862
J. M. Fuller,	Gallatin,	January 29, 1863
M. Graves,	Nashville,	December 16, 1862
T. W. Loving,	Nashville,	September 30, 1863

A. Lamphier,	Nashville,	January 7, 1863
L. Morris,	Nashville,	April 30, 1863
I. W. Moore,	Gallatin,	December 29, 1862
John Maxwell,	Scottsville,	November 9, 1862
Albert Nichols,	Nashville,	December 1, 1862
James Roney,	Nashville,	February 8, 1863
C. Van Burg,	Bowling Green,	December 23, 1862
M. Vincent,	Gallatin,	January 8, 1863
E. Woods,	Nashville,	November 29, 1862
E. Welch,	Stone River,	December 31, 1862
S. White,	Blunt's Farm,	May 2, 1863

NINETY-NINTH REGIMENT—COMPANY A.

D. F. Sawyer,	—— ——	February 12, 1863
O. E. Atkins,	Nickajack,	July 6, 1864
D. T. Burnham,	——————	August 21, 1864
J. Bartholomew,	Andersonville,	August 22, 1864
J. D. Clingham,	Huntsville,	July 11, 1864
H. A. Case,	La Grange,	March 10, 1863
James Foster,	Atlanta,	July 22, 1864
James Horton,	Atlanta,	July 22, 1864
H. H. Haskins,	Andersonville,	October 20, 1864
R. T. Harris,	La Grange,	March 11, 1863
John Lorey,	Black River,	September 21, 1863
Adam Mock,	Black River,	September 11, 1863
N. Newman,	Black River,	August 4, 1863
T. C. Pinnel,	La Grange,	February 7, 1863
Corydon Pierce,	Washington,	April, 1863
Albert Robbins,	——————	August 6, 1864
J. Schmidt,	Indianapolis,	July 28, 1863
J. Stickleman,	——————	September 23, 1864
A. Vandervert,	——————	March 19, 1863
M. Winand,	At home,	December 11, 1864

It seems singular that the four companies should have lost almost the same number of men. Company G, and

Company B, nineteen each; and the two A companies each twenty. Taking twenty per cent. as the general average, our whole loss would be two hundred men.

Terrible was that necessity that caused throughout the North the loss of so many young and valuable lives; and that appeal to arms on the part of the South, for the settlement of a long dispute, must be held responsible for a large amount of life-blood and treasure. We may well hope that the whole nation has been sufficiently taught not to kindle again the flames of fraternal strife. Multitudes of this generation, both North and South, will carry with them to their graves the dark shadows which passed over their souls, in those fearful years of the life struggles of a great nation, as loved ones so untimely fell; and, of these, young and loyal Lake may well claim to have her full share. Some proper estimate here ought to be placed on the value of a united and not a dissevered nation.

Although for four years of this decade the absorbing interest was the war, and the withdrawing of a thousand men from our industrial pursuits was at times sorely felt, yet prices advanced enormously, and all kinds of farm products found a ready and remunerative sale, and improvements and increase of inhabitants still went forward. In 1861 corn sold for seventeen cents a bushel, and a dull market. Before the close of the war, in 1864, corn sold for ninety cents a bushel at Dyer Station. Pork, which had also been low, as well as all other agricultural productions, advanced to sixteen dollars a hundred weight, and most other products in proportion. "Greenbacks" were issued by the Government, bounties and quarterly payments were sent home by the soldiers, and money became plenty.

Many good frame buildings were erected during the last ten years; but about 1860 commenced an era of a far better class of buildings. Henry Dittmers, who bought, in 1859, that farm on Cedar Lake, where the Ball family had for twenty-two years resided, erected one of the first of these in 1860. He bought common lumber in Chicago for seven dollars a thousand, and laid out in a house and barns some four thousand dollars. His example was followed by many others. Most of the best buildings now in the county, and especially of those in the towns and villages, have been erected since 1860.

In 1865 a new impulse was given to Crown Point, and to all the southern portion of the county, by the completion of the Cincinnati Air Line Railroad, known afterward as the Great Eastern, and now called Pittsburg, Cincinnati & St. Louis Railway. This road, passing through Crown Point, started it at once into new life. Railroad Addition was laid out and added to the town; a depot building was erected, grain houses were built, and a western railroad growth commenced.

In the same year (1865) an educational enterprise was started which accomplished something for the intellectual progress of the community. Block No. 1 in Rail Road Addition was obtained, a building was soon completed at a cost—building and furniture—of some $5,300, and in January, 1866, the building was occupied for school purposes. I place on record here, as a memento of what it was designed to be and was, its last advertisement, as published in the CASTALIAN, of March, 1870.

CROWN POINT INSTITUTE.

FOUNDERS

CROWN POINT INSTITUTE EDUCATIONAL COMPANY, ORGANIZED MAY 31, 1865.

Designed to furnish Collegiate Instruction for young ladies and young men, with a graduating course for the former, in

I.—Languages,
II.—Physical Sciences,
III.—Mathematics,

IV.—Philosophy,
V.—Belles-Lettres,
VI.—Ornamental Branches.

Preparatory and Primary Departments were also added. Instruction commenced September 11, 1865.

T. H. BALL, PROPRIETOR AND TRUSTEE.

LOCATION.

Crown Point is located on the Chicago, Columbus and Indiana Central Railroad, forty miles from Chicago, in Lake County, Indiana. It is noted for the healthfulness and beauty of its location. It is a county seat.

THE INSTITUTE.

Is now in its Fifth Year. The Fourth Term will commence April 25, 1870. Ten weeks in each Term—Four terms in a year. Pleasant rooms are furnished for self-boarders.

RATES OF TUITION, ETC., PER TERM, PAYABLE IN ADVANCE.

Primary Department............$3.00
Intermediate 4.00
Preparatory 5.00
Collegiate 6.00
Janitor's fees..................... .50
Room Rent (self-boarders)........ 2.50
Drawing Lessons 2.00
Painting, Water Colors........... 4.00

Bookkeeping $2.00
Music—Lessons and use of Instrument—
    Melodeon 8.00
    Piano 10.00
Board—washing and lights excluded 30.00
Or, per week 3.00

VACATIONS.

At Christmas, one week; in April, one week; Summer vacation, ten weeks.

RECREATIONS.

Besides the daily exercises and recreation, excursions sometimes to Cedar Lake, a beautiful sheet of water, distant five miles, and a few sleigh rides in the winter.

COURSE OF STUDY.

PRIMARY.

Spelling,
Reading,

Writing,
Geography.

Mental Arithmetic,
Readers, 1st, 2d, 3d & 4th.

INTERMEDIATE.

The same, adding Practical Arithmetic and Fifth Reader.

PREPARATORY.

Spelling,
Sixth Reader,
Intellectual Arithmetic,

Practical Arithmetic,
Geography,
English Grammar,

Algebra,
Latin Grammar, and
Reader.

COLLEGIATE.
YOUNG LADIES' COURSE.

FIRST YEAR—JUNIOR CLASS.

English Analysis and Scanning, Physical Geography, Algebra,	Physiology, History of the United States,	Composition and Rhetoric, Cæsar, Botany.

SECOND YEAR—MIDDLE CLASS.

Ancient Geography, History of England, Virgil,	Geometry, Natural Philosophy, Trigonometry,	Moral Science, Zoology, Cicero's Orations.

THIRD YEAR—SENIOR CLASS.

Political Economy, Horace, Logic, Mental Philosophy,	Chemistry, Ancient History, Elements of Criticism, Astronomy,	Modern History, Mineralogy and Geology, Evidences of Christianity. Butler's Analogy.

OPTIONAL IN THE COURSE, AND NOT NAMED ABOVE.

Bookkeeping, Drawing, Painting, Greek, German, Vocal and Instrumental Music, Sallust, Livy and Tacitus.

Rhetorical Exercises, Recitations and Compositions required in each department.

After taking out the musical instruments and some furniture, its academic work having been accomplished, the Institute property was sold, August 1, 1871, to the town of Crown Point for the sum of $3,600. Thus, like the Institute at Valparaiso, like the Female Institute at Indianapolis, like some other such private enterprises, it passed into the hands of the public, the prevailing disposition now in Indiana being to sustain only public graded and district schools. The following statements were published in the *Standard*, of Chicago, in July, 1872, which also, as a condensed view of things accomplished in the educational line, I place among these records.

The communication from which the extract is taken was signed by the former Principal of the Institute. After stating its origin and reason for its transfer to other hands the article proceeds:

"It educated, more or less, a few hundred students, who are now, so far as I know, in Nova Scotia, New

York, Kentucky, Virginia, Alabama, Indiana, Illinois, Kansas, Missouri, Iowa, and in the far West. Quite a number have engaged in teaching. Some are practicing law and medicine, some are clerks and in business, some are farmers and mechanics. One only is preparing for the ministry. Most of the young ladies have married, and a number of the young men. Some of the young ladies became leaders of church-music. All who have gone into life seem to be active and useful. Three of the young ladies have/ died. Seventeen of the students I baptized. Most of them received religious instruction. During one of the years there were some sixty boarders. Other years, not quite so many. The students were from the families of Baptists, Methodists, Presbyterians, Spiritualists, Lutherans, Catholics, and Jews.

"If labor for the mind and heart is profitable, if he who trains for activity and usefulness young minds achieves success, then I doubt not that when the involved radical of my strange earthly life is solved, the unknown quantities representing six years of varied labor here will come out in integers of determinate and real value. The equation is one which no mathematician at present can solve, although he perceives entering into it a minus one thousand. To sell was, for myself, financially, needful; for the cause of education it was a retrograde movement. There are those whose real interests should have perpetuated such a school as a living power for years yet to come."

The Institute also published a paper, the first literary and educational paper in the county, at first called the PIERIAN, and afterward its name was changed to CAS-

TALIAN. The educated reader will not need to be informed that these both are classic names. This periodical became an eight-page monthly, of good size and neat appearance. Of its literary character, Prof. Harkness, of Brown University, and others in the East, spoke very favorably; and the *Sun Beam*, in its Literary Review, naming a number of exchanges, said, "THE CASTALIAN, Crown Point, Ind., and *The Mount Auburn Index*, Cincinnati, Ohio, are educational monthlies worthy the patronage of every lover of learning."

Commencing November, 1867, its last issue was sent out in March, 1870. It may be that the teachers of the public schools would have done themselves credit and promoted their own interests by securing its continuance as an educational journal, but both it and the Institute are now among the things of the past.

The Pierian Society, conducted by the members of the Institute in its palmy days, the only society of the kind which has yet existed in the county, whose annual exhibitions were well attended, belongs alike to this period of educational progress.

The hundreds of former students, scattered widely now, will recall pleasant remembrances in connection with their academic life; and none of them will forget one, always so earnest and active in the Society, and in behalf of the CASTALIAN, the most thorough Latin and Greek scholar of the Institute, Henry Johnson, of Crown Point; nor will they be surprised that he, entering the Sophomore Class at Hanover College, took the honors of the class in the languages, graduated with credit, and is now pursuing a theological course in the seminary at

Chicago; and while the Dinwiddies and others are achieving success in farming, and J. B. Turner, and W. Weatherbee, and H. Nichols, and E. Bibler, and so many others are pressing on in business; and H. H. Pratt, H. Castle, and H. Pettibone are looking forward to distinction in the medical profession, scores of others, active men and women now, making their mark in the world; none will be surprised if Henry Johnson, in his lone pathway, as a *herald of the Cross*, should gain at last the highest honor of them all. For a prophet's pen has written, "And they that be wise shall shine as the brightness of the firmament; and they that turn many to righteousness, as the stars for ever and ever."

From the CASTALIAN of April, 1868, the following is taken, and it is again commended to all who are interested in education:

"The teaching which the Institute gives to its students:

1st. Prepare yourselves for usefulness.

2d. Prepare yourself for happiness.

3d. Do what you can to fit others for usefulness and happiness."

In the same year (1865) two ladies came from Illinois, Misses M. and K. Knight, and started a boarding and day school for girls in Crown Point. They erected a small building on East Street, which has since been removed to the south end of town. They have also erected on South Street a dwelling house, have admitted boys and some young men into their school, and seem to be quite prosperous.

In 1866 the first Teachers' Institute of the county was

held, conducted by W. W. Cheshire, then School Examiner. Pertaining to the Teachers' Institute, I find the following record taken from the Crown Point *Register*. As a fugitive production, belonging, probably, to 1867, it may interest the hundred teachers of the county to see it reproduced on a more permanent page.

" On Thursday evening the Social was well attended by both teachers and citizens. The exercises consisted of toasts, music, volunteer speeches, and reading. The following poem, prepared expressly for the occasion, was read by Mr. J. H. Ball:

> Fellow teachers and friends, we're assembled to-night
> To enjoy from stern science a social respite.
> A draft of nepenthe from study and care,
> Diversion to cheer us, kindred feelings to share.
> And though knowing all play "makes Jack a mere toy,"
> Still we think that all study " makes but a dull boy ";
> Hence, mirth, wit, and science we'd mingle together.
> Nor one from the other would too widely sever ;
> Yet of " Puss in the Corner," and " Blind Man's Buff,"
> Had we not in our childhood surely enough ?
> Above such enjoyment then, gently we'll mount,
> And sprinkle our pastimes from Piera's fount.
> In a parenthesis here to insert,
> Classical hearers, please do not feel hurt ;
> *Our* shoes may seem shoddy plodding *that* ground,
> But mayn't sense sometimes yield for the sake of the sound?
> Besides toasts, then, and music, and speech most profound,
> With our names, kindest friends, we'll acquaint you around.
> And the first to be found on the list or the roll,
> The two Arnolds of Merrillville quickly are told ;
> Not an Arnold of traitor extraction I ween,
> For a VIOLET never disloyal can seem.
> Next come the Bs, and the list not so small ;

There is Barton, and Bonnell, and Bothwell, and Ball ;
Bacon, and Boyd, and Barker, and Brannon ;
Gents and ladies in "pi" you'll observe by the scanning.
Craft, Cheshires, and Chapman, Cramer followed by Chase,
There's a Castle, a Coffin, and Death we must face ;
Dittmers and Davis, and with D we are done ;
And a Foster fills proudly F's column alone.
Gregg, Granger, and Gerloch, and then comes a Hyde,
Hayne, Hill, and a Holton who stands in his pride.
A Jackson, a Johns, a Miss Johns, ah, ha !
For a lady's name truly they've wandered afar.
A Kenny, a Knothe, a Lehman you see.
And skip "Ab," the invincible who never will flee.
The M's are so many we look out for the Mair,
To be lost in the list were an accident dire,
But no danger, that thought we quickly forestall,
For there stand the two Melvilles, both graceful and tall,
McClaren, McCracken, Merrill, Martins you scan,
Now introduce you a lady, yet surprising, a MANN !
Now Nichols from Lowell, stands alone in the line ;
Silver nickel is good, Hannah comes in good time.
Here is Palmer, and Pelton, a Pearce for the Post,
Rhea, Rundells, and Rollins, and in S stand a host ;
Sykes, Sales, Sasse, and Sheehan, Sturges, Sherman, and Starrs,
Like the bright flashing meteors, they've come from afar.
Now we're at tea with Tillotson and Tucker,
Wise, Whipple, Ward, Woods, Wood-*en* Williams we mutter.
And the last in our group is found in Dickens, short song,
A hope that his memory might ever be Young.
Thus showing you round, in front, left, and right,
We hope you'll enjoy yourselves hugely to-night,
And that never, down all of life's checkered lane,
May we sigh that these hours were hours spent in vain."

I return once more to the year 1865. On the 16th of September of that year was organized, at Crown Point, the Lake County Sunday School Convention, an organization which is yet living, and accomplished much, it is to be hoped, in promoting the moral culture of the young. Judge Ball, of Cedar Lake, was its first President, and continued to act as such, until, failing health laid him aside from active life. The convention holds each year, in the month of August, an anniversary meeting, which meetings have been largely attended and are very interesting.

In 1868, James H. Ball having been appointed School Examiner, held the Institute.

His first circular is placed here for preservation, and to show the progress now made.

"THIRD ANNUAL TEACHERS' INSTITUTE OF LAKE COUNTY

Will be held at Crown Point, commencing August 31, 1868, and continue five days. Classes and exercises will be conducted daily as follows:

Orthography and Reading.

English Grammar.—W. W. Cheshire, former Principal of Crown Point Graded School.

Physical and Descriptive Geography and Physiology.—Miss S. J. Walker, of Orleans, Indiana.

History.—Mrs. B. B. Cheshire.

Mathematics and Analysis of Language.—President T. H. Ball, of Crown Point Institute.

Political Geography.—T. J. Wood, Esq.

English Composition and Rhetoric.—Mrs. L. G. Bedell.

Calisthenics.—Miss C. A. Jackson.

Penmanship.—Miss M. J. Ball.

The following lecturers are expected to be in attendance: J. B. Hoag, M. D., of Knox, Indiana; A. S. Cutler, D. D. S., of Kankakee City, Illinois; W. Mendenhall, of Chicago, and others, giving a course of eight lectures."

While educational interests were thus striding onward and some of the educators were endeavoring to promote literary culture, although population was not increasing so rapidly as between '50 and '60, our towns were growing up at a rate unknown before; Lowell, without a railroad, Crown Point, and Hobart, and Dyer with railroad facilities, were erecting good buildings and sending off large amounts of produce; and the year '69 closed upon a region that had made a long stride in educational, social, and material progress.

CHAPTER VII.

BURIAL PLACES.

Different nations and tribes have devised different ways for disposing of the bodies of their dead. Some have embalmed them. Some have burned them and then preserved the ashes in an urn. Some have exposed them on scaffolds or heights that the flesh might be consumed by birds. Others have left them more or less exposed to be devoured by hyenas and other ravenous beasts. And still others have buried them as securely as possible within the earth.

The manner of disposing of the bodies of the dead marks the kind of civilization which a nation has attained. The practice of burning, though existing among nations of ancient civilization, is now called "barbarous."

Dr. Shaw says, of the present burying places of the East, which is the most populous portion of the globe, "They occupy a large space, a great extent of ground being allotted for the purpose. Each family has a portion of it walled in like a garden, where the bones of its ancestors have remained undisturbed for many generations. For in these inclosures the graves are all distinct and separate; each of them having a stone placed upright, both at the head and feet, inscribed with the name or title of the deceased, whilst the intermediate space is either planted with flowers, bordered round with stone, or paved with tiles." Kitto, page 359. Such cemeteries would indicate civilization.

I propose in this chapter to name ours, and briefly note their condition; considering that they belong to our progress and our civilization.

I—WEST CREEK TOWNSHIP.

1. A very retired, quiet resting-place over West Creek, on the Fuller place, where the dead of that neighborhood have been buried. Not fenced by itself nor deeded to trustees; but well cared for.

2. The Hayden Burial Place. Now West Creek. Not deeded. Protected.

3. The Methodist Church Burial Ground, near the bridge. Cared for, but too small.

4. Old Burial Ground near the Wilkinson place. Only some six graves. Private property. No special care, but not disturbed.

5. The Sanders Burial Ground. Probably not deeded to the public, but protected.

6. The Belshaw family ground, now owned by S. R. Tarr. Ought to be deeded to the County Commissioners. It is enclosed, contains some fine, large evergreens, but there is no security that it will remain undisturbed, and the dust of one of Lake Prairie's loveliest daughters, with several other once loved forms, is there reposing.

7. Lake Prairie Burial Ground. This is large, well protected and cared for; is on a sightly eminence, one of the best located cemeteries in the county. I can find no deed of this ground to trustees on record. It ought to be thus deeded.

II—CEDAR CREEK TOWNSHIP.

1. Lowell Cemetery. Fenced, cared for, and well filled with graves. Needs a gate.

2. Orchard Grove Burial Place. Well kept.

3. Tinkerville or Cedar Lake Cemetery. This is protected, is used as a public burial place, but is private property on the land of A. D. Palmer. It ought to be deeded to Trustees, or the Commissioners.

III—EAGLE CREEK TOWNSHIP.

1. Plum Grove Cemetery. Private as to ownership; public as to use. Needs fencing.

2. South East Grove Cemetery. Is near the school house, near where a church should be built; is fenced and deeded. It contains one of the finest gray marble monuments in the county, erected to the memory of Otto F. Benjamin, a very promising young man, who died suddenly, at the school house where he was teaching, in 1871. Only two burials at South East Grove up to the year 1843.

IV—WINFIELD TOWNSHIP.

1. Deer Creek Cemetery, near the school house. This place of burial, used for many years, seems to be properly kept.

2. Old Burial Ground at Hickory Point.

V—ROSS TOWNSHIP.

1. Cemetery at Ross.

2. Cemetery at Merrillville.

3. Family burial place at Deep River. This is, perhaps, the oldest in the county, having been first used in 1836. These are cared for.

4. An old burial place near the Wilkinson Ford of Deep River, from which some bodies have been removed, but where many yet remain. This old spot is now part of a cultivated field. It seems a pity that the little ground required to receive the dust of human forms may not remain undisturbed. This spot ought yet to be rescued from the plowshire, consecrated, as it has been, by the burial of old settlers; or the human remains there resting should be removed to a quiet cemetery which *is* sacred to repose.

5. A cemetery near the Joliet road, between Deep River and Merrillville. Tolerably protected.

6. Ground on the farm of W. T. Dennis contains some thirty graves. Here were buried many old settlers, as the Beebers, Dustins, Sturdeyvants, Clevelands, and others. Has not been used for burial purposes for five or six years. It ought to be protected and secured against desecration.

VI—HOBART TOWNSHIP.

1. Catholic Cemetery at Lake.

2. Protestant Cemetery at Lake; laid out in 1871. Unused at this date.

3. Hobart Cemetery. All these are properly cared for and kept.

4. An old burial ground that has been used for thirty years, south of Hobart, on a farm formerly owned by Wm. Banks. This is private property, the right of use for burial purposes being reserved when deeded by W. Banks, but not the land itself. It ought to be surrounded by a fence, as it is located in a road-side pasturage.

VII—ST. JOHN'S TOWNSHIP.

1. Hack Family Cemetery. A beautiful situation.
2. St. John's Cemetery.
3. Dyer Cemetery.

These, as consecrated grounds, are protected and kept in order.

4. An old burial place east of Shererville, on the east end of the sand ridge. Not protected by any fence, probably deeded to no trustees. It is Protestant ground, and shows neglect. The neighborhood interested ought at once to secure, by a suitable fence, this place, where for so many years their dead were buried.

VIII—HANOVER TOWNSHIP.

1. A burial place on the west side of West Creek. The ground belongs to the public, although undeeded, as it lies on a portion of land set apart for a highway, other land for the highway having been purchased beside it. This cemetery has been sadly neglected. It is the last resting-place of the remains of some old and highly respected citizens and deserves far better care.

2. The family cemetery of H. Sasse, Sen. This is well kept.

3. A little knoll near Cedar Lake, originally claimed by S. Russell, has been consecrated by occasional burials since the spring of 1837. The body of a little daughter of Solomon Russell, drowned in an unfinished well, was the first one there committed to the dust. A young Norwegian passing through this region, taken sick and dying at the Cox place, away from all friends and kindred, buried in December, 1837, was the second to find there a resting-place. Since then many residents

near Cedar Lake, have, during the past years, been added to those slumberers. This-knoll, by right, belongs to an uncle of that Norwegian, a man of intelligence and wealth, who came out from the city of New York many months afterwards, found the house in which his nephew died, the spot where he was buried, and who for that spot of ground paid Solomon Russell five dollars, the value then of four acres of land. H. Sasse, Sen., and myself have a knowledge of that purchase. John Meyer, of Hanover, is the present legal owner of this land; and I take the liberty to suggest that he ought, in consideration of its ancient purchase, and of its use for so many years as a place of burial, to deed the few rods in this little wooded knoll to the County Commissioners, that it may, in the language of the Statutes of Indiana, " be dedicated as a public burying place forever."

4. Hanover Centre Cemetery, consecrated; belonging to the Church of St. Martin.

5. A cemetery connected with the German Methodist Church.

IX—CENTRE TOWNSHIP.

1. Old Burying Ground.
2. Crown Point Cemetery.
3. Crown Point New Cemetery.
4. East Cedar Lake.
5. Old County-farm Cemetery.

Not one of these, I am sorry to make such a record, is cared for as it should be, except the new cemetery. The idea of removing the dead from place to place, not allowing even their bones to rest in peace, and the idea of leaving graves unprotected, or of running the plow-share over them, seem to me alike to do violence to the better impulses of our hearts; and I express here the hope that my fellow-citizens, in the different parts of the county, in other respects so considerate, so humane in feeling, so noble in disposition, so cultivated and intelligent, will awaken to a just sense of what, in regard to our thirty-eight burial places, their own civilization demands at their hands.

The metropolis of Great Britain comprises Westminster, London proper, and Southwark. The first two places, once a mile apart, are on one side of the Thames, and the last on the other side. In contrast with the burials in Westminster Abbey, where so many of the great and some of the good of England have been buried, a writer says: "Bunhill Fields is out of doors, a little plat of four acres in the heart of the great city, as plain and unpretending as a country church-yard. Yet it has a history as replete with interest as the more splendid depository of royalty and genius." One hundred and twenty thousand are said to have been buried in that city cemetery. Among them are John Bunyan, Daniel DeFoe, and Dr. Isaac Watts. In another cemetery across the street lie the remains of John Wesley. His mothers's dust reposes in Bunhill Fields, where also lie the remains of George Fox, the Quaker; of T. Fowell Buxton, the philanthropist, and of multitudes of others of renowned and unknown men.

When, one hundred years hence, Lake county having become densely populated, a large suburban town having spread out for miles around the present growing village, there will be no ancient, quiet church-yards into which observing travelers, and meditative poets, and studious antiquarians may enter and find the resting places of the noted ones of this generation, unless we change the present custom, and the prevailing popular taste. In view of the growth, and the love of research and meditation, which we may surely look for three generations hence, I earnestly recommend to the citizens of Crown Point, to purchase and fence the Old Cemetery—it is in a very good situation for a quiet summer morning retreat for thought and solitude—and set it apart as the resting place of the slumberers who are there, "forever," until the dead themselves shall awake. Then I earnestly entreat that they let the second one remain, re-fence it, and care for it, and let the two hundred sleeping bodies that *are* there *sleep on*. Let that once animated and honored dust lie where sorrowing friends, absent and scattered now, laid it away to rest. It is poor civilization to be continually moving the bones and ashes of the dead. Let the generations of the future see the very places where our bodies are moldering to the dust.

CHAPTER VIII.

TOWNS AND VILLAGES.

Leaving the resting places of the dead, and returning again to the abodes of the living, I present, in this chapter, a glance at the centres of business life, the villages, and the towns. They are arranged neither in the order of age or size; but partly in the order in which some of them were visited; and, partly, with the design of presenting as much variety as is practicable.

BRUNSWICK—1858.

This village is in Hanover Township, on the west side of West Creek, ten miles from Crown Point, nearly due west of the head of Cedar Lake. It was commenced by the location of a store, near the corner, in 1858. It contains eighteen families; one store, at which is sold annually some twelve thousand dollars worth of goods; two blacksmiths' shops; two wagon shops; two masons; one carpenter; one shoemaker; one harness maker, one physician, a homœpathist; and one horse doctor. It also has a two-story school building, which cost twelve hundred dollars; and a manufacturing establishment of water elevators. It contains the residences of H. C. Beckman, late County Commissioner; of Dr. C. Groman, J. H. Irish, J. Schmal, and A. Farwell. It seems to be prosperous, but not growing rapidly. It has no church building.

HANOVER CENTRE—1856.

This is east of Brunswick two miles, and eight miles southwest from Crown Point. It dates as a village back to about 1856. It contains ten families, one store, one wagon shop, one blacksmith's shop, one shoemaker, one carpenter, one dressmaker, and two saloons. It is the seat of the Church of St. Martin, belonging to which are five acres of land and a cemetery.

KLAASVILLE—1860.

This little village is pleasantly situated on the "Grand Prairie," about half a mile from the Illinois line, south and west from Brunswick, distant from Crown Point about twelve miles. It is near the summit of a slight elevation in the prairie, from whence one may look far away into the apparently boundless regions of Illinois. The village was founded by H. Klaas, who settled there in 1850, the first German in that vicinity. Here is located the Church of St. Anthony, erected in 1860, connected with which is a cemetery; and settled near are some ten or fifteen families, in the village proper about ten. Here is one store, and a school house; also a blacksmith, a carpenter, a wagon maker, a shoemaker, and a tailor. It is a quiet, thrifty, healthful place.

TINKERVILLE—1850.

The locality which bears this name, lying a little southeast of Cedar Lake, and distant from Crown Point about seven miles, is not a compact village. A store, and post office, and a blacksmith shop are near each other, and a few rods away are four dwelling houses. The school house is half a mile distant, on one of four corners, and within a circle of three quarters of a mile are ten other families. As a centre for evening and Sabbath gatherings, for schools and religious meetings, it is equal to a village of twenty families.

Here reside the descendants of the first settlers, on the east side of Cedar Lake, with other families who have settled among them, and nearly every family in this neighborhood is connected by ties of blood, or by marriage and intermarriage.

This settlement reached the village form about 1850. The Cedar Lake Baptist Church removed their meetings from the west side to the old School House in this place, and transferred the location of their Sabbath School at about this time, probably in 1849. Religious meetings have been held there, in the name of the Cedar Lake Church, by Elders Hunt, McKay, Brayton, Hitchcock, Whitehead, and Steadman, and thus this locality became the second Baptist centre in Lake County. No church edifice was erected; that church organization dissolved, and nothing remains to Tinkerville of that part of the past, except the Cedar Lake Sabbath School, one of the oldest organizations of its kind in the county. This locality is in Cedar Creek Township. It contains a cemetery. The store, blacksmith's shop, and post office have been already mentioned. Familiar names here are A. D. Palmer, Alfred Edgerton, Amasa Edgerton, and Obadiah Taylor. The McCarty family resided here for many years; B. McCarty, the father, and Smiley, William, Franklin, F. Asbury, Morgan, and Jonathon, the sons. One of these, FAYETTE ASBURY MCCARTY, going forth from Tinkerville, became the greatest traveler Lake has ever reared. He went into the Far West, beyond the Rocky Mountains, about twenty years ago. The maiden whom he had chosen to become his wife, fell with others a victim to Indian border strife just before the time set for their marriage. Lone in heart, he engaged for three years, in warfare against the Indians; was four times wounded by them; killed with his own hand twenty-one of the Red Wariors who had burned the dwelling, and killed the whole family of her whom he loved. Like Logan, the Mingo, against the whites, he could say, "I have killed *many*;" and then he commenced his wanderings. He went among the mines; he went up into Alaska, then Russian America; he went down into South America; he crossed the ocean—the Pacific; spent some time in China; visited the Sandwich Islands on his return; made money among the mines; and after fourteen years' absence, visited, some six or seven years ago, the haunts of his youth in Lake county. He found here some old friends; narrated to us his adventures; went to New York to take passage again for the mines; was taken sick, and died soon after reaching the gold region at Idaho. Successful in obtaining gold, noble in disposition, lonely in heart in the sad romance of his life, he leaves his name and memory to be carefully treasured up by the friends of his boyhood at Cedar Lake. I am glad to place here on record this brief tribute to the memory of our greatest traveler—F. Asbury McCarty.

TOLLESTON—1857.

Number of families, 80; population, 400; distance

from Crown Point, eighteen miles, on the P. & F.W. R. R. The men for the most part work on the railroad. The company pay out here, per month, about $2000. Stores, 4; carpenters, 3; blacksmith, 1; shoemaker, 1. This is a Lutheran village. It contains a Lutheran Church and parsonage, a good school house, and a few miles distant is a Chicago Club House. This is a neat looking building of wood, near the Calumet, erected by a company of sportsmen in Chicago, who occupy it as a boarding house country seat. The house and grounds have a city like appearance. Not far west of Tolleston, near the crossing of the Fort Wayne road and the Calumet, is said to be the highest sand hill around Lake Michigan. The wells in Tolleston are shallow, the soil very sandy, and the water not very cold. It is surface water. The number of families given here includes the suburbs.

CLARK—1858.

On Fort Wayne railroad. Number of families, 16; distant from Crown Point, 16 miles. Contains two ice houses, one hotel, and a school house. The principal industry is putting up and shipping ice.

MILLER,

On Michigan Southern Railroad; a station; number of families, 12. Contains a little grocery store, and school house. Distant from Crown Point, about 20 miles.

WHITNEY.

A station on Michigan Southern Railroad. Contains 15 families. No business except railroad work. Distant from Crown Point, some 20 miles.

GIBSON'S STATION—1850.

On Michigan Central Railroad. Families, 4; no business. Distant from Crown Point, 17 miles. Distant from Hessville, one mile.

PINE.

A station on Michigan Southern Railroad. Families, 4. Distant from Crown Point, 20 miles.

STATE LINE SLAUGHTER HOUSE.

On Michigan Central Railroad. Miles from Crown Point, 20. One store; one boarding house for workmen. The Slaughter House employs some eighteen men; ship three or four cars daily to Boston, loaded with beef, packed in ice.

CASSELLO—1858.

A station on Pittsburg & Fort Wayne Railroad. Very few families. Nearly destroyed by fire last fall.

CASSVILLE.

This place owes its existence to the Pittsburg, Cincinnati and St. Louis Railway. A grain house, a hay press, a store, and three dwelling houses comprise the buildings on this ground. The location was not favorable for the growth of a town; and some slight friction somewhere, preventing the opening of roads and the sale of town lots, has apparently retarded a growth that might have taken place. Cassville is about half way between Crown Point and Hebron, or six miles from Crown Point, in Eagle Creek Township, one of the youngest and smallest of all our villages. Yet its enterprising merchant, A Edgerton, does considerable business; a fair amount of grain is there bought and shipped by Z. F. Summers; near it reside J. Q. Benjamin, the McLaran family, and a few others; and around it lie lands owned by some wealthy non-residents, Dr. Cass, of Porter, and Judge Niles, of La Porte.

LAKE STATION—1852.

Number of families, 40 ; dry goods stores, 2 ; grocery stores, 3; blacksmith's shops, 2; railroad blacksmith's shop, 1 ; wagon shop, 1 ; saloons, 5 ; shoemaker's shop, 1 ; wind water elevators, for railroad, 2 ; boarding houses, 5 ; basket maker, 1 ; meat market, 1. It contains also one church, and one school house, the Audubon Hotel, large and roomy, and an engine house. Most of the inhabitants are connected with the railroad. The depot grounds are the largest and most tastefully laid out of any in the county. There are many neat looking buildings. Soil, sandy. Distant from Crown Point, 15 miles.

HESSVILLE—1858.

Joseph Hess, the proprietor of this village, settled in 1850, and kept cattle. Store opened about 1858. Families now here, 20. One store, one blacksmith's shop. The families here live by cutting wood, picking berries, and working on railroad. There are two carpenters. Hessville contains a school house in which are instructed some seventy scholars. A Sabbath School has been opened there this season, numbering thirty members, and Lutheran meetings are also held at the school house. This village is distant from Gibson's Station, one mile ; and from Crown Point, 16 miles. A good grazing region is near Hessville, and some inhabitants live near the village, but the most of North Township is as yet sparsely inhabited.

DEEP RIVER—1838.

This place is the home of John Wood, whose name appears among the records of the early settlers. No lots were ever laid out and sold, as the proprietor here, who had paid one thousand dollars for the quarter section, it being an Indian reservation, patented to Quashma, saw no other way successfully to keep out strong drink. It has therefore contained no saloon, and has formed a pleasant home for the Wood family, and a few others.

The present number of families is fourteen. It contains one store, owned by Augustus Wood, a saw mill and grist mill, conducted by Nathan Wood, a physician, Dr. Vincent, son-in-law of John Wood, a blacksmith's shop, and a shoemaker's shop. It did contain a very good school house, which was consumed by fire and has not been rebuilt.

The residence of Nathan Wood is of brick, very substantially built, and is one of the most city-like dwelling houses in the county. The saw mill here was erected in 1837; and the grist mill, in 1838. Deep River village joins the Porter County line, and its location as a mill seat has been very desirable. For years there was no other grist mill in the two counties. Distance from Crown Point, 10 miles.

CENTREVILLE—1842.

At Wiggins Point, near the present village of Centreville, was formerly an Indian village. The old burial ground and dancing ground still remain on the place now owned by E. Saxton. White settlers came here in 1835 and 1836, but I place the date of the commencement of the village when Miles Pierce built the first tavern here, and pouring out a bottle of whisky or breaking it upon the frame, after the manner of naming ships, called it "Centreville Hotel." Well would it have been for that village and many others, if all the whisky had gone the same way.

This village now contains twenty-three families, two taverns, and a two story brick school house, which is used for Sabbath school and for Religious meetings. It has no church. It has a store, blacksmith's shop, wagon shop, harness shop, a milliner, dress-maker, tailoress, two shoemakers, a sale stable, and one saloon. The post office is named Merrillville. The Indian name of the place was McGwinn's Village. McGwinn here lived, died, and was buried. The first settlers retained few Indian names. Distance from Crown Point, six miles.

ROSS—1857.

Forty acres of land are here laid out in town lots, all south of the railroad. Many lots are yet unimproved. The village lies on the Joliet Cut-Off, on which road it is a station. Number of families, 13. Store, 1; blacksmith, 1; shoemaker, 1; carpenter's shop, 1; plasterer, 1; *saloon, none*. This place is the residence of Amos Hornor, Esq., an early settler near Cedar Lake, who has here a clothes drier factory in successful operation, the machine being patented and of his own invention. Many families in the county have been supplied with these very useful machines.

There has also resided here for the last twelve years, Rev. George A. Woodbridge, who settled near A. Humphrey's, in the eastern part of Winfield, in 1839, and who spent two or three years in Crown Point. A native of Connecticut, a graduate of Yale, a New England Congregationalist, he has spent these years in almost entire seclusion from the busy and the religious world.

He has a large library—large for this region—and his books and periodicals have kept him well informed. In October he will be eighty years of age, and retains the use well of his senses and faculties, working in his garden with as much apparent activity as a man of sixty.

Ross is on a ridge of sand. The woods around abound in huckleberries, and some of the marshes in cranberries.

It is not a place of much business. It contains a school house, but no church. The wells are dug here, not driven. The water is partly soft, and is quite cold and good. Depth of wells from twelve to twenty-two feet. Distance of Ross from Crown Point, eight miles.

ROBERTSDALE STATION.

This is a small place of four or five families, on the Michigan Southern Railroad. No business done.

ST. JOHNS—1846.

Number of families, 27. One store, 1 tavern, 1 dressmake, 2 wagon shops, 2 blacksmiths' shops, 2 tailors, 3 carpenters, and 4 shoemakers. Distance from Crown Point, six miles. This is a Catholic village. Its one store does a large business. Prairie West, of which it is the business and religious centre, is thickly settled up with an industrious, thrifty, prospering German Catholic population. Near this village the first German family of the county settled; and not far from it, on a beautiful elevation in the prairie, the Hack family cemetery, containing one of the finest gray marble monuments in the county, arrests the eye of the traveler. In this village is the large brick Church of St. John, the Evangelist, with other church buildings, and here, on the Sabbath mornings, gathers the largest congregation in Lake county.

There are here some good, substantial dwelling houses, and many of the farm houses on the prairie are neat and tasty. Many evidences appear of the abundance and wealth of this community, of the existence and the practice of patient industry. All over Prairie West, once so destitute of fence, and house, and orchard, and grove, are seen its results.

SHERERVILLE—1866.

Miles from Crown Point, 7; number of families, 27; stores, 2; shoemakers, 2; saloons, 2; shippers of live stock, 2; a tin and hardware store, and of the following trades one each: Carpenter, tailor, cooper, plasterer, saddler; also, one contractor, and one physician, one grain warehouse, and a lumber yard. This village has grown up rapidly. It has a thrifty appearance. It is on the sand, and wells are obtained by "driving." The water is quite good.

LIVERPOOL—1836.

In 1835 or 1836 a company of three men, John C. Davis and Henry Frederickson, of Philadelphia, and John B. Chapman, a Western man, obtained an Indian float located on the Calumet, and laid out town lots for the founding of a western city. The location was considered to be favorable, at the head of boat navigation on the Calumet, and on the great route of travel.

In 1836 a sale of lots took place, and the sales, in three days, amounted to $16,000. J. Wood and a friend bought lots to the amount of $2,000. A deed of nine of these lots, made out by J. B. Niles, as attorney, and acknoweledged by Samuel C. Sample, the first Judge of Circuit Court in this region, is preserved among other papers at Deep River. In 1834 or 1835, a ferry boat was placed on the Calumet at Liverpool, and a hotel was there opened in 1835. The location of this town was about three miles westward and north from the present town of Hobart.

In 1836 George Earl, of Falmouth, England, then from Philadelphia, came with his family to Liverpool, and soon became the proprietor of all that region. He resided in Liverpool until 1847. For about nine months, probably in 1837, the stage route from Detroit to Chicago passed through this place. Also for six months, in 1837, a line of stages was run from Michigan City to Joliet. This line, not paying, was discontinued. The other was changed to the North Road. In 1837 the Pottawatomies, a powerful Indian tribe, passed through this place on their way to the more distant West.

In 1838—1839 a charter was secured from the Legislature for a toll bridge. A store was opened here about 1840. Few families, however, came.

In 1839 Liverpool became the county seat of Lake county. A court house was erected and nearly completed, but in 1840 a re-location took place; Crown Point, or rather as it then was, Solon, Robinson's rival village, obtained the location, and this building was sold, floated down the Calumet to Blue Island, and set up in 1846, for a tavern. "And with it," writes Solon Robinson, "has gone almost the last hope of a town at that place."

In 1847, the Earle family removed to what has since become the flourishing town of Hobart. At present two families reside at the old Liverpool site, and two others at the railroad crossing not far away.

INDIANA CITY—1836.

This was another of our early towns. I have been unable to find out exactly when it was commenced, but give it this date, as this was the era of western speculation, and four little places on Lake Michigan were about this time struggling for an existence. These were Chicago, Indiana City, City West, and Michigan City. The first was in Illinois, the second in Lake County, the third in Porter, the fourth in La Porte. To them might well be added the fifth—Liverpool, on the Calumet. And I have no hesitation in saying that no ordinary foresight of man could then, or *did then*, see much difference in their chances for success. Indiana City was laid out by a company from Columbus, Ohio. It was truly a "paper city." It was sold in 1841, for $14,000. As for inhabitants, I find no record that it ever had any. All these five places may be found on Colton's map of Indiana, compiled from "authentic sources," published in 1853. Of the four on the beach of the lake, Michigan City is now quite a place among its ever changing sand banks; Chicago has become indeed a city; City West ceased to be in about 1839; and Indiana City, except on paper, and as shown by laid out lots, never was. An Indian half-breed states that eighty-six years ago traders had a fur station at Liverpool. In less than half as many years to come there may be an Indiana City at the mouth of the old Calumet, exceeding in size and wealth all the existing towns and villages of Lake. Late explorations of the Calumet river serve to show that, as a location, it is favorably situated for the growth at some day of a commercial emporium.

DYER—1857.

This village is dated as commencing with the first store. Two or three houses were here many years before, and a tavern in 1837, or earlier. Present number of families, 50.

Dyer contains a large flouring mill, a grain house,— and it has the name of being the best grain market in the county—a lumber yard, a sash, door and blind factory, a wooden shoe factory, and a tannery; grocery, and dry goods stores, 2; taverns, 3; shoemakers, 2; furniture stores, 2; physicians, 2; builder, 1; wagon shop, 1; blacksmiths, 2; tinsmith, 1; butcher, 1; harness maker, 1; saloons, 4.

A fine Catholic Church and parsonage have been erected here, and there are two school houses. A. N. Hart, now doing business in Chicago, one of the large land owners of Lake county, resided here for many years with his family, and has done considerable to improve and build up the town. Dubriels' flouring mill at this place has done a good business.

Thorn Creek, a pretty little Illinois stream, enters this county at Dyer, but after winding about for a short distance, returns again to the lower prairie lands of Illinois.

HOBART—1849.

Number of families, 95; dry goods stores, 4; hardware, 1; drug store, 1; furniture, 1; agricultural implements, 1; bakery, 1: blacksmiths' shops, 2; wagon shop, 1; harness shop, 1; shoe store, 1; shoemakers' shops, 3; cooper's shop, 1; millinery store, 1; dress makers, 4; mill wright, 1; lawyer, 1: physicians, 3; carpenters, 3;

plasterer, 1 ; livery stable, 1 ; gardener, 1 ; notary publics, 2 ; hotels, 3 ; large flouring mill, 1.

Hobart contains ten brick buildings. It has a brick school house, a frame church, a brick church, and an art gallery. This gallery, the property of Geo. Earle, now of Philadelphia, contains about three hundred paintings. It is the only collection of the kind in the county, and has been visited by many admirers of the fine arts. It reflects much credit upon the taste of the cultivated and wealthy proprietor of this town.

ORGANIZATIONS IN HOBART.

Hobart Literary Society, organized in 1871 ; members, 50; meets in Methodist Church, Tuesday evenings.

M. L. McLellan Lodge, No. 357 ; members, 62 ; date of 1866. Value of property, $2000.

Earle Lodge, I. O. O. F. Number 333, date 1869. Value of property, $1000.

Hobart Real Estate and Building Company. Capital $3000. Dealers in real estate. W. H. Rifenburg & Co.

Band Association; members, 15 : property, $500.

Trotting Park Association ; capital, $200.

Hobart is located on the Pittsburg and Fort Wayne Railroad, and its great branch of industry is brickmaking. There are four yards which turn out of pressed brick per day some 60,000. These yards give employment to one hundred persons, and pay out per month to the workmen $4000.

The Railroad Company pays out monthly about $700. A wax candle factory has also been started at Hobart, which promises success. This factory, and the brick yards, and the art gallery, showing useful arts and fine arts, are well worth visiting.

There seems to be in Hobart the atmosphere of a city, It has changed remarkably from what it was in earlier days. Population now 500. Distant from Crown Point, twelve miles.

John G. Earle has erected here a fine dwelling house and makes this place his home. The senator of Lake and Porter counties, Hon. C. R. Wadge, also resides at Hobart.

LOWELL—1852.

M. A. HALSTED, who, with his wife and mother, came into this county from Dayton, Ohio, in 1845, and settled on a farm in West Creek Township, is the proper founder of the town of Lowell.

According to the Claim Register, one John P. Hoff, of New York City, purchased " Mill seat on Cedar Creek," Range 9, Town 33, Section 23, which is the section on which Lowell now stands, Oct. 7th, 1836. He registered his claim October 8th, and also claims for four others from New York City were registered the same day in sections 22, 23 and 24. None of these city men seem to have actually settled; instead of these I find the names of Wm. A. Purdy, H. R. Nichols, J. Mendenhall, and Jabez Clark. But the "mill seat" remained unimproved till about 1850. It is a somewhat singular coincidence that the first claimant of a mill seat on Sect. 23, T. 33, R. 9, should have been named Halstead. According to the claim register, Samuel Halstead first entered here " Timber and Mill-seat." The claim was made August, 1835, and was registered November 26, 1836. There is added, " This claim was sold to and registered by J. P. Hoff, October 8, who has not complied with his contract, and therefore forfeits his claim to it." And under date of November 29, 1836, the record is "Transferred to James M. Whitney and Mark Burroughs for $212."

Number of families, 106; dry-goods stores, 4; drug stores, 2; hardware stores, 2; millinery establishments, 2; dress makers, 2; jeweler, 1; shoemaker's shops, 2; barber's shops, 2; harness shop, 1; blacksmith's shops, 5; wagon shops, 3; cooper shop, 1; meat market, 1; bakery, 1; cabinet shop, 1; agricultural store, 1; saloons, 2; photograph gallery, 1; livery stable, 1; hotels, 2; notary publics, 2; attorney 1; physicians, 4; cigar factory, 1; churches, 3.

The flouring mill at this place does a large custom work and sends off quite an amount of flour. It has two runs of stone, and grinds in the spring time some 275 bushels of feed per day, and in a good season, 150 bushels of wheat on a single run of stone. Lepin and Westerman are the enterprising proprietors. A large factory building has been erected at this place at a cost of $8000. It is three stories high, 80 feet by 50, of brick, and is the largest building in the county.

The school house at Lowell is also of brick, a large two-story building, the largest and best furnished school house in the county. Cost of house and furniture $8,000. Both of these buildings were erected under the superintendence of M. A. Halsted. All of the churches in this town are of brick. Whole number of brick buildings eight. A printing office has been established here this year, which publishes the *Lowell Star*, edited by E. R. Beebe.

ASSOCIATIONS.

Colfax Lodge—Masonic; number 378; members, 60. Value of property, $1600.

Lowell Lodge I. O. O. F.; number 245; members. 60.

Temperance Lodge No. 22, Independent Order Good Templars. Members 160, and increasing quite rapidly.

Lowell Grange of Patrons of Husbandry, No. 6. Members 80.

The first store, and first tavern in the place were opened by J. Thorn, about 1852. It has now a growth of about twenty years. Its water power is good, supplied by three different ponds, Cedar Lake also being used as a water reservoir. It lacks an element which has so largely stimulated the growth of Hobart and Crown Point, railroad communication with the world. Distance from Crown Point, eleven miles. It is located in the heart of the best farming region of Lake. Population of Lowell 550. J. W. Viant and W. Sigler, have sold at this place large quantities of goods.

CROWN POINT—1840.

The early history of this town has been already given, and the growth to which it had attained in 1847, has been mentioned. Its growth, until the railroad came, was slow. M. M. Mills built what is now called the Rockwell House, in 1842. Joseph Jackson removed from West Creek to Crown Point, in October, 1846, renting that house for five years. In 1847, he was elected Auditor, and his son-in-law, Z. P. Farley, came up to town and went into the hotel. In 1848, Wm. Alton built the brick store-house now occupied by Meyers & Bierlin; and, in 1849, Z. P. Farley and Clinton Jackson built the bakery, also of brick, in the upper room of which was the first office of the REGISTER. These were the first business buildings built of brick.

In 1851, Z. P. Farley built the Hack House, and this hotel was kept by J. Jackson and Z. P. Farley, for the next five years.

The present Court House bears the date of 1849; George Earle, architect; Jeremy Hixon, builder.

In 1858, the following brick buildings were erected: The dwelling houses of Z. P. Farley, J. G. Hoffman, and J. Wheeler, and the three story building containing the REGISTER office and Masonic Hall. The county offices were built the following year. The brick school house also bears the date of 1859.

After the completion of the railroad, in 1865, good buildings went up quite rapidly. Dr. A. J. Pratt's residence, erected in 1868, covers an area of two thousand, three hundred and twenty-eight feet, and cost nearly $5,000. This, and the Nicholson mansion, built in 1869, are the two most costly dwelling houses as yet erected. The neat residences of J. H. Prier and W. Nicholson, the latter costing $4,000, were built in 1870. Among the more elegant dwellings erected in 1871, may be named the residences of F. S. Bedell, covering an area of two thousand and forty feet, costing about $4,000, and of Z. F. Summers, Judge Turner, and T. J. Wood, each costing some $3,000. The new dwellings of Hon. Martin Wood and Major E. Griffin, the latter not yet finished, belong to the year 1872.

In the spring of 1868 the town was duly incorporated, divided into three wards, and trustees and a marshal were elected by the citizens. Three School Trustees have the charge of the public schools. They employ four teachers at the "Brick," and two at the "Institute."

Number of families in Crown Point, 293; total population, 1300. Industrial and professional pursuits are represented thus:

Lumber yards, 2; brick yard, 1; broom factory, 1; brewery, 1; agricultural stores, 4; dry goods stores, 2; grocery stores, 3; general dealers, 3; merchant tailors, 2; confection shops, 2; clothing store, 1; hardware stores, 2; drug stores, 2; milliner shops, 3; ladies' furnishing, 1; harness shops, 2; bakeries, 2; furniture stores, 2; shoe store, 1; shoe shops, 4; wagon shops, 3; tannery, 1; blacksmiths' shops, 5; railroad repair shop, 1; door, sash, and blind factory, 1; planing mill, 1; grain houses, 2; hotels, 3; eating house, 1; jewelers and watchmakers, 2; egg and poultry dealer, 1; carpenters, 14; plasterers, 6; painters, 6; paint and oil store, 1; saloons, 8; photograph gallery, 1; meat markets, 2; hay barns and presses, 2; cooper shop, 1; coal yard, 1; gunsmith, 1; tin shops, 2; school buildings, 3; church buildings, 6; county officers residing in town, 6; clergymen in town, 6; newspapers published, 2; dentists, 2; practicing physicians, 4; lawyers, 13.

ORGANIZATIONS.

Lake Lodge, No. 157, F. & A. M.; organized 1853; value of property, $2500; number of members, 88.

Lincoln Chapter, No. 53, R. A. M.; date, 1865; number of members, 34; value of property, $1000.

Crown Point Lodge, No. 195, I. O. O. F.; value of property, $750; number of members, 50.

Grove City Encampment, No. 116, I. O. O. F.; number of members, 22; organized March 13, 1872.

Crown Point Sing Verein; organized in August, 1868; number of members, 32; value of property, $1000.

Crown Point Fire Company; organized January 1, 1872; engine and hose owned by the town; value, $2000; number of members, 40.

Band Company; number of members, 11.

SUMMARY.

Number of towns and villages, 25. Number of families residing in towns, 860. Number of town inhabitants, about 4400.

CHAPTER IX.

FACTS AND FIGURES.

In this chapter, and under this heading, will be found arranged, for preservation and reference, *facts* concerning our various social, literary, and religious organizations, and *figures* showing our past and present condition in material interests, all of which ought to be of general interest to the citizens. And if this chapter should not be considered at present as readable as some others, I apprehend that in future years many will refer to it with interest.

LAKE COUNTY TEMPERANCE SOCIETY.

In June, 1841, by the efforts of three individuals,—Solon Robinson, Norman Warriner, and Hervey Ball, a temperance society, bearing the above name, was organized at Crown Point. Its meetings were held in the log court house, and were very interesting and well attended. It accomplished, in its day, much good ; and, about 1849 or 1850, it was discontinued, the ground being then occupied by a division of the Sons of Temperance.

SONS OF TEMPERANCE.

About 1848, a division of this order was organized in Crown Point, which accomplished good in its day, accumulated some funds, completed its work and disbanded, leaving, on a memorial stone in the brick school house, the following as its last record:

"In memory of Crown Point Division No. 133, Sons of Temperance, who donated $1000 to the erection of this building, 1859."

GOOD TEMPLARS.

In December, 1855, the first lodge of Good Templars in the county was organized at Crown Point. This flourished for some time, but at length went down. Other lodges of the same order succeeded it in Crown Point, and in Hobart, Centreville, Tinkerville, and Lowell, none of which are now in existance, except Temperance Lodge, at Lowell.

THE ALLIANCE.

In 1871, the last temperance organization at Crown Point was formed, known as the Lake County Temperance Alliance.

"LAKE COUNTY AGRICULTURAL SOCIETY.

The first meeting to organize an Agricultural Society in Lake County was held at the Court House in Crown Point, August 27th, 1851. William Clark was President of the meeting, and Harvey Pettibone, Secretary. The meeting appointed a committee, consisting of Hervey Ball, John Church, and David Turner, to draft a Constitution and By-Laws for the government of the society. The meeting then adjourned to the 30th of the same month, when the committee reported a constitution, which was adopted. The meeting then adjourned until the next Thursday, when an election was held, and the following officers duly elected:

President—HERVEY BALL.
Vice-President—WILLIAM CLARK.
Treasurer—J. W. DINWIDDIE.
Secretary—JOSEPH P. SMITH.

Also the following Directors:

Center Township—HENRY WELLS.
West Creek—A. D. FOSTER.
Eagle Creek—MICHAEL PIERCE.
St. Johns—H. KEILMAN.
Winfield—AUGUSTINE HUMPHREY.
Ross—WILLIAM N. SYKES.

At a subsequent meeting it was agreed to hold the first Fair on Thursday, October 28th, 1852, and the sum of one hundred dollars was appropriated for premiums; but when the list was made out, it only amounted to $93.

The first Annual Fair was held as per order, on the 28th of October, 1852, and the total number of entries made was sixty-nine, and the total number of premiums awarded was thirty, amounting in all to the sum of $48. The printing for this Fair was done by Wm. C. Talcott, of Valparaiso, for which he presented a bill of $8, which was duly allowed. The same President and Secretary were re-elected each year, up to and including the sixth Annual Fair.

The second Fair continued two days, and was held on the 27th and 28th days of October, 1853; and the premiums awarded at that Fair amounted to $61.75.

During the 7th and 8th Annual Fairs, A. D. Foster was President, and E. M. Cramer, Secretary. The 8th Fair was held on the 4th, 5th, and 6th days of October, 1859, after the close of which, I find no record of any further meetings of the society until July 20th, 1867. In 1860, the political excitement ran high, and immediately thereafter the war of the Rebellion broke out, so that the attention of farmers was drawn away from agricultural fairs to the all-absorbing affairs of the nation. At the meeting of July 20th, 1867, the Society was re-organized, and elected Hiram Wason, President; Bartlett Woods, Vice-President; J. C. Sauerman, Treasurer, and A. E. Beattie, Secretary. Under the management of these officers the 9th Annual Fair was held on the 2d, 3d, and 4th days of October, 1867. Since then our Annual Fair has been one of the fixed institutions of the county, and has increased in interest and magnitude each year. The 14th Annual Fair is to be held on Wednesday, Thursday, and Friday, the 11th, 12th, and 13th of September, 1872.

JOB BARNARD."

LAKE COUNTY SABBATH SCHOOL CONVENTION.

Record.—" A few superintendants, teachers, and friends of Sabbath Schools in Lake County, met at Crown Point, September 16th, 1865, for the purpose of forming a Convention in accordance with a call given at the celebration at Cedar Lake. On motion, Rev. R. B. Young was called to the chair, and H. B. Austin chosen Secretary. * * * * Some articles for adoption were offered by Judge Ball, and the following were adopted. * * * * The officers elected were Hervey Ball, President; Rev. R. B. Young, Vice-President; Rev. J. L. Lower, Secretary; M. A. Halsted, Treasurer."

Rev. H. Wason was the second President; Rev. R. B. Young the third and the present one. Rev. T. H. Ball was elected Secretary in 1866, and has so continued until the present time.

The following table gives the names of the schools, or

places where held, of the present year, with the date of first organization, so far as known, and the present membership in round numbers.

	Date.	Members.
Crown Point Presbyterian	1840	75
Crown Point Methodist Episcopal	1843	100
Cedar Lake	1845	40
South East Grove	1845	40
Deer Creek	1846	55
Orchard Grove	1849	40
Cedar Lake (German)	1850	50
Buncombe Union	1851	30
Hobart	1851	70
Plum Grove	1852	Not in session.
Lowell Union	1857	Closed in 1871.
Lake Prairie	1857	40
Jones School House	1859	30
Crown Point Baptist	1860	40
Bryant's School House	1869	50
Centreville	—	30
Eagle Creek	—	25
Prairie View	—	60
Pleasant Prairie	—	50
Hurlburt School House	—	50
Vincent's School House	—	60
Hickory Top	—	40
Ensign's School House	—	25
Lake Station	—	25
Hessville	—	30
Fuller's School House	—	25
Livingston School House	—	40
Lowell Methodist Episcopal	1871	50
Robinson's Prairie	—	30
Underwood School House	—	60
Adam's School House	—	40
Total membership		1310

FACTS AND FIGURES. 171

Number of children between six and twenty-one years of age, in the townships, as reported officially for 1872. North, 592; Hobart, 299; Ross, 625; St. Johns, 585; Hanover, 376; Centre, 340; Winfield, 232; West Creek, 400; Cedar Creek, 465; Eagle Creek, 232; Town of Crown Point, 439. (The latter number would increase the number in Centre Township to 779). Total, 4585.

The order of the townships in population, estimated according to the number of children, will then be the following: Centre, Ross, North, St. Johns, Cedar Creek, West Creek, Hanover, Hobart; Winfield and Eagle Creek being the last in the order and equal in number.

The following table gives the names, so far as I have been able to obtain them, of those who have gone forth from our county to attend the higher institutions of learning.

Names of graduates are given first, with names of institution and date of graduating.

T. H. Ball ....Franklin College, 1850
Henry Humphrey................University of Michigan, 1851
Milton Blayney ....Wabash College, 1861
Henry Johnson........................Hanover College, 1872
Leila G. Robinson..............Phipps Union Seminary, 1857
Mary Jane Ball........................Ladoga Seminary, 1859
Henrietta Ball............Indianapolis Female Institute, 1861
Fannie C. Vanhouten ....   "   "   "   1862
Sarah J. Turner...............Oxford Female Seminary, 1868
Nannie Wason ....   "   "   "   1871

MEDICAL GRADUATES.

John Higgins ....La Porte Medical College, 1846
Samuel R. Pratt.............. University of Michigan, 1860
Stephen S. Farrington...........   "   "   "   1867
Frederick Castle ....   "   "   "   1869

J. W. Johns.............................Chicago Medical, 1869
A. Tillotson ....Bennett Medical, 1871
H. H. Pratt............................Rush Medical, 1872
H. A. Castle...........................Indiana Medical, 1872
A. Vincent ....Chicago Homœpathic, 1872
        THEOLOGICAL GRADUATES.
Henry Humphrey............................Princeton, 1860
T. H. Ball..............Newton Theological Institution, 1863
        LAW GRADUATES.
James H. Ball....................University of Chicago, 1871
T. S. Fancher...................University of Michigan, 1871
J. W. Youche ....   „   „   1872
Milton Barnard..................   „   „   1872
        NORMAL GRADUATES.
William Dubriel....................Englewood Normal, 1872
   NOW PURSUING A REGULAR LITERARY COURSE.
J. H. Dowd........Junior Class, State University, Bloomington
J. A. Burhans.....Sophomore Class, Indiana Asbury University
   ENTERED THEOLOGICAL SEMINARY AT CHICAGO.
Henry Johnson..1872
     LITERARY COURSE NOT COMPLETED.
E. J. Farwell..............................Wabash College
H. G. Bliss................................   "   "
Charles Ball...............................Franklin College
James H. Ball ....   "   "
John Wood..................................   "   "
Alex. McDonald.............................Notre Dame
Ambrose McDonald ....   "   "
O. Dinwiddie.........................University of Chicago
Milton Hart..........................University of Michigan
J. W. Hart ....   "   "   "
Abbott Wason...............................Wabash College
E. Ames ....   "   "
Charles Holton ....   "   "
Henry Pettibone............................Hanover College

COURSE NOT COMPLETED.

Mary E. Pelton	Ontario Female Seminary
Martha B. Sanger	" " "
Helen Clark	" " "
Lucina Brannon	Oxford Female Seminary
Annie Gerrish	" " "
Mary E. Merrill	Englewood Normal
Loe R. Thomas	Terre Haute Normal.

OXFORD STUDENTS OF THIS YEAR.

Cordelia Wood,	Emma Turner,
Ruth Ann Pettibone,	Mariah Wason,
Annie M. Turner,	Henrietta Bridgman.

EXTRACTS FROM THE MARRRIAGE RECORD OF LAKE COUNTY.

No. 1.—Solomon Russell to Rosina Barnard. Married March 9, 1837, by S. Robinson, J. P.

(The county was organized February 15, 1837. License obtained at Valparaiso).

No. 2.—Lorenzo O. Beebe to Betsey Prentice. March 12, 1837, by A. L. Ball, J. P.

No. 3.—John Russell to Harriet Holton. October 19, 1837, by William F. Talbot, V. D. M.

No. 4.—David M. Dille to Loretta Lilley. October 24, H. Taylor, J. P.

No. 6.—Charles Woods to Mary Ann Russell. March 15, 1838, by H. Taylor, J. P.

No. 10.—Thomas Clark and Harriet Lavina Farwell. January 23, 1839, by Hon. H. D. Palmer, Associate Judge.

No. 12.—Alfred D. Foster and Emeline Hathaway. April 4, 1839, by E. W. Bryant, J. P.

No. 25.—E. S. Townsend and Eliza Eddy. December 17, 1839, by Rev. W. R. Marshall, Minister of the Gospel, of La Porte.

Up to this time every marriage ceremony in the county except one had been performed by a civil officer. And afterwards no minister appears till number 49, November 25, 1841, when A. Morrison's name is recorded.

No. 50 is by Robert M. Hyde, M. G.

No. 55 is by Norman Warriner, March 3, 1842.

Up to this time it is to be inferred that ministers in this region were few.

November 28, 1842, is the first record of the name, as an officiating clergyman, of Rev. J. C. Brown; and December 22, 1842, is found the name of Rev. W. Blain.

FIRST MASONIC LODGE.

Dispensation dated November 11, 1853; six members: H. Ball, John Wood, H. S. Holton, W. A. Clark, W. G. McGlashon, and J. H. Luther. Charter granted May 24, 1854. Hervey Ball, W. M. from 1853 to 1857. Whole number of master masons up to this date, 164. First masonic burial was that of W. C. Farrington, in 1856. Sermon preached by Rev. T. H. Ball. Text, John xiv : 6. "Jesus saith unto him, I am the way, and the truth, and the life; no man cometh unto the Father but by me." Other masonic burials have been of the following members of Lake Lodge: John Wheeler, July, 1863; D. Crumbacker, 1864; Charles Ball, September, 1865; C. Kurtz, March, 1867; James B. Turner, August, 1867; Hervey Ball, October, 1868; A. E. Beattie, October, 1869; J. E. Fraas, May, 1871; A. Sanford, December, 1871; S. S. Farrington, May, 1872.

LITERARY SOCIETIES.

In countries that enjoy constitutional liberty, voluntary associations for intellectual improvement are common and useful. Next to schools for the young come their literary societies. Before either, in importance, are, sometimes, the home training and private reading.

In Lake County a number of these societies have been organized. I think that as early as 1840 a debating club met for some time at the house of Solon Robinson. But the first one organized for the young, and of which there are existing records, I suppose to be

THE CEDAR LAKE LYCEUM.

The date or its organization is February, 1846; and a grand day it was for the youth of Cedar Lake, Prarie West, and West Creek, when it started into existence. For a group of boys in these localities, at least five of whom are now active professional and business men, between the ages of thirty and fifty, in the East, the West, and the Far West, it accomplished, in the cultivation of a literary taste and in promoting a desire for thorough mental culture, what money could not purchase. A number of its members are dead; but the living can never forget its pleasant and profitable exercises. Next in order I name

THE CEDAR LAKE BELLES-LETTRES SOCIETY.

Which included girls also among its members, met only once each month, and required the chief attention of its members to be given to writing. The date of its organization is 1847.

One of the memorable addresses delivered before this

Society was by Solon Robinson, in which he paid a high compliment to the culture manifested in his note of invitation, and referred to his having met the Indians there, for some consultation, not many years before. The Corresponding Secretary at that time was noted for her beautiful penmanship. She afterwards became the wife of Munson Church, of Prairie West, and after discharging her duties for several years as a wife and mother, she many years ago, died. I think that not more than two girls in Lake county have ever excelled her in penmanship. Like many others of our early dead, she sleeps almost forgotten by the living. I record here her given name, the name of that rare but lovely virtue, CHARITY.

The third of these organizations was formed at Crown Point, in the log court house, by young persons from Cedar Lake and Prairie West, with a few at Crown Point. Date of organization, 1848.

This was designed to be a Lake County Literary Society, but there was not at that time a sufficient literary spirit at Crown Point to aid in keeping up such an organization, and its originators, therefore, let it die. In these later years there have been societies at Brunswick, Tinkerville, Lowell, Orchard Grove, Plum Grove, South East Grove, Hickory Point, Pleasant Prairie, Deep River, Merrillville, Hobart, and Crown Point, with the names and dates of which the secretaries have not thought to furnish me. At Crown Point I find:

I.—THE CROWN POINT LITERARY.

Organized in 1863. Among the active members were especially the three pastors in the town, one of these doing considerable of the literary work, aided nobly by a choice band of coadjutors; and J. E. Newhouse, and J. L. Lower, both teachers of vocal music, and amateur performers on the guitar, furnishing much excellent music. This Society met at the Brick School House, and its meetings were well attended by the citizens and by visitors. In musical talent it was highly favored, the two guitars and the accompanying voices producing rich melody.

II.—THE PIERIAN SOCIETY—1865.

This Society was composed exclusively of members of the Institute, and was the first, and only one of its class thus far, in this county. One of its programmes is placed here for preservation.

SECOND ANNUAL EXHIBITION

OF THE

PIERIAN SOCIETY.

PER ASPERA AD ASTRA.

CROWN POINT INSTITUTE, FRIDAY EVENING, APRIL 12, 1867.

CROWN POINT, INDIANA.

ORDER OF EXERCISES:

MUSIC.

PRAYER.

MUSIC.

Declamation— I. CUTLER.....................................Cedar Lake
Letter—Miss C. BARTON.....................................Yellow Head, Ill.
Essay—Freedom—T. F. PALMER.............................Burnettsville
Recitation—Miss A. EARLES.................................Crown Point

MUSIC.

Declamation— H. GRIFFIN....................................Crown Point
Address—Education—Miss M. FOSTER......................Crown Point
Oration—A Good Name—H. JOHNSON......................Crown Point

MUSIC.

Discussion ꜀ Did Pocahontas save ⸴Aff. U. J. FRY..........Lowell
⸴the life of John Smith? ꜀ Neg. J. DINWIDDIE..........Orchard Grove

MUSIC.

Declamation—P. Ebbert.. Chicago
Letter—Miss F. Starr... Eagle Creek
Essay—Future Prospects of our Country—J. B. Turner............... Crown Point
Recitation—Miss E. Millis... Door Village

MUSIC.

Declamation—W. Hill... Cedar Lake
Address—Study of the Languages—Miss B. F. Weatherlee.............. Chicago
Oration—Our Country—C. Holton..................................... Deep River

MUSIC.
BENEDICTION.

Its meetings were held weekly during term time, and it doubtless did a good work in cultivating a literary taste.

III.—THE WEBSTER SOCIETY—1869–1872.

Meetings held first at Fraas' Hall, and finally at the Court House. At this society could be found, each week, the largest and most cultivated audience of the town.

The societies here named are no longer organized bodies. Their work is done. They belong to the records of the past.

The society at Hobart is apparently the most permanent Literary Society now in the county.

Crown Point has about reached the transition state between literary societies and lecture associations. Its next organization in this line will probably be a Lecture Association, to secure for each winter a course of Lyceum Lectures.

As towns grow into cities this seems to be the sure result.

CHURCH ORGANIZATIONS.

There are in the county seven Catholic Churches, all having houses, and resident pastors or supplies. One more will soon be organized, and a chapel will be built at Lowell.

There are four Lutheran Churches, all having houses of worship.

There are two Presbyterian Churches also having houses erected.

There is one Christian Church, and building.

There are two German Methodist Churches, and buildings, one of these called Evangelical.

There are three Baptist Churches, and buildings; one building not yet completed.

There are four Methodist Episcopal Classes having church buildings; and classes at Deer Creek, Prairie View, Centreville, Underwood School House, Lake, Eagle Creek, Orchard Grove, and Jones' School House, having no church buildings. Whole number of classes, 12.

There is a German Methodist class and congregation at Centreville. No church building. Evangelical German Methodist classes also meet at Deer Creek, and at Crown Point, having no church edifices.

There is a Methodist Church, not Episcopal, at Vincent School House.

All these make, of church organizations in the county, and maintaining public worship, 35. Besides these thirty-five places of preaching, the pastor at Lake Prairie preaches at the Burhan's School House, the Livingtone School House, and the Fuller School House; the pastor of the Presbyterian Church at Hebron preaches at South East Grove, and Bryant's School House; the pastor of the North Street Church preaches at South East Grove, and Pleasant Prairie; and the minister supplying at Salem Presbyterian Church preaches at the Hurlburt School House.

The German Methodist pastor at Cedar Lake preaches at Lake Prairie, at Crown Point, and near Centreville.

The Lutheran pastor at Tolleston also preaches at Hessville.

The pastor of the Vincent Methodist Church preaches at Hickory Top.

There is also preaching this summer at the Adams School House, by Rev. R. Randolph, who has lately moved here from Michigan.

The pastor of the Covenanter Church in Porter county, also preaches at Hickory Point.

A German Methodist pastor at Valparaiso preaches at Hobart,

Number of places of religious meeting, 50.

TABULAR VIEW OF CHURCH BUILDINGS.

CATHOLIC CHURCHES.

Name of Church.	When Erected.	No. of families.	Value of property.
Church of St. John the Evangelist, at St. Johns	First Chapel, 1843. Present Church built of brick, 1856.	140	$18,000
Church of the Holy Apostles Peter and Paul, at Turkey Creek	First Log Church, about 1852. Present large building of Joliet stone, 1864.	40	8,000
Church of St. Anthony, at Klaasville	1861.	45	2,000
Church of St. Joseph, at Lake Station	1861.	20	2,000
Church of St. Joseph, at Dyer.	1867.	60	6,000
Church of St. Martin, at Hanover Centre	1860.	60	4,000
Church of the Blessed Virgin Mary, at Crown Point	1867.	60	5,400
		455	
Families at Hobart and at Lowell		45	
Total No. of families		500	
Whole No. of Churches, 7.			

LUTHERAN CHURCHES.

Zion's Church, in Hanover.	1850.	30	3,000
Trinity Church, Crown Point.	1869.	23	3,300
Tolleston.	1869.	65	2,800
Hobart.	1870.	25	2,500

The first three of these are German Lutheran; the fourth is Swedish Evangelical Lutheran, supplied from Bailey Town, and Chicago. No resident pastor.

METHODIST EPISCOPAL.

Hickory Point.	About 1844.	Now dilapidated.
Crown Point, 1st	1845–47.	
Crown Point, 2d	1860	6,000
Pleasant Grove	1853	500
Now Lowell	1870	6,500
West Creek, 1st	1843	
West Creek, 2d.	1869	2,000
Hobart	1872	4,000

Membership in the county, 450.

PRESBYTERIAN.

Crown Point	1845–47.	3,000
Lake Prairie	1872	1,500

Membership in the county, 124.

GERMAN METHODIST.

Cedar Lake	1855	2,000

GERMAN EVANGELICAL.

Cedar Lake	1858	800

CHRISTIAN.

At Lowell.	1870	6,000

BAPTIST.

Crown Point	1856	800
Lowell	1856	1,500
North Street, at Crown Point.	1872	1,500

Whole No. of members, 62.

In all 23 houses of worship now in the county. The Lutheran at Hobart, and "North Street," not finished.

CONDENSED VIEW.

Whole number of families, 2,500; Catholic families, 500; Lutheran, 225; Methodist Episcopal, 250; Presbyterian, 80; Christian, 45; Baptist, 40; German Methodist, 50; Non-Episcopal Methodists, 25; Covenanters, 10; total, 1,250.

PASTORS OF THE DIFFERENT DENOMINATIONS.

BAPTIST—AT CEDAR LAKE.

N. Warriner, ordained in June, 1840, 1838–'42; Wm. T. Bly, 1845–'46; Alex. Hastings, 1848; Thomas Hunt, December, 1851, November, 1852. Died in the county; buried July 22, 1853; Uriah McKay, October, 1853–'54. This Cedar Lake Baptist Church dismissed members to form a church at Thorn Grove, Illinois, in 1848; also dismissed members to form a church at West Creek, in 1848; and in December, 1851, dismissed members to form a church at Crown Point.

The population changing, new centres springing up, and many removing, considering its mission accomplished, this church disbanded January 17, 1856, having been organized June 17, 1838.

AT LOWELL.

T. H. Ball, 1856–'57; John Benny, 1857–'59; T. H. Ball, 1863–'64; G. Lewis, 1864–'65; J. Bruce, 1867–72.

A. E. Simons was pastor at Crown Point, from 1859 to 1862.

The Presbyterian Church at Crown Point was constituted, according to its session records, April 27, 1844.

PASTORS.

J. C. Brown, 1840–'46; Wm. Townley, 1846–'56; —— Shultz, 1857–'59; James L. Lower, 1859–'65; A. Y. Moore, 1866–'69; Samuel McKee, 1870–'71; S. Fleming, 1871.

The first pastor, Rev. J. C. Brown, D. D., resided at Valparaiso. He died chaplain of the 48th Regiment Indiana Volunteers, at Paducah, Kentucky, July 14, 1862. The second pastor, Rev. Wm. Townley, was instrumental in the erection of the first private school house in Crown Point, which is now the Presbyterian parsonage. He carried on a school himself for some years, and aided in giving quite an impulse to the cause of education. He was for some time School Examiner of the county, and conscientious in the discharge of duty. He died, during this year, in the State of Illinois.

PASTORS IN LAKE PRAIRIE.

H. Wason, 1857-'64; B. Wells, 1864-'68; E. H. Post, 1870-'72.

CHRISTIAN.

PASTORS.

N. Cofenburg, 1842-'52; C. Blackman, 1855-'57.

SUPPLIES.

Johnson, Russell, Jones, Goodman.

Rose, 1862-'67; Shortridge, 1869-'70; Wheeler, March, 1871.

LUTHERAN.

The church at Tolleston had supplies for some six years from Dalton, and Chicago. H. Wunderlich, resident pastor since August, 1871.

Zion's Church, in Hanover Township, Rev. P. Lehman, pastor 1859-'68. No pastor at present.

Church at Hobart supplied.

CHURCH AT CROWN POINT.—PASTORS.

C. F. W. Huge, 1870-'71; George Heintz, 1871.

NON-EPISCOPAL METHODIST PASTORS.

W. S. Hinds, 1871.

METHODIST EPISCOPAL PASTORS.

Lake and Porter, originally attached to La Porte, were a mission field, at first, of that circuit. Mission preachers were Jones and Beers.

CIRCUIT PREACHERS.

Robert Hyde, 1837-'38; Stagg, 1838-'39; Green, 1839-40; Wheeler, 1840-'40; W. Posey, 1840-41; W. J. Forbes, 1841-'42; Cozad, 1842-'43; D. Crumbacker, 1843-'44; J. Early, 1844-'45; S. B. Lamb, 1845-'47; Salisbury, 1847-'48; H. B. Ball, 1848-'49; Strite,

1849–'50; Casey, 1850–'51; L. Moore, 1851–'52; C. S. Burgner, 1852–'53.

The county was now divided into two circuits.

CROWN POINT CIRCUIT.

R. B. Young. 1853–'54; F. Cox, 1854–55; Brown, 1855–'56; Crawford, 1856–'57; C. B. Heath, 1857–'58; J. W. Green, 1858–'59.

CROWN POINT NOW MADE A STATION.

J. W. Green, 1859–'60. New church built. Morris, Robinson, and R. B. Young, 1860–'61; J. H. Claypool, 1861–'62; H. C. Fraley, 1862–'63; J. E. Newhouse, 1863–'64; B. H. Bradbury, 1864–'65; S. P. Colvin, 1865–'66; T. C. Stringer, 1866–'69; M. M. Stolz, 1869–'72.

LOWELL, OR WEST CREEK CIRCUIT.

D. Dunham, 1853–'55; C. B. Mawk, 1855–'56; McDaniels, 1856–'58; W. J. Forbes, 1858–'59; A. Haze and J. H. Ciscel, 1859–'60; W. W. Jones, and Brook, 1860–'62; J. H. Claypool, 1862–'63; Unsworth, 1863–'64; W. T. Jones, 1864–'65; D. Winegar, 1865–'66; Vickars, 1866–'67; E. W. Lawhorn, 1867–'69; J. J. Hines and R. B. Young, 1869–'71; J. Harrison, 1871–'72.

HOBART CIRCUIT.

N. B. Wood, 1866–'67; Vickars, 1867–'69; J. W. Crane, 1869–'70; Stafford, 1870–'72.

CATHOLIC PASTORS AT ST. JOHNS.

Francisco Antonio Carius, 1846–'49; F. Cointet, (S. S. C.,) 1849–'50, February; F. C. Schilling, 1850; B. J. Voors, 1851–'52; F. C. Schilling, 1853–'54, May; B. J. Voors, 1854–'57, June; A. Tursch, July, 1857–'58, March; Jacob Mayor, 1858–'58, April to September; B.

Rachor, September, 1858–'70. September; A. Heitmann, 1870.

AT KLAASVILLE.

Church consecrated May 12, 1861, by Right Reverend John Henry Luess, D. D., Bishop of this diocese. The present pastor has kindly furnished for me the following note: "Since the church's dedication, attended by Rev. Francis Nick, Rev. King, Rev. Frederick Fuchs, who died here, and is interred in the Catholic Cemetery of the congregation ; and he was succeeded by Rev. Henry Renssen ; and the church is now attended and pastored by the Rev. Francis Seigeluk, every Sunday, and holiday. As the congregation is fast increasing a new church will be built there ere long." The pastor at Klaasville resides at Hanover Centre, and is pastor of that church.

At Turkey Creek, and at Lake, no resident pastors at present.

AT DYER.

K. Schmidt, 1867–'71 ; B. Wedne, 1872.

AT CROWN POINT.

P. Wehrle ; L. Weiser, 1869–'70 ; H. Meissner, 1871.

I take the opportunity to acknowledge here the kindness and courtesy of the pastors at Hanover, St. Johns, and Crown Point, in furnishing to me information for these records ; and to express my gratification in regard to the pleasant acquaintances thus formed. Indeed, all the pastors of the different churches have aided me in this very kindly ; but some of us do not keep our own records in as good shape as do our Catholic brethren.

Population in 1870, 12,339. Present population about 12,500.

CHURCH MEMBERS.

(Some of these are estimated from the families.)

Catholic, 2500; Lutheran, 1125; Methodist Episcopal, 450; German Methodist, 120; Presbyterian, 124; Christian, 78; Baptist, 62; Evangelical, 50; Non-Episcopal Methodists, 40; Covenanters, 20; total, 4560.

Number of children in the townships, as enumerated for public school purposes, 4585.

Number of children in the Sabbath Schools, under twenty-one years of age, about 1000.

The Catholic and Lutheran children, who are religiously instructed with great care, would number about 1500.

Great changes have taken place in the religious organizations in the past thirty years. Four Baptist churches have disbanded, located at Cedar Lake, West Creek, Hobart, and Eagle Creek. Methodist churches or classes have ceased to exist, that were once flourishing, at Pleasant Grove, Centre Prairie, Hickory Point, Hickory Top, and probably other places; and Methodist preaching is discontinued also at Jones' School House, South East Grove, and the Butler School House. Flourishing United Brethren congregations have been scattered, and pastoral ministrations of this denomination have ceased. Yet the county, as a whole, is not falling back in regard to Christian civilization. Four resident Catholic pastors, two resident Lutheran, three Methodist pastors, and one Presbyterian, devote their time to the religious training and spiritual welfare of their flocks. Ten men devoting their whole time and energies to the upbuilding of Christianity in our townships ought to accomplish much. And there are five others, engaged in part in secular pursuits, to earn the necessaries of life, who may also be counted as laborers in the wide harvest field of which our domain forms a little part. Fifteen laborers in this "vineyard" ought to be able to secure a high state of cultivation. It will appear from the figures elsewhere given that one-fifth of the inhabitants of Lake county are Catholic, one-eleventh are Lutherans, and that, including these, one-half of the families are believers in what may be called orthodox Christianity.

Among the twelve hundred and fifty families making up the other half of our population, there are some Universalists, some Spiritualists, some Sceptics, some with no fixed religious belief; and among these families are *some* —I record it because believing it to be true, and that one truth will not suffer in consequence of another truth; and I record it also, believing intensely in pure Christianity, and disgusted thoroughly with some wicked things done professedly in the name of Christ, and professedly for his cause—among these non-evangelical families are *some* of the kindest, most obliging, most reliable, and best disposed of our citizens. How many, this record will not disclose.

Hoping to be able to give *honor to whom honor, and praise to whom praise is due*, and having had some large opportunities for ascertaining character, I make this record for the sake of justice, and truth, and for the suggestions which it may call forth. And I suppose it to be saying much for our evangelization to repeat, that one-half of the families of Lake are believers in one revealed religion, and in one inspired book; a book of whose teachings, Bonar, of England, one of the best Christian poets of our day, has said:

> "More durable they stand,
> Than the eternal hills;
> Far sweeter and more musical
> Than music of earth's rills.
>
> "Fairer in their fair hues,
> Than the fresh flowers of earth.
> More fragrant than the fragrant climes
> Where odors have their birth."

PHYSICIANS AT CROWN POINT.

The earliest regular physician in the county was Dr. H. D. Palmer, who settled north of Solon Robinson's location, in the winter of 1836. An irregular practitioner, Dr. Joseph F. Greene, settled soon after near Cedar Lake, practiced several years in that locality, was a great hunter and trapper, and died about 1847. Those residing at the county seat are the following: W. F. Farrington, 1840-'56; Andrew Stone, — '46; —— Cunningham,—; H. Pettibone, 1847; Wm. E. Vilmer, 1853-'61; A. J. Pratt, 1854; —— Finney, 1855-'58; J. Higgins, 1859; S. R. Pratt, 1860-'63; C. Groman, 1861-'63; O. Poppe, June, 1870.

DENTISTS.

O. H. Wilcox, 1864-'71; D. T. Quackenbush, 1871; G. E. Eastman, 1872.

Dr. J. Higgins went into the army as surgeon in 1861. At first he was connected with a United States regiment, but that becoming disorganized he received the position of surgeon of the 12th Cavalry, Illinois Volunteers. He remained in the service, a great part of the time as brigade surgeon, or in general hospitals at Chicago and Washington City, until 1865, early in which year he resumed practice at Crown Point. As an experienced, operative surgeon, he stands at the head of the ranks among the physicians of the county. Dr. Samuel R. Pratt also served as army surgeon; first in the 87th Regiment Indiana Volunteers, resigning on account of ill health; and afterward in the 12th Cavalry, remaining with this regiment until its return at the close of the war. He then located at Hebron, where as practicing physician, he still resides. Dr. Otto Poppe is a homœopathist, an intelligent, courteous German, comparatively young, but acquiring quite a practice.

Two physicians have died here, Drs. Farrington, and Wilmer. One resided here for a short time, Dr. Brownell, and removed to the neighborhood of Plum Grove, and died not many months ago.

The resident physicians are now four, all of whom for the last year or two have made their professional visits in two-horse covered carriages.

Dr. Bliss, a retired physician, also resides in town, keeping a drug store, and occasionally visiting, professionally, his particular friends.

PHYSICIANS AT LOWELL.

At the head of this list I place one of the oldest practicing physicians of this region, Dr. J. A. WOOD, who settled in Porter county, in June, 1837, and extended his rides into Lake, and removed to West Point, Cedar Lake, in the winter of 1840. In 1842 he removed to Center Prairie, and in 1847 to Lowell. He was, for eighteen months, Regimental Surgeon in the 12th Indiana Cavalry. Was much of the time in hospitals in positions above his nominal rank in the service. He built his present residence in the suburbs of Lowell in 1862.

Dr. John Farrington ; Dr. John Hunt, 1855–'57. He returned to La Porte county and died. Dr. S. B. Yeoman, 1856. Died at Lowell, January, 1864. Dr. A. A. Gerrish, 1865 ; Dr. S. B. Taylor, 1865–'69. Removed to Nebraska. Dr. E. R. Bacon, 1866 ; Dr. J. E. Davis, 1870.

PHYSICIANS AT BRUNSWICK.

M. Hoffman, 1857–'59 ; C. Schlemm ; ⸺ Walensky ; C. Schlemm ; H. Volke, 1865 ; C. Groman, 1865.

AT HOBART.

Dr. P. P. Gordon, 1866 ; Dr. H. Castle, 1872.

AT DEEP RIVER.

Dr. Vincent, 1871.

AT DYER.

Dr. S. W. Johns.

LAWYERS AT CROWN POINT.

A. McDonald, date of location, 1839 ; Martin Wood, 1848 ; E. Griffin. 1857 ; Charles N. Morton, 1858 ; James B. Turner, 1861 ; T. Cleveland, 1863 ; E. C. Field, April, 1865 ; Job Barnard, May, 1867 ; T. J. Wood, 1867 ; W. T. Horine, 1870 ; ⸺ McCarthy, 1870 ; T. S. Fancher, 1871 ; James H. Ball, 1871 ; Milton Barnard, 1872 ; J. W. Youche, 1872.

The first of these lawyers, Alexander McDonald, was an early settler in the south part of the county. Removing to Crown Point, in 1839, and entering upon the practice of law, he became the most eminent lawyer of the county, was a representative four or five terms at Indianapolis, and in the midst of a prosperous legal career, died in 1869.

The fifth, James B. Turner, was a son of Judge Samuel Turner, an old settler. He was a refined and courteous gentleman, of prepossessing personal appearance, a member of the Presbyterian Church, and an exemplary Christian lawyer. Leaving his practice at Crown Point, he went, with M. A. Halsted, to the South, at the close of the war, for the purpose of engaging in the cultivation of cotton, and died there in 1866. His remains were brought to his home, at Crown Point, for burial.

Charles N. Morton, and —— McCarthy, remained here but a short time. The others are still members of the Lake County Bar.

The names of a few lawyers who were here for a short time are omitted in the above record, among them —— Hewitt, in 1848, and perhaps 1849, and George Glossner, a partner for a few months of this year with T. S. Fancher; also A. G. Hardesty, and J. B. Peterson, residents for a few months of this summer, at the county seat.

An idea of our growth in some directions may be obtained from the following contrast:

A post office, as has been mentioned, was established at Crown Point under the name of Lake C. H., in 1836. The receipts of the office from March to October were $15. The next quarter the receipts were $8.87. Third quarter $21.49. In 1837 a weekly mail was brought from La Porte. The contract was taken at $450 for the year. Quarter ending June 30, the receipts were, $26.92; September 30, $43.50; December 31, $38.20; March 31, 1838. $51.33; June 30, $51.39. This last was the largest amount received in one quarter while Solon Robinson was postmaster. This one office then supplied the county, and each letter taken out cost twenty-five cents if coming from any great distance.

In this year, 1872, the following is the record of Crown Point post office, Z. P. Farley, postmaster:

There was received for money orders, issued from January 1st to July 1st, 1872, $9,075.81. There was paid out on money orders drawn on this office during the same time, $2,892.81, the balance, $6,183, being remitted to Chicago. The amount received for stamps sold during the six months ending July 1st, was $576.36. The number of mails received at this office each week, 28; number of mails sent out, 28.

Another contrast is furnished by the assessment records. The first assessment, made after the organization in 1837, includes 8,726 acres of land valued at $77,787. the tax upon it amounting to $894. There were 226 polls and 23 over age, making 249 assessed for taxation. The personal property tax, at high rates of valuation, amounted to $521; poll tax, $282.50; total tax, $1,697. The assessment of 1846 shows 600 persons assessed; 54,421 acres, valued at $78,792; personal property assessed, at very low rates of valuation, $95,849; tax upon all, $2.754.

In 1871 the number of acres assessed was 293,614. valued at $2,342,155; personal property, $723,160; number of polls, 1,796; tax, $53,358.66; railroad valuation, $548,040; tax on railroad property, $6,263.51. The tax of 1837 was brought up by high valuations, and by including 409 town lots in Liverpool assessed at $26,440, to $2,002, equaling more than two-thirds the tax of 1846.

It was ascertained, a fact which shows how unsettled that first squatter population was, that of the 249 first assessed 80 only remained in the county ten years afterwards; 27 had died; "so that" says he who then counted up the number, "142 have rolled on in that irresistible wave of western emigration that never will cease till it meets the resisting wave of the western ocean, which will cause the mighty tide to react upon itself until all the mountain sides and fertile plains of Mexico and Oregon are teeming with the Anglo-Saxon race."

And still a third contrast appears in the number of voters, and in the census returns of number of inhabitants. At the first election, which was held in March, 1837, 78 votes were polled. At the presidential election in 1844, votes 325; in 1868, 2,336. The estimated population in 1837 was 1,245.

In 1840 the United States census was taken by Lewis Warriner, of Cedar Lake. Population then, 1,468; in 1850, 3,991; in 1860, 9,145; in 1870 it reached 12,339; increase between 1840 and 1850, 2,523; between 1850 and 1860, 5,154; between 1860 and 1870, 3,194.

A fourth contrast appears in the amount of productions. A sufficient amount of food for home consumption was raised probably in the summer of 1838. In 1840 sales of produce may be said to have commenced. The first articles for market were grain and pork. As productions increased, and facilities for transportation were provided, we added to the grain and pork, butter, cheese, honey, potatoes, wool, poultry, eggs; horses, cattle, and hay.

The value of each of these now marketed in a year, I am sorry to be unable to give; but the following figures and facts will aid in forming an estimate: One dealer, H. C. Beckman, of Hanover Township, village of Brunswick, has bought in a single day, in the regular course of trade, thirty-seven hundred eggs, and about three hundred pounds of butter. In five months of this year he bought 5,600 dozen, and his amount for the year may be placed at 8,000 dozen. Amount of butter taken in during the year, 10,000 pounds.

The butter and egg trade of Lowell for a year is in dollars, $12,000; that of H. C. Beckman, about $3,000; A. D. Palmer, about $1,000; Crown Point, about $12,000; other places, probably $22,000; total, $50,000.

During the past year there have been shipped from this county, as near as can be ascertained, 160,000 bushels of corn; 360,000 bushels of oats; 2,200 tons of hay. Of pork, a large amount; the figures I cannot obtain; and many cattle have been sold for beef.

Some seventy horses were this summer taken to the New England markets. Many more went to Chicago. Total valuation of products sent out of the county, $300,000.

In manufactures also something is done. The wagon-making business at one shop in Crown Point, the shop owned by J. Hack, gives constant employment to eight workmen, and turns off in a year some fifty wagons, ten or twelve carriages and buggies, besides doing quite an amount of repair. Other shops at Crown Point and Lowell do a fair amount of work.

The broom factory of T. Fisher sends to Chicago yearly a large amount of brooms.

A fifth contrast, that exhibits one law of growth, is in the amount of land held by single individuals. The squatters allowed to one individual only two hundred acres. Many actual settlers entered only eighty or one hundred. The following table presents a view for 1872 of a few

LARGE LAND HOLDERS.

Of these some are non-residents. A. N. Hart, a resident at Dyer, but doing business in Chicago, holds some 15,000 acres. Estimated value of his estate, $500,000.

NON-RESIDENTS.

Dorsey & Cline, 10,000 or 12,000 acres; —— Forsyth, about 8,000; G. W. Cass, 9,577; J. B. Niles, about 1,800; Dr. Hittle, 1,200; D. C. Scofield, about 1,000.

RESIDENTS.

Estate of J. W. Dinwiddie, about 3,500; Wellington A. Clark, 1,320.

The value of the real estate of the county may be put down at $10,000,000. This would give, to each family, if equally divided, $4,000. But, as elsewhere in the world, property is here unequally divided. A few families hold real estate in round numbers, in the following amounts: A. N. Hart, $500,000; Mrs. M. J. Dinwiddie, $125,000.

NON-RESIDENTS.

Gen. Cass, $150,000; —— Forsyth, $250,000; Dorsey & Cline, $150,000; total, $1,175,000.

It thus appears that ten families own about one-sixth of the area of the county, and that six families own more than one-tenth, in value, of the real estate of the county.

Another great contrast appears in examining the district schools, the buildings, the teachers, the wages or salary paid, and the mode of licensing the teachers. In 1847 Solon Robinson wrote, referring back to 1841: "This year a frame school house was built in Crown Point, which was the first respectable one in the county, and I fear that the same remark is still too true; for a decent provision for schools has hardly yet been made in any district of the county. And I don't mean to be understood that the Crown Point school house is at all worthy the name of a decent one for the place, for it is not; although it is better than the little old blank log cabin which was in use previous to the building of this one." Now, if the writer of the above could look over the county, and see the eighty-four neat and commodious school houses, attend a teachers' examination, and an institute, and visit some of the schools when in session, he would find a very marked improvement. The days of the log school houses and the oiled paper windows in Lake county are past.

One more contrast may be presented. The registering of claims ceased in 1837; about five hundred names are attached to the Constitution of the Squatters' Union, some of these however were in what became Poter county; and of our five hundred square miles of surface, one hundred sections in the north part were considered for several years to be unfit for cultivation and almost worthless, and seventy-five more lay in the Kankakee marsh; yet, when I first looked over the county as a boy, in 1837, the large prairie region, of some two hundred and fifty square miles, was almost unbroken by fence or furrow. The smoke of no cabin curled upward over the open prairie, no domestic animal was seen at any distance from the groves and the woodland, all life except the wild life was confined to the sheltering shade of the oak and the hickory trees. But now, in the very centre of our largest prairies are farm houses, and gardens, and orchards, and the large pasture grounds of twenty years ago are all enclosed by fence or hedge. The droves of cattle first pressed outward over the green savannahs and man followed. The cattle destroyed the polar plants, and the prairie dock, and the immense beds of flowers, and cropped to the earth the grass that once grew so tall. The wild prairie beauty long since departed. Time was when we could roam these wilds along many and many a mile; the grass tall, waving, and trackless; the phlox of different colors, as elegant and as luxuriant as in Eastern cultivated garden beds, in almost boundless profusion; the other bright-colored native flowers abundant in July, and August, and September; the tall polar plant, with its sunflower stalk from five to seven feet in height, and its clusters of yellow blossoms, and its bottom leaves two and three feet in height, forming a continuous succession of rich forest-like herbage of bright yellow and green; every now and then scaring up the grouse, the quick, thundering sound of whose wings would startle both horse and rider; occasionally coming near to a wolf and sending him away on a low and not rapid lope; and again seeing at a distance the tall sand-hill cranes, and sometimes even a herd of bounding deer. But now all is changed except the contour of the ground. Lake Prairie was nearly all enclosed, no range left for stock, in 1870. The prairie, northeast of Crown Point, was so fenced up, as to make the road a continuous lane, in 1871.

And this year, 1872, with the long lines of wire and board fence erected by Judge Niles, and others, sees the broad southern portion of Robinson's Prairie nearly all enclosed. The appearance of the prairie of 1872 is vastly unlike that of 1834. Farms and neat residences dot it all over now. It was in its native wildness and beauty then. A sweeping prairie fire can be seen no more. The prairie hens find few places in which to make their nests, and are almost destroyed; the wolves have few mounds left in whose sides to make their dens. The timid deer has become a stranger to its old haunts and would not know its once safe retreats. The wild fowls in the spring and fall still darken our waters, but they rear their young amid the surroundings of other regions now. Among our northern sand hills is heard nearly every hour the steam whistle; across our prairies there courses rapidly and frequently the iron-horse; on the Kankakee islands and in the marsh itself settlements are now made; and soon the engines will be running and drawing their ponderous burdens through that once almost impenetrable morass that skirts our southern border. No wonder the wild geese and swan seek other summer haunts where they may rest in solitude and hear no screams except their own.

CHAPTER X.

INCIDENTS AND ITEMS.

In this chapter and under the above heading will be found a variety of facts that have found no place for insertion elsewhere, and yet seem to me worthy of record as carrying out the design of this work. Some of them are of special, and I trust most of them will prove to be of general interest. In the first sketch will be found a notice of one of our relics of the past.

CEDAR LAKE—1670 OR 1680.

Two hundred years ago! Who lived around those waters then? Who admired the summer and autumn beauty which nature has lavished so richly there? Who can tell anything of that dim past? The mementoes of that age are silent. They are the water and the sands upon the shore, the unchanged banks, the ancient oaks, the pebbles, and the few old rocks. From one of these majestic oaks a different memento and witness has been obtained.

THE NAIL.

It is called a nail, but for what it was made, or how, or by whom used, what human witness can testify? None. Surely none. It was found some twenty years ago in or near the heart of an oak, outside of which were layers of wood one hundred and seventy. According to the method of calculation employed by woodmen, about two hundred years ago this small instrument of steel, now in the possession of Mrs. M. J. Cutler, at Kankakee, found a lodging place in that then young oak. It is about one inch and a quarter in length. The shaft is round, about the size of the large end of a clay pipe stem. The head on the top is flat and very smooth, and, besides this surface, it has twelve small plain sides, each smooth and well wrought. The point end is not a point, but has an edge like an axe. It is supposed to be of European workmanship, but the hands that made it, unquestionably human hands and skillful hands, have long since been dust, and the shop where it was made has probably long ago ceased to be a European workshop. But how came it at Cedar Lake two hundred years ago? Did not Indians then roam through these woods, catch fish in the waters, paddle their canoes over the lake, and pitch their wigwams on its banks? It was only fifty years after the Pilgrims landed at Plymouth Rock. Had articles of English manufacture gone westward then a thousand miles? Had this identical piece of steel indeed come over in the May Flower, coming at length into the hands of descendants of the Puritans, who, some two hundred years after that landing sought a home in the free, wild West? It might have been so. Perhaps Indian women used it to cut holes in the deer hides and buffalo robes, in which to place the sinews or strips of bark with which they sewed together the coverings of their wigwams, the skins that formed their couches, the mantles for their winter covering. And perhaps some toil-worn mother, or young maiden learning the simple domestic handicraft that would fit her for the duties of a wife to a red warrior in the Red Cedar haunts, placed the instrument in the bark of a sapling, near the door of the wigwam, that it might be out of reach of the little boys eager to use and appropriate articles as rare as this must have there been; and, in the hurry of a sudden departure, when the tents were struck, and ponies loaded, this little instrument was forgotten. And having crossed the ocean, and penetrated a thousand miles into the deep American wilds, nature reclaimed its own, and not the earth but the wood, covered it from human eyes, took it out from the range of human hands. *Perhaps!* But who can tell its story? It has no tongue to speak; but it says white man made, European tools probably fashioned, hammer, and anvil, and forge gave it form. And the tree says, *about two hundred years!*

But again; perhaps white man's hands not only fashioned this instrument but also put it into the young oak. Perhaps a white man looked upon the lake of the Red Cedars within sixty years after the landing on Plymouth Rock. What says authentic history? A Genoese navigator, in Spanish vessels, discovered in 1492 the New World. An English explorer, a Cabot, in 1499, sailed along the North American coast. A Spanish settlement was first made in 1565. A permanent English settlement was commenced in 1607. The Dutch first settled on American soil in 1614. New England settlements began in 1620. But the English remained along the Atlantic coast. The Spanish kept along the Gulf and up the Mississippi. The Northwest seems to have been first explored by the French. By them Detroit was commenced in 1670, some two hundred years ago.

Two distinguished names of those then exploring Western wilds are La Salle and Hennepin. Louis Hennepin was a Franciscan. His name may be found in the records of events in Europe in the seventeenth century. He came to America. He joined La Salle's expedition, which set forth in 1679. The voyagers passed through lakes Erie, Huron, and Michigan, to the mouth of the St. Joseph's river. They ascended that river in canoes to the portage. They carried these across five or six miles to the Kankakee. They passed down that river, and down the Iroquois, to the Illinois, and to the place, or near the place, now called Peoria. La Salle returned to Fort Frontenac for supplies. He instructed Hennepin to explore. In February, 1680, Hennepin set out in a canoe on a voyage of discovery. He followed the Illinois to its mouth, ascended the Mississippi to the falls of St. Anthony, upon which he was the first European to look, reaching this point April 30, 1680. He traveled for some hundred and eighty miles along a river which he called, in honor of his patron, St. Francis, and visited the Sioux Indians. Remained about three months, according to his account a captive. He met then a party of Frenchmen who came by way of Lake Superior, returned with them to Canada, sailed from Quebec to France, and published, in 1683, an account of La Salle's expedition and his own explorations.

According to the calculations made it was about the time of this expedition, under La Salle, that our nail was placed in the young oak. But it does not appear that Hennepin saw Cedar Lake. He made a circuit around it, but his recorded route passed no nearer than some fifteen miles. Let us turn to La Salle. He left at or near Peoria to return to Erie, and Niagara, and Fort Frontenac. Did he return up the Kankakee? Or did he vary his route a little northward, arriving at the head of Cedar Lake, camping on that height for a night, and first among white men did he look upon that sheet of water? Or if not he, some others of those roving Frenchmen may have reached that spot in their expeditions, a spot from whence one might journey to Lake Erie through woods, almost continuous woods, and to the Mississippi without coming under the shadow of a tree, over a pathless prairie. The hand of a Frenchman evidently may have inserted this instrument of steel into the growing oak. But for what? Was it left by accident, or left by design? Was it intended as a signal for some other explorer, as a memento, as a token of some kind, to inform a brother of some mystic order, that another had there stood, or suffered, or sorrowed? Did its thirteen faces speak a language? Conjecture alone remains. Recorded history says nothing that will offer an explanation. It may tell of useful work, of weeks and months of toilsome wanderings, of bloodshed, of massacre, of a human life going out there in sight of the blue water two hundred years ago.

This much is sure. French explorers passed near Cedar Lake at that time; the Indians certainly lived there and had some intercourse with the French. I imagine La Salle himself, standing on that height, and for some purpose, which we can never know, inserting that instrument of steel within the bark of the young oak. And now, two hundred years afterward, into the hands of children of the West, descendants of English Puritans and French Huguenots, that durable metallic memento has come, perchance, from the hand of that noted explorer, the French La Salle.

EXTRACTS FROM THE FIRST RECORD BOOK OF BOARD OF COMMISSIONERS OF LAKE COUNTY.

"MEMORANDUM—FORMATION OF THE COUNTY.

"By an act of the Legislature approved on the 28th day of January, 1836, the county of Lake was erected out of the counties of Porter and Newton, and comprises all that tract lying west of the centre of Range seven West, and North of the Kankakee River, which contains about Five Hundred Sections of land."

Until February 15, 1837, it was attached to Porter county.

ORGANIZATION OF THE COUNTY.

By an act of the Legislature, approved on the 18th day of January, 1837, the county was declared to be an independent county after the 15th day of February, 1837.

On the 8th day of March, 1837, Henry Wells was commissioned Sheriff, and by order of a writ of election to him directed, due notice as the law directs, being given, an election was held on the 28th day of March, at the house of Samuel D. Bryant, under the direction of E. W. Bryant, inspector; and at the house of R. Eddy, under the direction of William Clark, inspector; and at the house of A. L. Ball, under the direction of Wm. S. Thornbury, inspector; for the purpose of electing a Clerk of the Circuit Court, and a Recorder of the County, and two Associate Judges, and three Commissioners of the County.

By the returns from the several polls, duly made to the Sheriff, on Wednesday, the 29th of March, it appeared that for the office of Clerk, Solon Robinson had thirty-eight votes; D. Y. Bond had twenty-one votes; and L. A. Fowler had seventeen votes; and Solon Robinson was declared to be duly elected.

For the office of Recorder, William A. W. Holton had fifty votes, and J. V. Johns had twenty-two votes. And said Holton was declared duly elected.

For the offices of Associate Judges, William B. Crooks had fifty-one votes; William Clark had fifty votes; Samuel D. Bryant had twenty-eight votes; Horace Taylor, one vote; and said Crooks and Clark were declared duly elected.

For the offices of County Commissioners, Amsi L. Ball had seventy-eight votes; S. P. Stringham, and Thos. Wiles each had fifty-nine votes. The tie being decided by lot as the law directs. Amsi L. Ball was declared duly elected for the term of three years; Thomas Wiles was declared duly elected for the term of two years; S. P. Stringham was declared duly elected for the term of one year. The said Commissioners, being duly commissioned by the Sheriff, appointed the 5th day of April for the first meeting of the board to be held at the house of Solon Robinson, the place appointed by law for holding the Courts of the County.

"S. P. STRINGHAM, P. B."

The first meeting of this first Board of Commissioners was held April 5, 1837.

They appointed Solon Robinson for their Clerk; adopted a county seal; appointed John Russell Assessor; divided the county into three commissioner's districts and three townships, the townships having the same bounds as the districts and being named North, Centre, and South; ordered elections for Justice of the Peace in each township; appointed Inspectors, and Constables, and Fence Viewers, and Overseers of the Poor for each township; and formed road districts and appointed Supervisors. They also, at their second day's session fixed the constable's bonds at three hundred dollars; appointed J W. Holton Treasurer of the County, and Milo Robinson Trustee of the Seminary Fund, and Agent of the Three per Cent. Fund, fixing the bond of the latter, as Agent, at three thousand dollars, and as Trustee at two hundred, and of the former, as Treasurer, at two thousand dollars. They ordered the Clerk to issue a summons to Samuel Haviland to show cause why his ferry license should not be abated, and made provision for county maps.

They ordered a bounty of one dollar on wolf scalps.

They instructed the Sheriff to prevent any person from taking pine timber away from the public or school lands of the county, and to bring such offenders to justice.

They made arrangements for Grand, and Petit Jurors for a fall term of Circuit Court, gave some special instructions to the Clerk, and adjourned until May of the same year.

A certificate of one dollar wolf scalp bounty was granted to W. W. Paine, April 20, 1837, payable April 1, 1839.

At the May Term the Commissioners granted a license to Vincent Matthews, to keep a ferry across the Calumet River, charging for the license two dollars, and establishing rates of toll, for a footman six and a fourth cents; for man and horse twelve and a half; for a horse and wagon and passengers, twenty-five cents; for two horses and the same, thirty-seven and a half cents; and for cattle, horses, sheep, and hogs, three cents per head. This ferry was near the Illinois line.

They also granted license to Henry Frederickson, Nathaniel Davis, and John B. Chapman, proprietors, of Liverpool, "to keep a ferry on and over Deep River, in said town," charging them ten dollars, and fixing some ower rates of toll; and they granted license to A. P.. Bucklin, and Foster Murdock, to keep a tavern in the ltown of Liverpool. This license fee was also ten dollars

They appointed Wm. N. Sykes County Surveyor, and Henry Wells, Collector of State and County Revenue.

They granted licenses to keep tavern on the "Beach of Lake Michigan" and "the shore of Lake Michigan," to Horace Stevens, John Craig, and Hannah Berry, on the payment of six dollars each.

I am unable to ascertain where Hannah Berry kept her tavern, but perhaps it was near Berry Lake, called on some maps, as I think inaccurately, Lake George. The proper Lake George is laid down north-east from Dyer, "water from one to eight feet deep." See Colton's Map of Indiana.

The Commissioners also granted licenses to S. J. Cady, and David Gibson, for six dollars each, to keep taverns on the Sand Ridge Road. These two names and places are yet quite well known. The tavern stands on the shore of Lake Michigan are obliterated.

The Commissioners also appointed Township Trustees for the following Congressional townships:

Thirty-two, Range nine, Simeon Beedle, John McLain, Horace Wood.

Thirty-three, Range nine, Jacob Mendenhall, Thomas Wiles, D. M. Dille.

Thirty-four, Range nine, P. S. Mason, David Hornor, Daniel May.

Thirty-three, Range eight, E. W. Bryant, Ephraim Hitchcock, Orrin Smith.

Thirty-four, Range eight, Joseph P. Smith, J. W. Holton, Milo Robinson.

Thirty-five, Range eight, Jonathan Brown, H. D. Palmer, Jeremiah Wiggins.

Thirty-four, Range seven, L. Hixon, —— Thayer, —— Lindsey.

Thirty-five, Range seven, John Wood, Robert Wilkinson, Wm. Hodson.

Thirty-six, Range nine, George Whittemore, S. J. Cady, and Wm. N. Sykes.

Road Viewers were also appointed to serve without compensation.

One Stephen Smith was found retailing spiritous liquors without license, and the Sheriff was ordered to attend to him. Arrangements were made for building bridges, and other matters were arranged, and the Board adjourned. Record. "May 15. Smith appeared and demanded a license on an insufficient petition. Refused."

May 29.—Licenses granted to Stephen Smith, J. S. Dille, and Thomas M. Dustin, to sell foreign and domestic groceries, and to Robinson & Co., and Calvin Lilley, to sell foreign and domestic groceries, and dry goods. Cost of each license, five dollars. License was also granted to Calvin Lilley to keep a tavern at Cedar Lake. Cost, fifteen dollars. Why he was required to pay more than the others does not appear. His was probably a large hotel.

On the same day the sum of forty-five dollars was allowed to John Russell for assessing the county.

May 30.—Joseph P. Smith was appointed School Commissioner, and S. P. Stringham, Surplus Revenue Agent.

June 19.—Permit granted to Russel Stilson to retail goods, and keep a tavern in Liverpool.

July 17.—Permit granted to Benjamin Rich to keep a tavern in Liverpool.

July 31.—Permit to Samuel Miller to retail foreign merchandise at his store on Deep River.

In August, 1837, was held the first general election. Candidates for State Senator that year were: J. H. Bradley, who received forty-nine votes; and C. Cathcart, who received eighty-six votes.

The candidates for Representatives were: J. Hammell, of Porter, who received sixty-five votes; and A. L. Ball, of Lake, who received seventy votes.

The candidates for Probate Judge were: Peleg S. Mason, who received thirty-five votes; and R. Wilkinson, who received sixty-six votes.

H. S. Pelton was elected School Commissioner, and Luman A. Fowler, Sheriff.

Milo Robinson had been appointed County Agent June 5th.

November 16.—Liverpool ferry license revoked.

November 17.—Abner Stillson, Jr., was appointed, under certain provisions, to keep the Liverpool ferry.

The same day a new county seal was adopted, " the impress of which represents a ship under full sail upon water, and a foreground with a plow and sheaf, and surrounded by these words, 'Lake County Circuit Court, Indiana.'"

January 1, 1838.—Joseph Jackson received a license to retail foreign goods and dry groceries, in the southwest part of the county, " on a capital not exceeding one thousand dollars." Cost of license five dollars. This seems to be the first of the early merchants whose capital the Commissioners saw fit to limit.

PETER OLSEN DIJSTERND.

Under date of this same, January 1, I find the following :

" That the Board will take the several accounts of the Overseers of the Poor of Centre Township, presented for expense of a transient pauper, deceased, at Aaron Cox's, under advisement until to-morrow morning."

January 2.—*Ordered*, "That the sum of thirteen dollars be allowed Aaron Cox; that the sum of twelve dollars be allowed Jonathan Griffin ; that the sum of four dollars be allowed Horace Egerton ; that the sum of two dollars be allowed Calvin Lilly ; in all, thirty-one dollars, on account expense of Peter Oleson, a transient pauper, under charge of Overseers of Poor of Centre Township."

REMARKS.

I am sorry to see, with my knowledge of the facts, the

names of old neighbors and friends in such an account as the above. For their sakes I would gladly have left it in oblivion; but justice and right are sacred things, and I propose to do that justice to Peter O. Dijsternd, which I would wish, in like circumstances, paid to my own memory. He was a young Norwegian, of fine appearance, well connected in life, passing through this region as a traveler, endeavoring to reach a settlement further on towards the southwest. He was traveling with another man in a buggy, and, being too sick to continue his journey, was left at the house of Aaron Cox. The other traveler went on his way. Peter O. Dijsternd was unable to talk English; he might have had better care and attention than he did receive; and in a few days he died. I saw his body buried, and, as an observing and pitying boy of eleven years of age heard some of the side remarks. All the care and attention which he received was no more, was not so much in fact, surely no more than Western hospitality demanded from strangers to a sick and suffering stranger. And more. Aaron Cox soon afterward went southward, and after he returned, in some conversation where I was a boy listener, he, in mentioning inquiries or remarks about this young Norwegian, made where he had been, dropped the expression that he "never let on." It was then to me a new hoosierism, and I wondered what it meant. I know its meaning and can guess its significancy now. Surmises only I do not propose here to give. But still more. When the news of Olsen's death reached his uncle in New York City, that uncle, Peter Sather, a broker of means, intelligence, and culture, came to Cedar Lake;

learned what particulars he could concerning his nephew's sickness, death, and burial; purchased, as elsewhere stated, the ground where he was buried; and returned to New York. Before me now lies the slip on which he wrote his own address, " Peter Sather. Exchange Broker, 164 Nassau street, New York;" and his nephew's full name, " Peder Olsen Dijsternd, from Norway." Now, I am sure that the uncle who would leave his business as an exchange broker, in New York, and incur the expense of a journey to Cedar Lake, at that early day, to learn something about the death and burial of a young nephew who was probably just over from Norway and penetrating into the West to find a home, was not the man to have refused to pay any proper charges connected with a lone, friendless, sickness, death, and burial; and the young Norwegian stranger, whose dust reposes in a mound near Cedar Lake, having such an uncle, was not a man whose mutilated name ought to stand upon our official records as a "*transient pauper*," whose sickness, and medical attendance, and burial, cost the county of Lake the sum of *thirty-one dollars*. It must have been a *pauper's* care and a *pauper's* burial that he received. It is not reasonable that this young Norwegian left his uncle's office in New York, to journey westward, without money or its equivalent. What became of his means I know not; but I propose here to take out his name from the list of the paupers of Lake. Justice was not done to him by those in whose hands he died. I claim for his memory and resting place the respect and care which are justly and richly due. Well as I remember that first burial witnessed at Cedar Lake, but a day or two after I became a resident of the county, and how much a small group of new settlers pitied the sad, untimely, death of that fine appearing young foreigner; and distinctly as I remember the circumstances of the visit of the courteous, gentlemanly broker from New York; I had no thought, till reaching the written page before me, that such accounts were ever presented to our Commissioners. I hope not to die among those who cannot understand my speech; or among those who could not give me shelter for three or four days, and then commit my lifeless dust to the earth, without calling me a transient pauper. For the credit of Lake county civilization I disclaim this record.

I here close the Commissioners' Record Book.

FROM A PAGE OF THE CLAIM REGISTER.
"LAKE COUNTY.

"This county contains 508 sections of land, about 400 of which are dry, tillable ground. To find the exact geographical centre of the county draw a line east and west through the centre of Section 8, Town 34, Range 8, and it will be found that the south part contains three sections more than the north half. Then draw a line north and south through the centre of the same Section 8, and it will be found that the west half contains 69 sections more than the east half. Now take the N. E. quarter of the county as divided by the aforesaid supposed lines, which contains 108¼ sections, and add it to the S. W. quarter, which contains 144¾ sections, and 253 sections will be found as the quantity contained in these two quarters of the county.

"Then take the S. E. quarter, which contains 110¾ sections, and add it to the N. W. quarter, which contains

144¼ sections, and 255 sections will be found as the quantity contained in these two quarters of the county; which is a difference of only two sections from making the aforesaid centre of Section 8, the true geographical centre of the county.

"The tillable land is as equally divided between the aforesaid supposed quarters of the county."

THE TEN MILE LINE.

In some of the deeds to be found in the Recorder's Office is the following boundary description:

"South of Ten Mile Line on Section Thirty-two." A question arises, What is meant by this Ten Mile Line?

On Field Note Records in the Recorder's Office, page 53, is the following explanation of a line drawn east and west, "South Boundary of Ten Mile Purchase." On page 54 of the same Records this same line is called "Indiana Boundary Line." The following is evidently the explanation of the two names for the one line. In the Constitution of Indiana, Article XIV., Boundaries, it is ordained and declared that the State of Indiana is bounded on the east by the western meridian line of Ohio; on the south by the Ohio River from the Great Miami to the Wabash; on the west by the Wabash River till leaving the main bank on a line due north from Vincennes, "thence, by a due north line, until the same shall intersect an east and west line, drawn through a point ten miles north of the southern extreme of Lake Michigan; on the north, by said east and west line, until the same shall intersect the first-mentioned meridian line, which forms the western boundary of the State of Ohio." It is to be supposed that the originators of this west boundary line expected that the northwest corner of Indiana would be on or near the shore of Lake Michigan, but it happens to be some distance out in the lake. The line drawn from the extreme south part of Lake Michigan to the west line of the State is therefore an " Indiana Boundary Line" and a Ten Mile Line, being the bound from which we are to measure ten miles northward into Lake Michigan to find our true northern limit.

Again. In 1828 there was acquired by treaty with the Pottawatomies a strip of land ten miles in width along the northern boundary of Indiana extending, in a narrow strip, to the extreme south limit of Lake Michigan. The northern boundary of the State being then the same as defined by the Constitution, it is evident that the line bounding the southern limit of this first purchase would meet that other line at the south limit of Lake Michigan, and so both would form a continuous straight line. The eastern part of this line in our county is therefore justly called "South Boundary of Ten Mile Purchase."

According to Colton's Map of Indiana, "compiled from United States surveys," a north and south line in Indiana has quite a different direction from a north and south line in Illinois. If our west line had the direction from the Wabash River northward of an Illinois north and south line, South Chicago would be included in Lake county. As it now is, the northern boundary of our county, instead of being, as stated in Chapter I, of this book, the beach line of Lake Michigan, is a line due east and west on the surface of that lake ten miles north of our noted "Ten Mile Line." All the fish therefore and fisheries connected with some one hundred and twenty-five miles of Lake Michigan belong, evidently, to the inhabitants of Lake.

INDIAN FLOATS.

An Indian "float" was something like a soldiers' land warrant. When this region was purchased from the Indians, instead of their reserving certain definite tracts or parcels of land, the United States issued to some of their head men a number of land warrants or documents called "floats," by the possesion of which they were authorized to select and own so much land within the purchase, under certain restrictions. It is said that section eight, on which Crown Point now stands, was selected by an Indian or his agent, and a float laid upon it; but certain influences induced the Land Office Agent at La Porte to slip the float over, in his record, on to section seventeen. So eight was entered and seventeen, joining it on the south, went into the hands of a great fur trader. Floats were laid on only some ten or twelve sections of land in the county, and most of these were near the Calumet.

INDIAN MOUNDS.

Several of these were mentioned in Chapter III. I have since ascertained that there were very many in the county, on the islands of the Kankakee Marsh, on West Creek, west and northwest of Centreville, and probably elsewhere. Their actual number no one can now determine. Some have been opened, and very large human bones have been exhumed.

VIEWS.

For a prairie region we have a few picturesque, and many beautiful, and some grand landscape views. Near Lake Station, from the summit of a sand hill, on the east side of the road, the northward view on a clear summer's afternoon, contains picturesque elements. The eye rests upon a part of the valley of Deep River; and just beyond is the village of Lake, surrounded by hills and woods, the fans for raising water reminding one of Don Quixote's windmills, and the vegetation giving evidence of the beds of sand from which it derives its nourishment.

The railroad grounds are the largest and neatest in the county, and the distance is just sufficient to give to the buildings a fine effect.

Another landscape view, picturesque and truly pretty, appears from an eminence near the residence of W. T. Dennis. The northward view is of a small section of Deep River Valley, which there resembles a New England meadow; thick trees skirt the river, a part of the interval is covered with willows and grape vines, another part is a rich harvest field and meadow land, and over the whole scene the summer's sun spreads light and beauty amid the green herbage, and foliage, and waving grain. Of those views containing more fully the elements of beauty may be named a few from the hill-tops of North Township, the sweep of vision from these taking in a portion of Lake Michigan's blue waters, and the pines, and sand hills, and valleys of the shore.

Along the ridge between Deep River and Turkey Creek, as one comes westward, near the Red School House, are some fine views. Northward the eye glances over the woodland ridges running parallel with the Calumet, and southward and westward it takes in a broad sweep of slightly undulating prairie. From this ridge, across prairie and valley, Crown Point presents a very pleasant picture, as it stands forth in the sunlight upon its prairie and wood-crowned height. This town also presents a fine appearance, against the blue woods back of it, from a summit near the eastern limit of the county. South of the east line of Crown Point, along the north and south road on the prairie, are some very fine, perhaps grand, landscape views, extending over a magnificently rolling prairie, and across the dry and wet marsh to the Kankakee timber, which in the distance presents a long line of blue. On Lake Prairie also are some beautiful prospects, from some of the large eminences, the range of vision taking in the whole of that lovely prairie, bounded by that same blue line on the south, woods on the west, Cedar Creek woods on the east, and a glimpse being obtained from some heights of the bright water of Cedar Lake on the northeast, if the sun should then be shining down on its crystal depths.

Another beautiful prospect appears, amid the summer's sunshine, on the Joliet road, one-half mile west of Centreville. From the Stone Church on the northeast around the horizon, till the eye rests on the grove and valley in which was once McGwinne's Indian village on the east, the whole view is beautiful. And yet one more may be named; the landscape that suddenly spreads out before one, who is coming northward in Eagle Creek, and emerges from the shrubbery on an eminence overlooking the region of Cassville.

We have not, like the lands of the Old World, any ancient historic records or traditions, linked with grove, or stream, or prairie slope, or even with the Lake of the

Red Cedars. The Red Men's remains are all of human hopes and fears, that are associated with morass, or hilltop, lake, woodland, or plain, beyond the experiences of this generation. Leave them out of thought, and they are almost out of our knowledge, and our region, for its long great past, reminds us only of primeval nature.

Amid such scenes, in whose vastness and wildness we laid foundations, the primative influence which natural scenery is said to exert upon the style and the taste of individuals may have moulded some minds into a peculiar love for untrodden wilds, and for freedom, and for magnificence. If it be true, as a certain critic, Gilfillan, states: "We firmly believe that the scenery of one's youth gives a permanent bias and coloring to the genius, the taste, and the style; that is, if there be an intellect to receive an impulse, or a taste to catch a tone:"—then, in some respects, the impressible youth of this county have enjoyed in the past, and may still enjoy in the future, advantages for cultivating a love of native beauty, and a love for an enlarged freedom. One reared amid our prairie prospects, accustomed to a broad range of vision, should take no narrow views of life's relations or life's duties.

If the moors and mountain scenery of Scotland had much to do in forming the taste of a Pollok, the beauties of this region may yet form the taste of some noble mind in giving to the world immortal verse.

GRANGES.

Among our social orders is one, comparatively new, known as "Patrons of Husbandry." The individual organizations are called Granges.

This order was organized in Washington City, in August, 1867. It now comprises a National Grange, State Granges, and Subordinate Granges. It is a secret organization, designed for the pecuniary, social, intellectual, and moral improvement of the agricultural community. It seems to be rapidly gaining favor in this country. In February, 1872, the State Grange of Indiana, and seventy-nine Subordinate Granges were organized. In this county are now three of these organizations:

Eagle Grange, No. 4, organized June 28, 1871; number of members, 80. Lowell Grange, No. 6, October 12, 1871: number of members, 80. Leroy Grange, No. —, ———, 1872; number of members, 26.

The organization in this county owes its existence to the enterprising spirit of Oscar Dinwiddie, First Special Deputy, who is still active in carrying it on, aided very much by the earnest zeal of C. L. Templeton, and other energetic farmers. O. Dinwiddie, and C. L. Templeton are both officers in the State Grange, and members of its Executive Committee.

I am at liberty to say that the Grange has a beautiful ritual, and that its practical teachings are fitted to improve and ennoble the families of the owners and cultivators of the soil; and the Grange influence in the south part of the county, where some of our wealthiest, most intelligent, and most energetic farmers reside, is certainly a felt and living power.

STATE GRANGE OFFICERS.

O. Dinwiddie, Overseer; C. L. Templeton, Treasurer; E. M. Robertson, Gate-Keeper.

There are other *ex-officio* State Grange officers in the county.

There have been Grange burials of the following members of the order: Charles A. Kenney, burial November 1, 1871; religious services conducted by Rev. J. Harrison. Norman Stone, burial September 24, 1872; religious services by Rev. T. H. Ball. The Grange Burial Service is touching, instructive, and impressive; but Christianity only can give a certain answer to that great question, "If a man die shall he live again?"

The Grange interest is on the increase in the county. It is probable other Granges will soon be organized. It is time that the farmers were more energetic and united in promoting their interests, cultivating their social natures, and gaining useful knowledge. To the Granges of Lake I take the liberty of dedicating the following little poem:

"THE INDEPENDENT FARMER.

"Let sailors sing of the windy deep,
 Let soldiers praise their armor,
But in my heart this toast I'll keep
 'The Independent Farmer.'
When first the rose in robe of green,
 Unfolds its crimson lining,
And round his cottage porch is seen
 The honeysuckle twining;
When banks of bloom their sweetness yield,
 To bees that gather honey,
He drives his team across the field,
 Where skies are soft and sunny.

"The blackbird clucks behind the plow,
 The quail pipes loud and clearly,
Yon orchard hides behind its bough
 The home he loves so dearly;
The gray old barn, whose doors enfold

His ample store in measure,
More rich than heaps of hoarded gold,
   A precious, blessed treasure ;
But yonder in the porch there stands,
   His wife, the lovely charmer,
The sweetest rose on all his lands—
   ' The Independent Farmer.'

" To him the spring comes dancingly,
   To him the summer blushes.
The autumn smiles with mellow ray ;
   He sleeps, old winter hushes.
He cares not how the world may move
   No doubts nor fears confound him ;
His little flocks are linked in love,
   And household angels round him :
He trusts in God and loves his wife,
   Nor griefs, nor ills may harm her ;
He's nature nobleman in life—
   ' The Independent Farmer.' "

WEATHER RECORD.

1835.

Winter mild until February ; then exceedingly severe weather. April 4th, "A most terrible snow storm."

1836.

A very wet summer.

1837.

"A most excessive wet one."

1838.

A summer " of severe drouth and great sickness." So scarce was water that musk rats, " driven out of their usual haunts * * * were found wandering about in search of" it ; and even went into houses and about wells to find some water to quench their thirst. One of these animals entering the house of Solon Robinson, " never so much as asked," he says, " for a drink of whisky," but went directly to the water bucket. " During the continuance of the drouth winter commenced."

1839.

February 20.—Early in the morning a shower of rain. Cleared off warm. 21st—Very warm and cloudy. 22d— During the night a hard thunder-storm; continued in showers all day; very warm like April. 23d—Raining during the night; showers in the day time; very warm and foggy 24th—Rain continued; warm and foggy. 25th—Cooler, but cloudy and foggy. 26th—Cloudy, no prospect of fair weather.

In March, some cold weather. March 12th—A very hard thunder storm last night. 18th—Some thunder last night; showers all day. 19th.—Very pleasant all day. 20th—Rainy and showers. 29th—Rain all night; showers all day. From these extracts I conclude that February and March of 1839 were warm and wet.

April 3d.—Commenced gardening. The winter of 1840 seems also to have been quite mild. I make the following extracts: January 1, 2, 3, 4, 6, 7, pleasant. 10th—Cloudy, foggy, and rainy. 11th—Rained; some cold weather followed. 29th—Rained.

February 9th.—Cloudy, spring weather; snow almost gone. 18th—Rainy and cloudy. 19th—Warm and rainy. 20th—Forenoon rainy. 22d—Cloudy and foggy. 23d—Thawy and pleasant. 28th—Warm. 29th—Very warm.

March 25th and 26th.—Plowing.

1841.

January 31.—Very pleasant weather for some days; seems spring-like.

March 22.—The first rain this year of any amount; frost nearly out of the ground; the snow has been gone some time; the lake can be crossed with a boat, until within a day or two it could be crossed on the ice.

The winter of 1842–43 was called *the hard winter*, one, it was said, that would long be remembered. Many cattle starved to death. The winter commenced the middle of November. November 17th—Wm. Wells, "a very steady, sober, and stout, healthy man," perished with cold in a severe snow while returning home from mill. His residence was near West Creek, and he had been to the mill at Wilmington, ih Illinois. He perished on the Illinois prairie. January 6th—A rain commenced; a thaw followed. 22d—Snow entirely gone; frost nearly out of the ground. 31st—A very severe snow storm all day.

February 18th—The weather contiues severely cold without intermission; sleighing good; forage for cattle scarce and cattle in many places dying.

April 1.—Snow deeper than at any time before this winter; from fifteen to eighteen inches in the woods. 12th—Alfred Edgerton crossed Cedar Lake on the ice. 16th—The lake is yet completely covered with ice, except at the shore; no grass for cattle. 19th—Muddy. 27th—Comfortably warm, but frequent heavy rains.

May 8.—Vegetation but slightly advanced; cattle barely find sufficient food. And so ended, at last, " the hard winter."

Winter of 1843–'44, mild; summer of 1844 very wet.

Winter of 1844–'45, unusually mild. May 6th and 7th, hard frosts. Winter of 1845–'46, less mild but "not at all severe." Summer of 1846 very dry. Long continued hot weather; very sickly. Of those who died this summer a few were: Cornelius Cook, at Crown Point, June 21, and on the same day, at the Belshaw Grove, Ann Belshaw, of Lake Prairie; September 28, at Cedar Lake, Mrs. Rasgen; and, also at Cedar Lake, October 25, Mrs. Elizabeth Horton, mother of Mrs. J. A. H. Ball, who came from the city of New York, in 1838, to reside with the Ball family at Cedar Lake.

The summer of 1838 and 1846 are the two most noted for sickness in the annals of Lake. Both were very dry seasons. The fall of 1846 was late and warm. Some apple blossoms opened. October 13th—A light frost. 20th—A hard frost. November 17th—Weather continues mild, seldom any frost. 25th—The ground not yet frozen.

Winter of 1846–'47, mild. Summer of 1849 wet. High waters in July. The cholera prevailed in the west.

1852.

February and March were mild; rain in each month. Muddy in February. In March it became cold. April 3d—Snow fell about four inches. 5th—Snowed all day. 11th—No grass or plowing; cold and backward spring. 20th—Grass not sufficient for cattle to do well.

May 1.—Cattle do not get filled on grass, yet can live.

1853.

Another backward spring. Diary entries. April 12th—It has been very dry; to-day heavy rain; grass grows slowly; cattle can barely live; out of hay. 26th—Grass is not sufficient, yet cattle live.

May 1.—Peach trees in blossom this morning. 11th—This is the fourteenth day in succession it has rained. The sun has not shone twelve hours during the time.

Winter of 1855-'56 snowy and cold. Winter of 1856-'57 severe, with deep, drifting snows.

1857.

Crops were unusually late in the summer of 1857; corn very small July 4th. No winter grain, rye or wheat, cut till in August; the yield was nevertheless good. The crop of spring wheat was considered the best ever raised in the county. S. Ames, from three acres sowed May 1st, gathered ninety-six bushels. Some raised forty bushels on an acre. Corn was sold that season for fifteen cents a bushel.

1858.

A wet spring and summer. The wild geese left the last of January and returned March 10th. 14th—Frogs appeared; rain and thunder 16th and 17th; hard rain from southwest.

May 14.—Very wet time. 23d to 30th—Unusual showers, with thunder. 24th—Very wet till June 4th.

June 10.—Flood of rain. Cold afterward.

July 8th and 9th.—Mercury 100.° 11th—Good rain. 31st and August 2d—Hard showers, hail and wind. 26th—Hard rain.

September 8.—Very great rain. 10th—A splendid comet appeared; very brilliant for several weeks.

October 6.—Hard rain.

November 27th and 28th.—Heavy fall of snow, rain, and sleet.

December 3.—Snow storm. 4th—Hard rain; high water.

1859.

A cold and backward spring. April 8th to 14th, snow.

June 5.—Very white frost. 11th—Frost.

July 4.—Light frost. Afterward hot. 12th—Mercury 104° from 10 A. M. to 4 P. M. 13th, 104°. 15th, 105° at noon. 16th, 102° from 12 M. to 5 P. M. 17th, 100° at 1 P. M. 18th, 104° at 1 P. M.

In September light frosts.

In October hard frost; cold, some snow.

1860.

January 1.—Mercury—22°. 2d—24°. 5th—17°; 6th—hard sleet; trees bent down.

April 27.—Hard frost.

June 1.—Light frost.

August 10, 12, 14.—Light frosts.

1861.

May 2.—Hard frost. 3d—Heavy rain; 4th—Hard frost. 5th—Tornado, hail and rain. 30th—White frost.

July 2.—Light frost.

October 13.—Frost. 24th—A freeze.

1862.

March 20 and 21.—Snow fell for twenty-four hours.

April 2.—Terrible wind and rain. 4th—Severe hail, stones larger than hickory nuts. 21st—Hard snow storm. 22d.—Ground white.

May 20.—Hard frost.

June 9.—White frost.

July 19.—Terrible storm.

December.—Mild; no sleighing.

1863.

January 1.—Rain. 2d—Terrible rain; mercury ranging from 6° to 50°. Wild geese around; cranes and wild geese occasionally all winter. A cool summer followed. Frost every month this year. August 2d—Mercury 98°. 3d, 100°. 8th, 99°. 30th—Hard frost; killed vines and corn.

October 30.—Snow storm. 31st—Snow three or four inches in depth.

1864.

January 1.—An intensely severe day; known as the cold New Years. Wind and snow; mercury—20°. 2d—Mercury—18°. 3d and 4th—Mercury 0. 5th—6°. 6th and 7th—20°. 8th—16°. 9th—7°. 11th—5°. 12th, 22°. Winter weather till 23d, when snow disappeared. From 23d to 29th mercury from 30° to 64°; April weather. 31st—Rain; frost out of the ground. Like spring till February 16th.

March 1 to 10.—Pleasant; robins, blue birds, larks and frogs around.

April 14.—Hot, cold, rain, hail. Mercury from 60° to 40°.

July 16.—Mercury 100°. Frosts in September. In November, Indian summer. In December mercury below zero, six different times from four degrees to sixteen degrees below.

1865.

February was a mild and pleasant month. Last week in March and first week in April very fine and warm.

June 20.—Terrible hail, wind, and rain; much damage was done. Marks of the hail storm remained for years.

July 1 to 9.—Warm. 9th and 10th—Cold rain. 15th—Cold rain. Most of the month wet and cold.

August 2.—Terrible rain, thunder, and lightning.

October 19 and 20.—First frost to nip vines. 28th—A snow storm. Indian summer in November. A fine month for corn husking.

1866.

February a cold month. Mercury below zero on several days. 16th—22°.

March 19.—Four inches of snow. 20th—Rain, hail, and thunder.

May 22, 23, 24.—Frosts. 26th and 27th—Hard rain; had been dry before.

September 1 to 15.—Wet and Cold. 22d—Frost that killed vines and injured corn.

December 10.—Mercury—3°. 16th—Seven inches of snow. 31st—Mercury—4°.

1867.

January 17.—Mercury—13°.

February 10.—12°.

May 1.—Hard frost. Last of May and first of June very warm.

June 7.—Mercury 100°. June a warm and dry month.

July 23.—Mercury 100°.

August.—A very dry and warm month. 9th to 12th—Mercury 100°. 31st.—A fine rain.

September 15.—Mercury 94°. Again dry; some showers.

October.—Some showers. The month for the most part dry and pleasant.

November 3.—Thunder, hail and rain. A wild month. 24th—Very warm. 29th—Grew cold.

In December some cold weather. 27th—Mercury at 54. Still very dry. Thus closed a remarkable season.

1868.

January was a month of steady cold weather.

February a dry month.

March a warm, pleasant month. 4th to 12th—Frogs, blue birds, robins, and all signs of spring abundant.

First week in April, cold.

May 11 to 20.—Very warm. Mercury 90° to 96°.

A very dry June, yet crops looked well.

July was a very hot month, with frequent showers. Mercury at 94, 96, 99, 102, 103, and July 15, 105°.

First week in September pleasant and dry; afterwards rain. 17th—A hard frost, killed everything. Frosts also on the 18th, 21st and 23.

December 10.—Mercury—18°. 11th—16°. December closed with rain.

1869.

January.—The trees were for some days heavily loaded with ice; many were broken. The month mild. 4th—Mercury at 47°. Wild geese in this month.

First half of February mostly pleasant. 7th, 8th and 9th—Cloudy and warm. 11th to 14th—Frogs, snakes, larks, etc., around as in April. Afterward some cold weather. Birds returned the latter part of March. In April trees again covered with ice.

April was a cold and wet month.

May and June wet.

July was a very wet month.

This summer may well be called the Wet Summer. It was a very poor corn season.

The following are two records taken from THE CASTALIAN

"JANUARY—1869.

"The month just closing has been remarkable, in the county of Lake, for its even temperature, its amount of sunshine, its mild winds, its general, uniform pleasantness. No snow of any amount since the sheet of ice of the first week, and very little mud. Excellent wheeling, no rain, no storm, day after day, week after week. South wind, southeast wind, west wind, north wind, east wind— still pleasant weather. It is said that such a January has not been experienced for some thirty years. For a winter month it has been truly delightful."

"Cedar Lake, having been covered with one strong sheet of ice, then again all open, can now, in the latter part of March, be crossed with loaded teams. Quite an unusual occurrence."

The following is another CASTALIAN record: "During the year 1867 there was in our county one cloudless day, September 28th. On the 27th a speck of cloud was visible before sunrise, on the 29th one was visible after sunset. During 1868 no cloudless day was observed by a close observer. At Rochester, New York, some years ago, eighteen such days were observed in one year, and thirteen in another. There are few such days at the south end of Lake Michigan; yet there are many delightful ones, the sky as deeply blue as that over Mount Auburn, and fleecy clouds as beautiful and lovely as float anywhere."

1870.

January came in mild. Was noted for its rain storms of the 11th, 14th, and 16th; the last attended with thunder and wind. January 12th—Wild geese appeared. Mercury at 45°.

May 4.—Mercury at 94°. May was a very warm and dry month.

In June, some showers.

July a warm and dry month.

August also warm and dry.

Killing frosts in September.

October was a fine month. An excellent practical farmer makes this note. "Our best corn year."

1871.

In January of this year were those remarkable days, commencing with rain and frost, and continuing so changeless, that gave us the most magnificent ice views, so far as records show, ever witnessed in this latitude. Commencing January 14, the sheet of ice continued over everything for two weeks. Immense damage was done to forest trees. Fruit trees were broken very much, but the injury to them did not prove to be serious. The winter scenery during those two weeks was indescribably grand. All the boughs of all vegetation were covered with ice that weighed the evergreens and smaller trees almost to the earth, and when the sun shone the brilliant crystals everywhere almost dazzled the eyes of the beholder. One evening, during those two weeks, the rays of the setting sun, with the redness of a glowing summer brightness, shone upon the tree-tops, and they flashed in that red light as though hung all over with myriads of rubies. Such a scene of resplendent beauty none here ever saw before. The temperature day after day was mild; very little wind; considerable sunshine; but the whole world around seemed bound in unyielding fetters of ice. It was like living in a fairy land, or in arctic regions without the cold and the darkness. Existence itself, amid such beauty, was a great delight. But rare elements of the magnificent in nature seemed to be combined, when at length motion again commenced in the outer world. Then at midday, in the usually silent winter groves, the continuous roar of the ponderous, falling, crystal masses, the breaking of loaded boughs as the wind began to rise and try their strength, the danger to which one was constantly exposed, were sufficient to rouse into excitement the dullest nature.

Between Crown Point and Cedar Lake the road was rendered impassable for days by an icy blockade; all our woods still show the marks of the giant power that was laid upon them; the like in our history was never known before. The ice sheet extended from Southern Michigan in a south-westerly direction into Illinois; its width being some twenty or thirty miles, and Crown Point lay near the centre of its course. At Chicago snow fell to quite a depth instead of the rain which here froze at the surface of the earth.

February, like January, was a mild month.

March 2d, mercury at 68°.

In June the locusts came in immense swarms, keeping themselves mostly upon the forest trees. They were especially numerous in the woods north of Lowell; south and southwest of Crown Point; and in the eastern portion of the county. These locusts stung the timber, but no serious results followed.

In October strong winds prevailed. The summer was very dry, and unusual fires raged along the marsh and in the islands of timber. It seemed as though what the ice and the locusts had left unharmed, the fires were commissioned to destroy. The October fires of 1871, in and out of Lake, will long be remembered.

Although a very dry season, and many wells failed, and cattle suffered severely from thirst, yet the corn crop was good, the oat crop was good, and grass was abundant.

1872.

The winter commenced with no heavy fall rains and no mud. In January there came quite a fall of snow and a few cold days, but on the whole the winter was mild. Spring came, and yet very little rain, no mud, no bad roads. Showers in the summer: very little rain. Vegetation grows, but cattle suffer, wells dry up, and it seems as though the fountains in the earth would fail. Since 1869 we have almost forgotten what a rain storm is or a muddy road. The summer of 1872 has proved an unusually abundant fruit season. The corn crop has been abundant, the oat crop fair, and the grass crop good. A late and pleasant autumn with but little rain and no mud. No bad roads since the spring of 1870.

And thus ends our weather record, extending through thirty-eight years, kept with more or less fullness by Solon Robinson, at Crown Point, the Ball family at Cedar Lake, and H. Wason, on Lake Prairie. At Cedar Lake thermometrical and barometrical observations were made and recorded for a series of years; the former made at sunrise, noon, and sunset. Meteorological records ought to be continued in the county, as they may prove of interest and use amid the advances of science in the coming years.

CAPTURING TIMBER STEALERS IN NORTH TOWNSHIP.

In our earlier years, when Chicago was beginning to grow, and builders wanted pine timber, the report reached the county officers that a party of their men were stealing some valuable trees among the sand hills. The proper papers, it is supposed, were made out, the civil officer summoned his posse, and as considerable force might be needed, the independent military company of those days, Joseph P. Smith, Captain, was taken into this service. The party took dinner at Liverpool, and in the afternoon or next day, proceeded with *great caution*, with drum and fife sounding (and, probably colors flying, how could the military march without), to the place where the trespass was committed. But to their great surprise the men with the axes were not to be found. The idea of meeting a charge led on with martial music, was too much for their courage, and they had ingloriously fled. George Earle footed the bills, which amount the Commissioners afterwards refunded, and the party returned laurelless to Crown Point. The timber, doubtless, soon after went into the Illinois city, and no money came to the lords of the soil.

In contrast with the above item, in contrast as to manner and success, I place

A NEST OF TIMBER THIEVES ALONG THE KANKAKEE.

In later years, during that wet summer of 1869, the Kankakee River being unusually high and affording great facilities for rafting off the timber, a number of men were said to be trespassing upon those wooded islands which were miles away from the abodes of civilized men. The high water seemed to secure these timber stealers from the observation of the owners of the islands. The trees were cut in water some four feet in depth, and floated down to Momence, out of the jurisdiction of the State. Hearing of these depredations, a party of land-owners went out in boats to ascertain the facts and bring the culprits to justice. A number of rafts had gone into Illinois, but they found nine then in the river, of choice timber, from fifty to one hundred feet in length. One division had left the edge of the marsh about ten o'clock ta night. The moon went down as they neared the channel of the river. The navigation up the stream became laborious and dangerous, requiring one in the prow constantly to watch the current, and one to steer, while the others rowed. Thus, in the silent hours of night they were approaching the camp of the unsuspecting trespassers. Some of the oarsmen becoming exhausted, they finally moored to a willow in the edge of the current and lay on their oars and slept. Again pursuing their voyage they reached Red Oak Island after daylight dawned. Four men were arrested and taken to Lowell for trial.

Another division of this party, with three boats, made in the day about thirty miles of marsh and river navigation. They met with some interesting incidents by way of variety. One of the boatmen, "poling" his boat along, lost his balance, and succeeded in regaining it from the bottom of the marsh into which he of course plunged. Others met with similar mishaps. When about to leave the river, one young man, who had succeeded in keeping dry all day, proposing to perform one more feat, pushed out in a small trapper boat to try a shot at some ducks.

Drawing sufficiently near, he stood up and fired. The reaction of the gun, in that frail bark, sent him backwards into the water, holding on still as he disappeared, to the destructive weapon. He secured a *duck* and also a *ducking*, to the great amusement of those who had met with like accidents during the day.

If not so successful as they hoped to be, the party put some stop to the rafting of their timber down to Momence.

The first settler at West Creek, R. Wilkinson, first Probate Judge, had some rather provoking experiences with the Indians. He was raising the walls of his cabin, log by log, with the assistance of his son Noah and his wife, when fifteen or twenty stout Indians gathered round and looked on. As, by means of hand-spikes and mechanical contrivances, the three succeeded in getting the logs in place, the Indians stood round and laughed. And when a greater effort than usual was needful to raise some heavy stick, and it seemed likely to slide back upon the tugging toilers, the Indians continued to stand round and laugh; until the vexed settler felt inclined to walk in among them with a hand-spike. They did not seem to realize the fact that a little help just then from their stout arms would have been very acceptable. They certainly had not read the anecdote about Washington, how he once took hold and lifted; nor could they have read Sir Walter Scott's Black Dwarf; or they would have acted with more consideration. The scene at that cabin-raising, if amusing and not very creditable to the Red Mens' thoughtfulness, is yet instructive. The three toiling whites, genuine pioneers in civilization, rearing for themselves a cabin on choice hunting grounds, surrounded by some twenty laughing savages, show the difference between the White and Red families of man, or rather between man now native and man instructed; and the moralist would read a deeper lesson, the difference between providing by effort for present and future wants and thriftless negligence. The log cabins have been replaced by some stately mansions; but where are now the laughing Pottawatomies?

This same settler returning from the Wabash region with a wagon load of provisions, drawn by oxen, and accompanied by one of his sons, having been absent many days longer than was anticipated, reached the bank of West Creek near night-fall, and found the water so high that his team could not ford the stream. Leaving the oxen to look out for themselves, and his son to sleep in the wagon, with some corn meal in a sack strapped on his head, he swam the creek and reached his home, distant some half mile from the bank, and supplied the most pressing home want. The next day, trying in vain to borrow some good canoes from his Indian neighbors, who although not troublesome, do not seem to have been obliging, he brought his son over in a little "dug-out," and also an additional supply of provisions, and left the wagon for some two weeks, until the water abated.

LONG HIGHWAYS.

There is an old saying, "It is a long lane that never turns." Of the various wagon roads crossing the county in different directions, three are on continuous straight lines for many miles.

The north and south road, from near Hickory Top, through Winfield, on a section line one mile west of the Porter county line, is straight and continuous for about eight miles.

The north and south road on the east line of Sections Eight and Seventeen, passing along-side of Crown Point, is straight for more than ten miles.

The east and west road, the continuation of North Street, eastward towards Valparaiso, runs from the west side of Section Eight, on section lines, due east to the limit of the county, and continues on the same line till it reaches the Gates' place, from whence it bears northeast for a few miles into the city of Valparaiso. Length in this county, eight miles.

BRICK DWELLING HOUSES.

Of these there are few in the towns. Of farm houses built of brick, there are nine. Jacob Wise built in 1856. Thomas Hayward built in 1860. John Sturdevant burnt a kiln of brick and erected a house in 1861 or 1862 at a cost of $3000. It is now owned by W. T. Dennis. Jabez Clark built a flat-roof brick on Lake Prairie in 1861. Jonas Rhodes built about 1866. Dates of the others not known.

NORTH TOWNSHIP.

This portion of the territory of Lake is not productive in grain, nor in wool, nor has it any special manufacturing interest; but its exports bring in a large amount of money. These exports are wild fruits, huckleberries, cranberries, and wintergreen berries; also wild game. It is asserted by good authority that the fruit crop of North amounts to more in a season than the whole grain crop of Centre Township. Its natural features, as formerly mentioned, are the sand hills, and marshes, and the winding Calumet, and that great blue lake. The proximity of the northwestern part of it to Chicago, especially to South Chicago, is making the land quite valuable; and when Indiana City starts again into existence and sixteen or twenty miles of the Calumet River—a great inland lake harbor—are, like the Chicago River, dotted with the white sails of commerce, and plowed by the noisy little steam tugs, those waste miles of North, that we used to consider so dreary and desolate, will be worth thousands and even millions of dollars.

A glance at the map will suggest that, if the waters fail not, the ducks and the musk-rats, the hunters and trappers, must retire before the advancing interests and forces of commerce.

The first white girl born in Lake county, so far as is known, was Samantha J. Fuller, born May 5, 1837, a daughter of Oliver Fuller, who became a resident in February, 1837.

The first brick kiln, near Crown Point, was burned in 1841, by Dr. Farrington and C. M. Mason. Before this time the chimneys had been built of sticks and mud. Now brick chimneys began to appear.

The first regular 4th of July celebration at Crown Point, on record, was in 1841, and S. Robinson's memorandum of it, connected with a notice of the Temperance Society, is as follows: "And the celebration of the 4th of July with cold water and a pic-nic dinner was the happiest one, to some three hundred men, women, and children, that I ever saw."

The first mapping in the county was done by Solon Robinson; the maps being colored by Mrs. J. A. H. Ball, the first resident painter in water-colors. It seems strange that not a solitary one of the hundreds of those first maps, colored at Cedar Lake, can now be found in the county.

The first cheese factory in our limits was started, in 1867, by Wellington A. Clark, on his large West Creek farm. In one season he has made 20,000 pounds of cheese. He is still carrying it on successfully.

In the fall of 1869, John Brookman, from Australia and England, came in with capital and enterprise, bought the thousand acre farm of W. A. Clark, north, of Crown Point, two miles from town, and erected a cheese factory. This was kept in operation for two seasons, and this year it has been lying still.

The first butter factory was erected by D. C. Scofield, of Elgin, Illinois, in 1869 and 1870. The factory has been in the charge of H. Boyd and family, and has been doing a good business.

This county has large tracts of excellent grazing land, and is well adapted for the raising of stock and for furnishing dairy products. The amount of butter exported from the county annually, is one of the large sources of profit to the farmers. When the Kankakee low lands become sufficiently dry for general pasturage, they can be dotted over with herds and factories.

SCHOOLS.

The first school in this county was kept by Mrs. HARRIET HOLTON, the mother of W. A. W. and J. W. Holton. She is still living, with one of her sons, about six miles from Crown Point, and is now in her ninetieth year. Her school was kept in a private house, near what is now the Crown Point Depot, in the winter of 1835-1836. Number of scholars, three.

In the winter of 1836-1837, it is probable that two or three other schools were commenced, but concerning them I find no records.

In 1838 one of the largest, and one of the best log school houses of the county was built at Cedar Lake on the land then held as a claim by Hervey Ball. In this house, which afterwards became private property, and which is still standing near the stately mansion of Henry H. Dittmers, were organized the Cedar Lake Lyceum, the Belles-Lettres Society, and the Cedar Lake Church; and here for several years their meetings were held. The public use of this house extends from the spring of 1838 to the fall of 1848. Many associations cluster about that well-built log edifice.

June 10, 1839, Mrs. J. A. H. BALL opened a school at Cedar Lake, which became the first boarding-school of the county. Here were taught, besides elementary branches, elegant penmanship, drawing and painting, botany, natural philosophy, and "Polite Learning"—the name of a little valuable text-book which is now rarely seen—here, too, surveying and algebra, Latin and Greek were studied. A few students of this county, and from Porter and La Porte counties attended this school. In penmanship, drawing, painting in water-colors, and in botany, the teacher has had in this region no equal. The boarders here were, Maria Bradley, and John Selkirk, of La Porte county; Ann Nickerson, and Melissa Gossett, of Porter county; and Augustus Wood, Abby Wood, and Sophia Cutler, of Lake county. There were some self-boarders and many day scholars. During some of the winters the school was taught by Hervey Ball, and day scholars came from the east side of Cedar Lake, from Prairie West, and from the west side of West Creek. Schools being commenced at other points, regular winter schools were not continued after about 1849 or 1850; but summer schools continued till about 1855. The Cedar Lake school therefore continued some sixteen years. It sent six students to colleges and seminaries, and fitted many for the business and the duties of life.

The next boarding and academic school of the county was opened at Crown Point by Rev. WM. TOWNLEY, about 1848. This school was commenced in a room of the dwelling-house which he erected, the house on Court street, where Andrew Krimbill now resides, in which room for a short time Sabbath meetings were also held, and then it was transferred to the academy building, which has since become the Presbyterian parsonage. A number of students attended, boarders and day scholars,— some well known names are among the list of students here—and this school achieved in its day a good success. In the winter of 1853 and 1854 this school was taught by Miss E. H. Ball, who had been teaching for some few years at the South, and returned to spend one more year of life in the home of her youth. In this school instrumental music was first taught, a piano, probably the second one in the county, being obtained for the school and music teachers procured. One of these teachers was Miss Sarah Bloomfield, from New Jersey, a thorough music teacher, who afterwards married Almon Foster, who came in the fall of 1855. In 1856 this school closed, Rev. W. Townley soon after leaving for the West.

The next select and academic school at Crown Point was carried on by Miss MARY E. PARSONS. She was a graduate of the Mt. Holyoke Seminary, an earnest and enthusiastic friend of that system, following closely in the views and principles of Miss Mary Lyon; had taught one year at Oxford, Ohio; some three years at Greensburg; and came to Crown Point with the hope of founding a Holyoke school, in 1856. She did not find all the encouragement she desired, there were other and different interests then beginning to unfold, but she opened an excellent school in a room of the Townley building, then owned by Judge Turner, and afterward in the hall room of J. H. Luther. With the exception of one summer, during which she visited Iowa, this school continued till closed by her sickness and death. She died November 14, 1860. The school thus suddenly and sadly closed, accomplished much for the cause of Christian education. By her death Crown Point and Lake county lost a most conscientious, devoted, self-denying, thorough, Christian teacher. Had circumstances favored her, and had life been continued, she might have accomplished much more; but she did what she could. She was one of a choice few. She spent her last years among us; and her name should not be forgotten.

In that same year of 1856 Dr. W. C. Farrington, with some others, was arranging for the founding of an academy on East street, but he died, and that plan was not carried out.

The next schools, therefore, coming into this record, were those of 1865, which have been elsewhere mentioned.

The growth of the public schools, from one to eighty-four, has been indirectly noticed.

Several of the teachers of these have taught select schools in the public buildings, when the public schools were not in session.

A primary select school in Crown Point, conducted by Mrs. Sarah J. Robinson, deserves special mention. Mrs. Robinson was one of the best teachers of children that we have ever had in Crown Point; kind, patient, loving, unselfish, and truly Christian. Her neatly furnished room was on Court street, north of the Rockwell House. She closed her labors here and, in July, 1864, went to Nashville, and entered the hospital in the service of the Christian Commission. She was also at Memphis, Vicksburg, New Orleans, and again at Memphis. She returned to Crown Point in September, 1865, in company with Miss E. Hodson, of our county, who had been for nine months in the same service in the hospitals at Memphis. These two, among the noblest of the Christian women of the land, were our only representatives in the Christian Commission service among the hospitals of the Union army. Mrs. Robinson disposed of her school furniture to the Crown Point Institute, married Dr. Wm. H. Harrison, an army surgeon, in 1866, and went with her husband to Mexico.

One other school remains to be mentioned. About 1866, A. Vander Naillen, a French mathematician, opened a school near Tolleston, in which he taught Civil Engineering. In December, 1869, he removed to the City of Chicago, transferring to that place his school interests.

FIRST NORMAL CLASS IN LAKE COUNTY—OPENED AUG. 19, 1872.

NAMES OF MEMBERS.

Ida Toothill, Inez Wilcox, Emma G. Sherman, Louisa Hornor, Olive Kenney, Herbert S. Ball, Myron B. Smith. Course of instruction included thirty lectures on important subjects, besides an outline of United States History, notes on Orthography and Geography, and some text-book recitations. Instruction was given in Physiology and English Analysis, and about one thousand selected words were written in spelling exercises. Length of session, thirteen weeks; teacher, T. H. Ball.

WOLVES.

For many years the prairie wolves were abundant and annoying. The early settlers became very familiar with some of their habits and their depredations. Genuine inhabitants of the prairies, as their name denotes, they were also found in the neighboring woods; and were often seen by day and quite regularly heard by night. Pigs, lambs, and sheep, melons and green corn, suffered from their voracious appetites. Although not considered very dangerous to human beings, the boy alone upon the prairie after nightfall, when he heard the quick, sharp, bark which he had learned to know so well, would naturally quicken his homeward pace. These troublesome, but romantic neighbors, were hunted down with dogs and horses, and shot, and trapped, as opportunity offered. But opportunity for trapping did not occur every night. After many trials one was securely caught on the west side of Cedar Lake. The trap was dragged quite a distance, but the wolf was found in the afternoon of the next day, killed and scalped, and a bounty obtained. The dead body was taken off by living wolves a night or two afterwards, but what they did with it could never be ascertained. No more were trapped in that vicinity. One was aftewards shot, in the early morning, by a Cedar Lake hunter boy, who was taking his morning ramble, rifle in hand, and he returned home to report, quite elated with his success. He was accustomed to carry a trusty rifle and was noted for his unerring aim. Large quantities of game fell by his sure hand.

A more successful wolf-trapper lived in the Myrick Settlement, south of Crown Point, SMITH SNYDER, who says he caught in a trap several prairie wolves, one of them, having learned to spring the trap, being at last captured, when human thoughtfulness, more than a match for wolfish sagacity, set the trap bottom upwards. The wolf turning the trap over, it is supposed, as usual, to spring it, found to his astonishment that it sprung the wrong way.

THE WILD CAT.

No really ferocious animals have been known in this region, but a true wild-cat or lynx was caught in 1837 or 1838, in an alder thicket, then almost impenetrable, at the head of Cedar Lake. It was a fierce and formidable looking animal; the fur was taken East by Job Worthington, then living at H. Ball's claim, on the lake; and the thicket was long know as the Wild Cat Swamp. Its recesses seemed almost impervious to the sunlight, and in mid summer it was covered with beautiful running roses. It has been, by its last owner, all cut down, and no trace is left of the wild-cat's ancient lair.

THE WHITE OWL.

During one of the very cold and snowy winters of our early times, a large white owl, not a native of this region, was shot on the west side of Cedar Lake. The bird seemed, from its appearance, so thoroughly protected was it from cold, and so white, to be a mountain or an Arctic denizen; and it was agreed to call it a Rocky Mountain Owl, brought out of its usual range and haunts by the great westerly storm. I think no such owls have been seen in this longitude since that severe winter.

THE BALD EAGLE.

In 1857 a bald eagle was shot on the west side of Cedar Lake by David Martin, which measured from tip to tip of the wings, some seven and a half feet. These American birds, formerly frequent visitors at that lake, have been rarely shot, and are now seldom seen. This is supposed to have been the last one killed around that lake.

THE SWAN.

In 1869, HERBERT S. BALL, a boy thirteen years of age, coming up to his home at Crown Point, through the woods east of Cedar Lake, met a magnificent water-fowl which he captured and killed. The plumage was of snowy whiteness, very pure and beautiful. The wings extended from tip to tip nearly eight feet. The head was almost twice the length, and some three times the magnitude of the head of a wild goose. Its neck was very long. Its wings were broad and strong. The long bone of the wing was in length nearly eleven inches. When examined at Crown Point this majestic bird was unhesitatingly pronounced to be an American Wild Swan, of which a few individuals were shot in Cedar Lake by Alfred Edgerton, a number of years ago. This is supposed to have been the last swan killed in this county, only a few flocks ever having been seen by the earliest settlers at Cedar Lake.

The regular yearly visitors and sojourners at this sheet of water were various species of ducks, gulls, brants, wild geese, sand-hill cranes, blue herons, white cranes, mud hens, pelicans, loons, and, around it, fish hawks, and bald eagles. It is no figure of speech to say that some of them darkened the waters, and that others covered it with snowy whiteness.

PERIODICALS.

The first printing in the county was done by Solon Robinson, who obtained a small press and some type and issued a little sheet occasionally. Some hand-bills and extras were also printed. The name of this occasional sheet is supposed to have been *The Ranger* or *Western Ranger*. No effort was made to establish this as a paper.

In 1857, perhaps as early as 1856, Rodney Dunning commenced the publication of a weekly sheet called *The Crown Point Herald*. After issuing it for six months he sold to J. S. Holton, who discontinued its publication. He, in 1857, sold to John Wheeler and Z. F. Summers, who resumed the publication, changing the name to *Crown Point Register*. In 1862 Wheeler and Summers sold to B. D. Harper and A. E. Beattie. In April, 1867, Harper sold to Samuel E. Ball, who September 19, 1869, sold his interest to F. S. Bedell; Bedell and Beattie continued the publication of the *Register* until the death of A. E. Beattie, in October, 1860, when F. S. Bedell purchased the remaining interest and has since been sole editor and proprietor. The *Register* has a circulation of nearly 800, and the number of subscribers is rapidly increasing. It is Republican in politics. Its motto is, " With Malice toward None—With Charity for All."

While J. Wheeler and Z. F. Summers were publishing the *Register* in 1860 or 1861, B. D. Harper commenced editing and issuing a Democratic paper called *The Jeffersonian*. It was printed on the south side of the public square, then removed to the "Chapman House," on the west side, and soon after was discontinued, the editor purchasing a half interest in the *Register*.

In November, 1867, the Pierian Society of the Crown Point Institute commenced the publication of a literary journal called *The Pierian*. In April, 1868, the name was changed to *Castalian*, and the publication was continued by the Institute. It became an eight-page monthly, size of page sixteen inches by eleven, printed at first at the *Register* office, and afterward at Chicago. Its literary character has been elsewhere mentioned. It exchanged with some of the best college papers in the land. Its last issue was March, 1870. At the next Teachers' Institute a proposal was made to revive this publication, and the following circular was sent to the teachers of the county:

"TO THE TEACHERS OF LAKE COUNTY.

" Permit us to call your attention to the proposal made, near the close of our late session as an Institute, in regard to our adopting the *Castalian* as our periodical and organ of communication with each other. You will remember the vote was taken to accept the proposal as there made. After a consultation held on Saturday afternoon, January 7th, we propose to change the name *Castalian* to *Teacher's Repository*, to have a change made in the character of the paper corresponding to its new relations; to introduce Educational, Literary, and Scientific Departments; a story for children in each number, and Queries, and to make it the organ of the teachers and schools of our county, and an efficient aid in cultivating our literary taste, and our capabilities as teachers. We also propose to make it of general interest as a literary paper for family reading. We now request you to take an active interest in the enterprise, to send your own name and the names of as many subscribers as you can obtain, accompanied by the subscription price, to Mr. J. W. Youche, according to the following rates:

SINGLE COPIES FOR ONE YEAR.

To teachers and students........................50 cents.
Other subscribers..............................75 "

Teachers of Lake, remember your mottoes, act with diligence, and let us do something worthy of ourselves and of our enterprising age.

J. W. Youche,	Jas. T. Herrick,	A. J. Beatie,
Mary Martin,	N. A. Sturges,	O. F. Benjamin,
Jennie Belshaw,	C. R. Jarvis,	F. McDonald,
M. A. Foster,	Clemmon Granger,	Anna Wilcox,
Helen Granger,	L. R. Thomas,	M. L. Clark,
Jas. M. Wise,	Charlotte Holton,	E. Lathrop,
E. McCaulay,	S. S. Erb,	Henry Sasse, Jr.
W. E. Abbott,	A. L. Thompson,	A. F. Coffin."

A sufficient number of responses failing to come, the publication of the *Teacher's Repository* was given up.

At Hobart a little sheet was published for a short time by Moses Hull, in the years 1868 and 1869. Its circulation was confined to the vicinity of Hobart, and it was probably not designed to be a permanent publication.

In this year, 1872, E. R. Beebe started a weekly political and local paper, at Lowell, called *The Lowell Star*. It is an eight-page sheet, one side printed in Chicago, neat in its appearance, well edited, and apparently well sustained. It is Republican as to politics, and bids fair to live and prosper.

In this same year, also, W. H. Ingram came to Crown Point and started a weekly political paper, under Democratic patronage, called *The Crown Point Herald*. This paper advocated earnestly the election of Horace Greeley for President of the United States; and soon after the result of the election was known it was sold to T. Cleveland, Esq., who is now carrying it on as a Republican paper. The size of sheet is the same as the *Register*, twenty-four inches by seventeen, four pages, and its motto is, "Independent in all Things—Neutral in Nothing." T. Cleveland, editor and proprietor.

No records have been kept concerning the annual mortality in the county. The following persons, however, were known to have died between the spring of 1846— the sickly season—and the spring of 1847 : Isaiah L. Beebee, David Currin, Dr. Joseph F. Greene, Thomas Henderson, Myiel Pierce, John R. Simmons, Thomas Gibson, Jeremiah Green, John Hack, Jr., Cornelius F. Cooke, Judge Samuel F. Turner, —— Hollingshead, S. C. Beebee, David E. Bryant, —— Miller, Royal Barton, John Smith, Ambrose Williams, ——Livinggood, —— Simons.

MINISTERS OF THE GOSPEL ORDAINED IN LAKE COUNTY.

N. Warriner, at Cedar Lake, in 1840; T. H. Ball, at Crown Point, in 1855; G. Lewis, at Lowell, in 1865.

MINISTERS DYING IN LAKE COUNTY.

Thomas L. Hunt, died July 21, 1853. He was pastor of the Baptist Church at Cedar Lake, and afterwards pastor at Crown Point. He was very self-denying and earnest in efforts to do good, and overtasked his powers of physical endurance. He was highly esteemed by all who knew him, and was the first and only pastor dying in the county. He died at the residence of his brother, James Hunt, and was buried in the Sanders Burial Ground in West Creek Township. His age was thirty-one years.

PHILIP REED, died January 3, 1863. He was an excellent man, a minister of the Moravian or United Brethren denomination, had a farm near Lowell, and often preached at that place. He went into the Union army and was First Lieutenant, Company A, 73d Regiment Indiana Volunteers. His dust also reposes in the Sanders Burial Ground in West Creek.

CHARLES BARTON, a Methodist Episcopal local preacher, residing at Centerville, died in February, 1872, in the 85th year of his age. He had been quite active and vigorous, walked to Crown Point and back, a distance of twelve miles, the summer before his death, was a man of strong constitution, a native of New England, and had lived in the county some twenty-five years. He was a man of decided and strong views, an exemplary and consistent Christian.

OTHER LOCAL PREACHERS.

GEORGE W. TAYLOR came to Pleasant Grove in May, 1845, having a family of three sons and nine daughters, and opened a store in the grove where a villiage was beginning to grow. He was a Methodist Episcopal local preacher. Three of the family married in this county; one is now residing at Crown Point, the wife of Hon. Martin Wood. In March, 1849, G. W. Taylor removed to Valparaiso, and September 13th, of the same year, died.

M. ALLMAN, a native of England, came from Michigan to Crown Point, in the summer of 1843. He was by trade a tailor, but soon entered official life, holding the office of County Recorder from 1845 to 1856, during two terms. He was instrumental in organizing the Methodist Sunday School; with Rev. W. Townley, S. Robinson, H. Ball, and a few others, formed at Crown Point an evangelical library association; and preached frequently. In April, 1856, he removed to Michigan, and died there in December, 1858, at the age of sixty-nine years.

D. CRUMBACKER, who was, in 1843, on the circuit, returned to the county in 1846, lived at South East Grove a few years, and then returned to Crown Point. He was clerk in the store of J. W. Dinwiddie, then a member of the Indiana Constitutional Convention in the wfnter of 1850 and 1851, and afterward County Auditor. He and Rev. M. Allman were for years associated together, and were influential men in the county. He died at Washington City, March 17, 1865, and was buried in the Crown Point Cemetery. He had gone to Washington with his family, after the Civil War began, and was holding a clerkship there at the time of his death.

Both Rev. Mr. ALLMAN and Rev. D. CRUMBACKER were more than ordinary men. Much of their active life was spent here, and they were efficient aid in building up good institutions. They were efficient preachers, and very helpful co-workers with the preacher in charge. The former was short and thick-set, in person, was an active member and President of the Lake County Temperance Society, often acted as Chaplain on public days, at the gatherings of the people, and was noted for his evangelical prayers. The latter was tall and rather spare in person, enthusiastic in temperament, a popular speaker, and was a general favorite for preaching funeral sermons. Associated for a number of years together here in public and religious life, we may suppose them to be associated together now where men rest from labors and where works follow.

R. B. YOUNG, was on the circuit here in 1853. He soon after settled in Crown Point, kept a drug store for several years, and became the owner of a farm. He is a strong temperance man, a bold and fearless advocate of what he believes to be truth, an earnest preacher, and a man of firm Christian principle. Although past the meridian of life he is actively engaged amid the realities of our daily life, and enters heartily into any great moral or religious movement.

SMITH TARR came into Winfield Township about 1848. He resided there for several years, and has now for some years been a resident in West Creek, on the McLane or Belshaw place. He is a man of firm religious principle, and preaches occasionally, as duty seems to call. He has conducted the Sabbath School this summer at the Burhan's School House.

GEORGE A. EADUS, a Protestant Methodist preacher, came into the county about 1859. He resided for a time at South East Grove, afterward he lived near the McCarty mill, and now resides in Pleasant Grove, on the Cleveland place, having married Mrs. Cleveland.

R. RANDOLPH came from Michigan last year, and now resides at Centreville. He is comparatively young, and enters earnestly into the duties of active life.

RESIDENCES.

The five most costly country dwelling-houses, I would name thus: the Dittmers mansion, the Sturdeyvant brick dwelling, the residences of George Willey, of J. A. Crawford, and of Mrs. M. J. Dinwiddie, buildings costing from twenty-five hundred to three thousand dollars each.

At first we built, without any iron, or brick, or lime, the small log cabins with "shake" roofs, mud and stick chimneys, and puncheon floors. Sometimes a few nails would find their way into a window frame or into a door, but none on the roof, and none in the floor. Less than forty years have passed, and neat $3000 houses can be found on the prairies. The $30,000 residences may be found in forty years more. The best building materials of the United States may now be quite readily obtained.

THE KANKAKEE DETECTIVES.

A number of years ago it became necessary for the inhabitants along the marsh to secure themselves against depredators whom the locality seemed to invite. One hundred men were organized in a band under the above name. These met with a number of adventures, brought several men to justice, and established law and order in the community.

———

Andrew Moore, who came in September, 1838, had quite a new country experience in going to mill. He went in November to Vale's mill, near Michigan City. The roads were very bad. His load was fourteen and a half bushels of wheat and one of corn. He was gone ten days. Spent fourteen dollars. Returned home, and, in a few days, the flour was all loaned to neighbors.

WELLS AND SPRINGS.

Nearly all of the early settlers used "surface water." That "spring" besides which Solon Robinson first pitched his tent was not living water, and the first settlers did not suppose there were, in this prairie region, any real springs. Probably the first well of which anything can now be known, was dug by Warner Holton, in 1835. He lived on what is now "Railroad Addition," near the present depot. He dug four feet. Water came in which supplied other families. When the water failed he dug deeper, and finally reached a depth of about twelve feet.

Probably the same season, Judge Clark, who lived on Section Eight, near Dr. Pratt's place, dug some sixty feet and failed to obtain water. A well of some depth was not long afterward dug on the Pelton place, now Dr. Pettibone's, and water obtained.

At Cedar Lake, on the Russell claim, a well was dug to quite a depth, and mineral water reached. It was used by different families, but was not pleasant to the taste. Other families therefore dug shallow wells, ten or twelve feet in depth, in the low places. In the dry seasons the hooks or poles with which the water was drawn would sometimes be hidden, and some were actually compelled to steal water in order to quench thirst. But as the surface wells failed and brick began to be made, permanent wells were dug. The depth of these wells varies from some fifteen to seventy feet.

At Shererville the wells are driven. The sand comes to the surface. The wells are shallow but the water is good. At Ross and Tolleston, and other villages on the sand ridges, the wells are also shallow.

The dry weather of the last two years has caused many new wells to be dug. Some of these and a few others, possess some peculiarities.

Thomas C. Goodrich, in the fall of 1871 dug, on the side hill of that broad ridge south of Turkey Creek, and near the base of the hill, twenty-seven feet, and then bored eighteen feet and reached water. The brick were then laid up about three feet, the bored orifice having been closed, and the workmen rested for the night. The next morning the well was filled with water to within ten feet of the surface, the supply seemed inexhaustible, and the walling up was abandoned. A second was dug, about ten feet up the hill, rise of ground about one foot, to the depth of twenty-seven feet. On boring twenty inches water was reached, the brick were laid, and the water came up to about eleven feet from the surface. The water is excellent in quality and abundant in quantity.

A well on the Dittmers' place is impregnated with some mineral resembling Epsom salts. It is a very agreeable, healthful water.

The well at the cheese factory, north of Crown Point, was dug sixty-five feet, then bored twenty-seven feet. The water came up to within some fifty feet of the surface.

J. H. Ball has lately dug two wells on his lots in Railroad Addition. The first is twenty-four feet in depth, in which the water rose eleven and a half feet and there remains. The second is fourteen and a half feet, furnishing a supply, but no rise of water. These are about two hundred feet apart. Water is reached at different depths, but will generally rise several feet on Railroad Addition.

The first springs discovered by the settlers were probably on the west bank of Cedar Lake. One was on the Brown claim, and furnished sufficient water for one family for several years. The water was clear, pure, cold, and good.

A second was known as the Gray spring. It furnished a large amount of water, which was sometimes carried more than a mile in barrels, conveyed across the lake in boats, and supplied several families. This water was cold and good, but strongly impregnated with iron.

Springs were afterward discovered in various localities. Along West Creek, along Deep River, and even on the prairie. Some of these are quite large, but they send forth no bold streams. This is not a region of running waters and gushing fountains; the streams are often sluggish, yet are there among the grassy meads some sunny brooks, and quiet rivulets.

SOUTH EAST GROVE.

This grove is one of the largest and finest in the county outside of the Kankakee Marsh. In form it is circular, covering about one section of land. The corner of sections One and Two, Eleven and Twelve, Township 33, Range 8, is not far from the school house, in the southern half of the grove. The timber is mostly hickory and oak, much of it at present young and thrifty. Some of the earliest settlers here have been already mentioned. There were two Flint families, the families of O. V. Servis, Gibson, Parkinson, Orrin Smith, —— Morris, and some few others. In the spring of 1840, Alexander F. Brown came to the grove, from the State of New York. He brought with him three hired men. He secured a choice location and commenced extensive improvements. While carrying on his plans, and having the ambition and resolution which would have been likely to have secured a large success, his prosperous course was suddenly terminated by an accidental death. At work one day, his horses took fright, he was thrown from his wagon, and died in about a week, October 21, 1849. His sons, John Brown, and W. Barringer Brown, at their father's death, boys of nine and six years of age, are now among the most intelligent and enterprising business young men of the county. The former is now county treasurer, the other remains at the grove, on the farm.

Other energetic business men settled at and around South East Grove. Wm. Brown, late a County Commissioner and now Township Trustee, came in 1843. John A. Crawford in 1844. H. Kingsbury came about 1847. James Doak came in the spring of 1852. George Doak came April 21, 1855. He taught at Plum Grove, West Creek, Orchard Grove, and again at Plum Grove. He married a daughter of H. Kingsbury, and now resides on the Kingsbury place, one of the best winter wheat farms in this region.

Several other families reside in the neighborhood who have bought farms in later years, and the congregation meeting at the Grove School House for Sabbath worship is noted for intelligence, good order, and generous hospitality.

ORCHARD GROVE

Is smaller than the one named above; is pleasantly situated near the edge of the marsh; and gives a name to the post office, store, and school house, of an intelligent, prosperous, farming community. The two Kenney, the Woodruff, the Handley, and Warner families, have long resided here; and a number of other families in easy circumstances are living on the choice farms of this locality.

PLUM GROVE

Is east and a little north from Orchard, distant about two miles. It is small, is near the marsh, and now contains more crab apple than wild plum trees. The families of the neighborhood are the following: Mrs. M. Pearce, J. Pearce, O. V. Servis, Sen., W. Buchanan; Mrs. M. J. Dinwiddie, J. Dinwiddie, F. Westman, H. Deters; J. Hamilton, M. Nichols, J. Hildarbiddle, Mrs. Hale; W. V. Fuller, J. Filsinger, J. Alyea, Earl Brownell, Charles Brownell; A. Mitch, C. A. Hale, C. Emmerling, M. Jordan, S. Hogan, and A. J. McCann.

LOST ON THE PRAIRIE.

Two have been mentioned who perished on the prairie from exposure to the cold. Many others were lost, but their wanderings and hair-breadth escapes are for the most part also lost.

T. Fisher was returning in the spring of the year from Door Prairie, with a load of broom corn, and was overtaken by the darkness of a cloudy night on the prairie between Hickory Point and South East Grove. Some dangerous sloughs lay in that region. Missing the course in the gathering darkness, the horses soon came to a halt. To urge them forward into the slough that lay before them was risky, and he turned back and endeavored by careful examination to find some safe passage across the barrier. Leaving his wagon, to ascertain, if possible, his bearings, he barely succeeded in finding his way back in the darkness. Again driving onward, the horses once more stopped. Giving up at length the hope of reaching home that night, he unharnessed the horses, tied them to the wagon, and spreading a buffalo skin on the ground, waited for the morning light.

In the thick darkness of the spring and summer it is not pleasant to be lost all night; but amid the piercing wind and freezing cold of a winter night, to wander, as some have done, on the trackless prairie, is terrible.

In the winter of 1838 or 1839, H. Ball was returning from Michigan City to Cedar Lake, the night-fall found him on the open area of Twenty Mile Prairie. The snow clouds obscured the sky, the wind blew, the horses missed the track, and he was lost. No houses were near. It was to him a night of suffering and danger. Two or three circumstances combined to save his life. A star shone out for a moment and kept him from taking a direction that led yet further away from human abodes. Finding it useless to continue wandering around on the bleak prairie, having with him fortunately a bolt of satinet, and having a pair of large and powerful horses, one of which was remarkably sagacious, he wound the cloth around him and stood between the heads of the horses to seek some shelter from the wind and to share some warmth from their breath. To grow weary and seek rest, or to lie down in the sleigh there and become benumbed, was to perish. And so he remained between the heads of those noble horses amid the bitter cold, until a shrill sound, the distant crowing of a rooster before the morning dawned, indicated the direction of a human dwelling. Proceeding toward that cheering sound he reached a house, and found shelter, and warmth, and rest. It was a night which he never forgot, the winter night spent on Twenty Mile Prairie.

NATIVE WILD ANIMALS.

Most of our wild animals have been incidentally named. Of the fur-bearing tribes there originally were musk-rats, mink, otter, and beaver. The latter disappeared before the white men came. Of other quadrupeds there were deer, and wolves, and wild-cats, fox squirrels, and rabbits. On one island in the marsh, black squirrels are found. Chipmunks, gophers, and ground squirrels abounded. There was found in Cedar Lake a pair of large horns, supposed to be elk, indicating that they were once in this region.

The wolves were very abundant here, as were most of the other animals, when the settlers came. Two boys out from home one day saw as many as a dozen, and two followed them within half a mile of their home. On winter mornings the new fallen snow would be marked with a multitude of their tracks. Men would chase them sometimes with horses, and, among the grubs, the wolf has been known to look saucily up at the rider, as much as to say, "Catch me if you can." A physician, on his rides, has sometimes given them chase; and even a well-mounted pioneer minister, on the way from one appointment to another, has been tempted to follow the unscared wolf, and only missed capturing him by his wolfship at length taking refuge in a marsh where the swift horse could not follow.

A few large gray wolves have occasionally visited our prairies, even as lately as this present year; but they are not considered to be native.

Of feathered animals, the grouse, or prairie chickens, were those that gave character to the prairies; the waterfowls have been named in connection with Cedar Lake; the usual varieties of little birds were in the groves; and the crow, the hawk, and the eagle, were native inhabitants.

Of wild life, without ferocious animals, there was no lack. The waters swarmed with fish; and the groves, and the prairies, and the marshes were alive with their appropriate inhabitants. The larger marshes, and even small ones, in the midst of the dryest prairie, contained some fish, and multitudes of small shell-bearing animals, called snails or periwinkles. The prairie crawfish abounded. The rattlesnakes and other venomous and harmless serpents were on almost every rood of land; and ox flies and horse flies seemed to drive the domestic cattle nearly to distraction.

But these smaller animals, and the venomous serpents, and many of the other denizens of the region, have already disappeared; and few comparatively remain amid our present civilization. It is ever so, that the children of nature retire before the cultivated races. A few more years and we may scarcely have anything that comes under the name of game.

I close the items in this chapter with some specimens of our Fine Arts. From the amateur painters, musicians, and gardeners, nothing can be obtained capable of being set up in type; but the amateur poets furnish me with some specimens of their art which I transfer to these pages. It is not to be expected that in a region where forty years ago the Indian hunters were sole occupants, and where the squatter and the settler have toiled early and late to secure the comforts of life, there should be—without any city growth—the wealth, or leisure, or talent even, to accomplish anything in this line which would attract the attention of a connoisseur. Nevertheless I place on these pages for preservation a few specimens from true children of Lake.

"TO THE WHIP-POOR-WILL.

"Strange bird of the evening, we love thy pure tone,
    That comes over valley and hill,
When the wind from the southland utters its moan,
And Winter's chill wings from the wild wood have flown;
Thy voice in the dark hours then, plaintive and lone,
    Sings ever its clear whip-poor-will.

" Shy bird, dost thou know how we list to thy note,
    When sounds of the day are all still?
The deep chords of feeling are touched when there floats
On the still evening air from woodland remote,

Thy voice, sad and mournful, yet strong, that denotes
   Thy true faith, thou lone whip-poor-will.

"But why dost thou sing, all through night's lonely hours?
   Hast thou too, a mission to fill?
Does earth's gloom, through sympathy, call forth thy powers,
And when from *our hearts* are gone sunshine and flowers,
While night-dews are chill, and star-beams gem thy bowers,
   Canst cheer with thy shrill whip-poor-will?

"Ah! brave heart and true, that can hopefully beat,
   Though sorrows earth's chalice doth fill,
And find 'mid the dark hours of life a retreat,
And sing, "songs in the night," with deep joy replete,
And with sunshine of soul the morning, can greet,
   Like the night-bird, the loved whip-poor-will.
                                 A. A. A."

"THE SEASIDE RECLUSE.

[Lines suggested by an Engraving in Mrs. ——'s drawing-room, and to her respectfully dedicated.]

BY J. H. B.

"Lovely vision! maidens fair!
Unbound tresses! flowing hair!
By the rocks, and by the sea;
Emblems sweet of purity!
Painter's hands portray you well!
Is it here you ever dwell?
Or come you to hear the beat
Of ocean throbbing 'neath your feet?

"Mountain nymphs or water naiads,
Tell me how long here you've staid,
If indeed of human mould
What sad sorrows all untold
May have crossed your pathway bright?

For if now I judge aright,
Anxious cares once filled your breast,
Though now so calm, serene, at rest.

" Imagination tunes her ear ;
I listen now and seem to hear.
Voices blending, sad and sweet,
As echoes in the woodlands meet,
Plaintive, mournful, soft and low,
Like purling streams that gently flow ;
Noting words while still I may,
Much like this they seem to say :

" 'I have found your retreat, by the surf-beaten shore,
   Ah ! these cold granite stones look too sombre and grim,
Here the sea breeze is damp, much too damp for you more,
   Hasten home with me then, ere is sung our night hymn.
'Melia, gaze not so sad on the ocean's dark crest,
   There is much yet in life, although mixed with alloy.
Then dismiss your dark thoughts, bid your moaning heart rest,
   There are pleasures still left, if you would but enjoy.'

" Oh ! Theresa, dear friend, I'm resigned to my fate,
   All repinings long since, have departed my breast,
Yet I love to sit here, by these gray rocks, and wait,
   While one faint ray of light lingers still in the west.
Yes, 'tis here, while in listening to the waters' low moan,
   My brow fanned by the sea breeze that nightly sets in,
That I care not for life, all I'd live for seems flown,
   All earth's joys set for me when I parted with him.'

" ' Now I think of the Past, and my mem'ry goes back
   To the time when we wandered here, free from all care,
Treading lightly our path, by yon rivulet's track,
   In the eventide cool, or by morn fresh and fair,
All unconscious of sorrow, of suff'ring, of pain,
   Fearing naught, dreading naught, knowing naught of life's ills,

Fondly dreaming these pleasure would ever remain,
    Drank the full cup of bliss, and yet sighed for it still.'

"'Now the Present looks dark, very dark to my eyes,
    And each purpose in life seems vague, dim and uncertain,
On the grandeur of ocean, on the blue-vaulted skies,
    I find solace in musing, while night spreads her curtain,
I people the mists, with gentle forms, and sweet voices,
    Now the sad, and the gay, I commingle together,
And oh! with what a thrill my heart often rejoices,
    That there's one at my bidding, that comes to me ever.'

"'Wrap this mantle around you and sit down awhile,
    For the dark clouds are breaking, the sunset is bright,
And perchance from old sorrows my mind 'twill beguile,
    Should I tell you a vision I saw but last night.
It was later than this, I had gazed long, so long,
    On the waters' weird face, after twilight's last ray,
The darkness had deepened, and the night-breeze blew strong,
    And beneath moaned the surge, as it dashed its wild spray.'

"'A lone ship seemed to move, phantom-like on the wave,
    I could plainly distinguish the sails and the shrouds,
As a transient light seemed the sea's surface to lave,
    Like the moon breaking forth out of dark-rifted clouds.
A group on the deck were peering out on the gloom,
    With anxiety descrying the face of the land,
Now awaiting in silence and with fear the sad doom,
    Should their vessel on some of these unknown rocks strand.'

"'At the helm there stood one with lips firmly compressed,
    Self-reliant and calmly he guided their way,
And each movement he made close observed by the rest,
    As all waited his nod or command to obey.
All so perfect, so real, it then to me seemed,
    The proud bearing, the mien, was Brusabo's alone,
Could there be but truth in it, and though I have dreamed,
    Might I think he still lived, that he yet would come home

"'Six long years have now passed since that wild, gloomy day,
    Years of longing, and hoping, and watching, and prayer,
When they called him a convict, and bore him away,
    And my heart seemed to sink in the wildest despair.
One thought then sustained me, is upholding me still—
    When in agony's calmness he bade me farewell,
'Oh! believe me,' he said, 'and I trust that you will,
    All this dark tale is false that against me they tell.'"

"'Oh! I knew 'twas so false to charge him with a crime,
    It was jealousy, malice! 'twas envy or hate,
He could do nothing wrong with a spirit so fine!
    Ah! they drove him to madness, then laughed at his fate!
His proud spirit soon sunk 'neath the blow and the chain,
    As in bondage awhile with the chained-gang he trod,
Then he sickened and died, and was laid in the main,
    As the ship passed in sight of our own native sod.'

"'When I think what his hopes were, so glowing and bright,
    How his life's sun arose with no clouds in the sky,
Then so sudden went down in such darkness of night,
    Murm'ring thoughts to subdue, it seems vain that I try!
He was all things to me, there's naught ever can fill,
    In my wounded and bruised heart, the aching void left,
Oft I strive to forget, but I think of him still,
    And in anguish my heart moans, 'Bereft! Oh! bereft!'

"'Oh! Amelia, remember, though poignant the grief,
    This one thought, that our Father permitted the blow,
Our repinings should still, to our hearts bring relief,
    For He deals but in wisdom to mortals below.
Then dispel all this gloom, look on life's brighter side,
    Though the pathway seems dark, light is shining beyond,
With each duty performed we no ills need betide,
    But sink sweetly to rest when declines the day's sun.'

"'I feel all that you say, to its truth I attest,
    And the strange cup I drink, I accept what is given,

> Calmness now fills my breast, but not rest, no, not rest,
>   I will find that alone when I find it in Heaven!
> Yes, beyond the cold tide and the mists of life's ocean,
>   Loved Brusabo awaits, standing on the dim shore,
> In the twilight oft, oft, he is seeming to motion
>   For me there to join him where are sorrows no more.'"

I place next, not as a model epithalamium, a little piece, slightly revised, written and read at the marriage of Dr. Andrew S. Cutler and Miss Mary Jane Ball, December 16, 1869.

> On a lovely prairie in the State of Ind.
> In a pleasant home well sheltered from the wind,
> Two little flowers appeared not many years ago,
> Growing in the sunshine and dreading not the snow.
>
> Like the lily opening, like the rose, they grew,
> Showing forth alike the sweet, the pure, the true;
> Like twins indeed they seemed on one rich rose stalk set,
> Fed by the self-same showers, by the same dew-drops wet.
>
> Fast they grew and lovely thus growing side by side;
> But lovely things and pleasant may not long abide;
> The one was taken up within the gates of light,
> The other blooms in beauty here with us to-night.
>
> Said I two little flowers? Oh no, two gentle birds,
> Came to that prairie home, I change two little words;
> One came in glowing autumn, mid October's sun;
> The other in December, this the youngest one.
>
> I know not whence they came, but I am very sure
> They seemed to us like doves and like the robins pure.
> Were they birds of passage? or were they birds of song?
> One flew to Paradise; may this one tarry long.
>
> Did I say flowers and birds? They were my sisters dear,
> Who for some twenty years were seldom severed here;

Alike they grew in knowledge and alike in love,
Were they gentle visitants sent us from above?

They were the household pets, the youngest of our band;
(There are not "seven" to-night together here to stand;)
It has been said, the youngest never do grow old;
'Tis sure that loving natures never need grow cold.

Joy for that flown and freed one. Perfect joy and love
Are where we trust she dwells among the good above.
And joy to this young bride, unmingled by earth's fear;
Though perfect joy and perfect bliss are not the dwellers here.

Yet to sister Mary and brother Andrew joy!
May life for them be bright with little to annoy.
No tears are shed to-night around our household tree;
For hope, and peace, and love, go with the truly free.

The two sisters referred to above were Mary Jane and Henrietta Ball, both born at Cedar Lake, and in their childhood and youth almost inseperable companions in every occupation. The younger, HENRIETTA, considered by all who knew her as being richly endowed in all the qualities and capabilities that gave promise of a noble womanhood, graduating at the Indianapolis Female Institute in 1861, died at Cedar Lake, January 27, 1863, being twenty-one years of age.

"MYTH AND TRUTH; OR, PAST AND FUTURE GLORY.

"I have read the ancient stories,
　Fables, legends, fiction, truth;
Read of many wondrous glories,
　Told of nations in their youth.

"Read of Eastern pomp and splendor,
　Read of warriors true and bold;

Of a noted witch of Endor,
    And a temple bright with gold.

" Read of peace and read of slaughter,
    Written in the Book of books;
Moses found by Pharaoh's daughter,
    Strong in faith and fair in looks.

" Of the Shepherd boy so fearless,
    Smiting with a sling and stone,
'Mong the warrior poets peerless,
    King at length on Judah's throne.

" Read of gifted prophets many,
    Those so grand, and true, and wise,
Unexcelled on earth by any,
    Seeing distant glories rise.

" Prophets, poets, seers and sages,
    Shepherds, soldiers, priests and kings:
Earth still holds these deathless pages,
    Earth still with their record rings.

" I have read the myths and fables,
    That arose in ancient time,
Like that tale of Augean stables,
    Fictions most of love and crime.

" Persian, Hindoo, Scald or Norseman,
    All these have their legends old;
Romans tell of two twin horsemen,
    Pollux, Castor, swift and bold.

" Romans tell of many a hero,
    Who has borne him well in fight;
Long before the bloody Nero,
    Rome had fabled gods of might.

" Greek and Arab lack not fable,
    And they give us stories rare,

> Arthur's Knights and his Round Table,
> Scarcely with them can compare.
>
> " Myths and legends all might perish,
> They are powerless on the heart ;
> Sacred truth the world should cherish,
> Never with it can it part.
>
> " Still in future myths may linger,
> Will be read by students o'er,
> But there points an index finger,
> Ever to the sacred lore ;
>
> " Saying to earth's children ever,
> Listen to these words divine,
> Lay aside the prophets never,
> Future glories soon will shine.
>
> " Buried in the depths of ages,
> Lies the greatness myths declare ;
> Promised on the sacred pages,
> Future greatness looms forth fair.
>
> " Let earth's children read and ponder,
> Let them earnest workers be,
> For the day dawns, see it yonder !
> Soon earth's millions will be free.
>
> " Soon will come the Latter Glory ;
> Ours a glory *yet to be*,
> When each fabled mythic story
> Sinks beneath oblivion's sea.   Y. N. L."

I place last, among these selections, a little piece read at the marriage of Dr. H. H. Pratt and Miss Carrie R. Jarvis, May 15, 1872, and to them affectionately dedicated.

A NEW PSALM OF LIFE.

Our life is what we make it.
Then if we could only know,
How to take the ebb and flow
Of the mighty currents round,
Bearing swiftly, without sound,
To the dark unfathomed deep,
It might be grand and glorious.
Death is not an endless sleep.

Listen to the words, "What cheer?"
Cheer to thee amid the gloom!
Cheer to thee amid the strife!
Through the many struggles here,
That may lead to endless life!
Through the dark, and through the bright,
Those still steadfast to the right,
Whisper to each other cheer.

Ah! 'tis not alone to breathe,
Not to eat and drink alone,
That make up life, something more—
Things that live beyond time's shore.
Life is more, yes, more than meat,
More than raiment too, is life.
Sit at the Great Teacher's feet,
Learn the worth of toil and strife.

Yes, life is what we make it;
Our life is as we take it,
Marked with brightness, love and joy,
Worthless with some base alloy.
And alas! how very mean,
How sad, how vainly wasted,
Its sweets almost untasted,
Is the life of many a queen.

From the highest to the low,
From the throne to peasant's cot,
Few solve aright life's mystery,
Few that share a blessed lot.
For life is what we make it,
And we do not make it bright ;
Our life is as we take it,
And we do not take it right.

It may lead us up on high,
Through the blue and lovely sky,
To the gift of a white stone,
To a super-human throne,
To a new name written bright,
And to mansions fair as light ;
To the gates of endless day,
Where no loved ones pass away.

CHAPTER XI.

SKETCHES OF EARLY SETTLERS.

"MEN DIE BUT PRINCIPLES LIVE."

"Better to weave in the web of life
    A bright and golden filling,
And to do God's will with a ready heart,
    And hands that are swift and willing,
Than to snap the minute, delicate threads
    Of our curious life asunder,
And then blame heaven for the tangled ends,
    And sit, and grieve and wonder."

Lord Bacon, it is said, assigns the highest meed of earthly fame to the founders of States, to those whom the Romans called *conditores imperiorum*. The early settlers of the United States, especially those world-renowned men, the Pilgrim Fathers of New England, doubtless belong to the class and merit the fame of "Founders of States" or *conditores imperiorum;* but those who first penetrated the Western wilds, like Daniel Boone, when Kentucky was the "dark and bloody ground," pioneer men in their home-spun, and with their rifles, certainly deserve some of the credit and honor belonging to builders and founders. And our own early settlers, who first woke the echoes of civilization in Northwestern Indiana, who endured hardships, and privations, and exposures, to establish a county and found a small republic, although not exposed to the Indian tomahawk, are nevertheless justly entitled to some meed of fame as men who truly belonged to the class of builders. Lake county was a wild when they entered it, beautiful and fertile, it is true, like primeval nature, but inhabited by wild animals innumerable and the lingering Pottawatomies.

Taking possession, for the generations of the future, of five hundred square miles of surface, they at once began to build for the benefit of posterity. Law and order, and material comforts; and social, and intellectual, and religious institutions, rapidly grew up under their fostering care. Few of them now remain among us, and no full sketches can here be given even of those most distinguished in our earliest annals. For a notice of some, however, I possess more ample material than I do concerning others; and in the brief sketches that follow I hope to do none injustice.

SOLON ROBINSON.

The readers of these chapters have already become somewhat familiar with the name written above. Although not quite the first settler, yet of right, the first sketch should be of him whose name is so fully interwoven with our early records. From 1834 to 1851, Solon Robinson was intimately identified with the interests of Lake. A native of Connecticut, he spent some years in the southern part of Indiana. Removing with a young family into this beautiful wild, away from civilized man, he was active in forming the Squatters' Union; was the first recorder of claims; after the organization of the county was elected clerk; was clerk and general manager

of the board of commissioners; at his house the first
courts were held; and by means of his situation, his opportunities,
his intelligence, his capabilities, and his talent,
he to so great an extent controlled the affairs of the
settlers that he gained the title of "Squatter King of
Lake." I am not aware that he was disposed to be arbitrary,
or despotic, or overbearing;—he was himself, then,
but a squatter among squatters, and although soon by
means of his *pen* he began to shape for himself a new
line of life; he was affable, familiar, plain, hospitable,
kind and accommodating;—but he doubtless liked to
wield influence, and was then entering upon a career
that gained for him no little celebrity. Practically, he
was not much of a farmer. His garden spot, where the
Indians had raised maize, formed the common garden of
the summer of 1835 of the four families of the settlement;
and although he in common with them "broke up"
the prairie sod and commenced making farms, his official
duties and merchandising soon engrossed his time, and
that Indian garden spot became his principal sphere of
actual farming operations. Yet he took an interest in
agriculture and commenced writing for the *Cultivator*.
The first article which I find, on a somewhat careful examination
of some bound volumes, is dated Lake C. H.,
July 12, 1837. It is headed, "Nutmeg Potatoes—Lake
Superior Corn." It speaks of sending "prairie flower
seeds," is short, and reads like the communication of a
new correspondent. A longer communication is in a
succeeding number, dated August 29, which contains a
proposition to increase the circulation of the *Cultivator*,
and the proposition is accompanied with a five dollar

subscription for gratuitous distribution. In 1838 and 1839 other communications followed. In 1840, I find twelve; in 1841, fifteen; in 1842, seven; in 1843, five; *Cultivator* communications.

In 1843 Solon Robinson was removed from the office of postmaster, which he had for so long a time held. As he expressed it, see *Cultivator*, "in the operations of Tylerism I have lately lost the franking privilege"; and he assigns this as a reason for not writing so many letters as formerly. He feared his friends would not consider them worth the postage. Letters cost in those days, and were not generally prepaid. He says: "For the same reason my communications to the numerous agricultural papers will be less frequent than formerly." For what other papers he wrote I am not informed. These contributions to the *Cultivator* are on a variety of topics of interest to farmers, and some of them are sketches of life in the West at that early period; and some of them are addressed to "Western Emigrants." In one of these he says well, "An able general selects a small portion of a large army for pioneers because of the peculiar fitness of that small part for that arduous and important service. It is my opinion that a much smaller portion of the community are fit for pioneers in settling a new country." He therefore does not advise everybody to come West.

These various articles, by their style and from their locality, secured many readers, gained for their author much celebrity, and made his name familiar in very many farmer homes. They secured for him also many correspondents.

As early as March, 1838, he made the proposal to form

an "American Society of Agriculture." This subject he agitated considerably, and in April, 1841, he wrote " an address to the farmers of the United States," which went out through the columns of the *Cultivator*. In April, of the same year, he wrote to the editors of the *Cultivator* the following:

"I now have in contemplation to make an extensive agricuitural tour during the coming summer, and it would be a great pleasure to me, and I have reason to believe it would be equally so to some of your readers, to form a personal acquaintance with them as far as practicable; and as I shall ' take notes,' and you will ' print them,' it may also conduce to our mutual improvement. I have, therefore, thought proper to make this public announcement of my intentions and route."

He then names the places through which he will pass, and individuals upon whom he expects to call, along quite a route of travel. That trip he took. The October *Cultivator* contains the following editorial:

"It gives us great pleasure to state that our friend Solon Robinson, Esq., the zealous and able promoter of industry, and the original projector of a National Agricultural Society, has safely arrived at Washington, and that on the fourth of September a meeting was held in the Hall of the Patent Office, at which the incipient steps for the formation of such a society were taken." After giving proceedings they add: " We here gladly insert the remarks of Mr. Robinson, accompanying and explaining the report of the proceedings, in preference to anything we could add ourselves in enforcing the propriety and necessity of such an organization. It is indeed probable that before this sheet goes to the press, Mr. Robinson will have been among us; and we cannot doubt his reception among his agricultural friends in the east and north, will be such as to convince him that they will not be behind those of any portion of the Union, in a cordial support to his great undertaking."

It thus appears that the credit of forming a National Agricultural Society belongs to the County of Lake. Those "remarks" that followed are too lengthy to be here given.

To his neighbors and acquaintances, here, it was quite entertaining to see how distinguished and popular their fellow citizen had become abroad, and especially when they looked upon his little farm in the garden and knew that practically he was not a farmer at all. They had not fully learned that the *pen* was "mightier than the sword," or even then the heavy plows which *they* followed, and the scythes and the cradles which *they* swung.

Solon Robinson returned home to Crown Point; staid a little longer among us; represented our State in a large convention at Chicago among such men as Tom Corwin, Horace Greeley, and other notables of the land, in about 1845; made a tour, as a Western agricultural writer, through the Southern States; and made a visit to New York. He found a position that seemed to suit him better than holding office in Lake County. He left his family here, a wife, two sons, and two daughters; made to Judge Turner, of Crown Point, a deed of his real estate in Lake and La Porte Counties for the benefit of his wife; and they separated by *mutual agreement*.

He took a position in connection with the *New York Tribune.*

His life in New York it is not a part of my present task to give. It is sufficient on this to say that his moral principles were not of the Puritanical school, and that the man who would abandon such a woman as was Mrs. Maria Robinson could not be expected afterwards to lead a very exemplary life.

HIS LITERARY PRODUCTIONS.

The first of these, so far as here known, was a story of Indian and border life, called "The Will." The scene was laid, on the Indian side, at Cedar Lake, other incidents transpired in the bounds of the county. It is quite an interesting story. The next was called, "The Last of the Buffaloes." This I have not read. These two were written and published while he was residing at Crown Point. After he became established at New York he published, in book form, "Hot Corn," "Green Mountain Girls," and "A Dime a Day, or Economy of Living Well;" also a story in the *Weekly Tribune* called, "Mewon-i-toc," the scene of which was laid in Lake County. He also edited a large work of some four or five hundred pages, called "Farmers' Encyclopædia."

In or about 1868 he left the Tribune office and made his home at Jacksonville, Florida. He is understood to be in easy circumstances, even what here we would call wealthy, having an income of some four or five thousand dollars a year.

In person he is rather tall, spare, dignified; accustomed to the ways of society. His hair was white thirty-five years ago, and it has not grown dark since. His age is sixty-eight. Although the *pen* has been his special instrument, and that to which in a great degree he owes his celebrity and position and wealth; yet he can speak easily and readily; and has evidently possessed a shrewd and cultivated intellect; cultivated not by the learning and drill of the schools, but by thought and effort in actual life.

In one article to Western Emigrants he says: "Happiness and not wealth should be the aim of all, though no man should allow himself to be happy without he is doing some good in the world—promoting the happiness of his fellow creatures as well as himself."

In closing up his last address to the Lake County Temperance Society, in the year 1847, Solon Robinson gave utterance to the following words:

"And as for myself I will ask no prouder monument to my fame than to be assured that the members of this society will stand as mourners around my grave, and, pointing to the lifeless form beneath the falling sods, shall truly say, 'There lies a brother who in this life had an ardent desire to promote the happiness of his fellow creatures. May his historian be able to record that in the latter years of his life he was eminently successful in this.'"

Scattered and dead as most of the members of that society now are, and far away from this region as he who uttered these words now resides, himself an aged man, it is not probable any of these associates will aid in laying his lifeless form away to rest. And I fear, if rumor be true, that in these "latter years," he, like too many of us, has forgotten sometimes the happiness of his fellow creatures in the pursuit and enjoyment of merely selfish gratifications. But well, evidently, has Solon Robinson known *how*, and *for what*, men ought to live. The Perfect Records will show at the last whether he has achieved an *eminent success*.

GEORGE EARLE.

The town of Liverpool, so noted in our early history, was on an Indian reservation, or on land selected under an Indian float. In the Recorder's Office is a copy of the patent, signed by Andrew Jackson, President of the United States, June 16, 1836, conveying to John B. Chapman Section 24, Township 36, Range 8, being 603.60 acres, in accordance with the third article of the treaty made on the Tippecanoe River with the chiefs and warriors of the Pottawatomies in 1832. The town plat as recorded bears the date January 30, 1836. In this town George Earle, from the City of Philadelphia, a native of Falmouth, England, became a resident in the year 1836. Prominent as he soon became among the settlers, he was not himself a squatter. He was at first agent for the proprietors of the town, he was afterwards County Agent, and purchasing one interest after another, he became owner of a large tract of land. Section 18, T. 36, R. 7, was bought by John B. Chapman, one of the original proprietors of Liverpool, for $800, of Re-re-mo-sau, or Parish, also written Parrish, as the deed says, "once a chief but now an Indian of the Pottawatomies." So near as I have ascertained some ten or twelve sections of land came at length into the hands of the County Agent. Across this land railroads were at length built. The towns of Lake and Hobart were laid out and grew up upon it, and the owner became wealthy.

A personal friend, yet at the same time a rival of Solon Robinson for the location of the county seat, gaining it at first and losing the location afterward, his agency in the naming of the permanent county seat and sale of the lots has been already mentioned. After the question of location was finally settled the proprietor of Liverpool continued to improve that place. It was claimed to be the head of navigation on the river, and a large boat was built in 1840–'41 to carry produce to Chicago and to open inland commerce. The navigation proved difficult. The boat was taken in 1841 by horse-power to Chicago, was remodeled into a schooner, and, while making a voyage, was wrecked near Michigan City. The time had not then come for the boat navigation of our marshy rivers. Finding that Liverpool was not likely to become a city, its proprietor in the spring of 1845 commenced building mills at Hobart, distant some three miles. The dam and saw mill were completed in 1846, a grist mill was soon in operation, and the family removed to that place in 1847. The town was laid out in 1848.

In 1854 the proprietor of Liverpool, and Lake, and Hobart, returned to Philadelphia, leaving his son, John Earle, to manage the property interests in the county.

The resemblances and the contrasts between Solon Robinson and George Earle are somewhat singular and marked. Both remained some sixteen or seventeen years in this county. One founded a town and secured the county seat; the other obtained the county seat but lost it, and laid out and established other towns. The one retired to New York; the other to Philadelphia. The one, well as he knew the lands of the county, invested but little in land, and left here the owner of none, depending for his future fortune upon his talent and his pen; the other made selections of land that proved profitable investments, and retired to use the pencil and the brush, to draw architect's plans and place forms of beauty on canvas. The one seems carefully to avoid revisiting the scenes of his settler days; the other frequently returns to his former home in his railroad town. Both had talent and intelligence, both have now the reputation of possessing ample means; but their early training, native tastes, and circumstances in life, have led to different results. In 1855 George Earle revisited his native place in England. He made a second visit in 1865, and a third in 1868. While there he caused to be erected a home for the poor and aged of the town of Falmouth, at a cost of $30,000, and made a donation of it to the town. Fond of architecture and painting, he in his home at Philadelphia, sometimes made architectural designs, combining profit with pleasure; and in leisure hours painted a number of pictures which have been placed upon the walls of the art-gallery which he erected at Hobart in 1858. He made a visit of several weeks during this summer, at the residence of his son, and will probably soon revisit the shores of England. He is tall in person, dignified and courteous in manners, manifesting the bearing of an American and English gentleman.

HON. LEWIS WARRINER.

Lewis Warriner was born in West Springfield, Massachuetts, in June, 1792. He settled on the east side of

Cedar Lake, November 9, 1837, having lived until that year in his native town, near the west bank of the Connecticut.

His wife, an estimable woman, Mrs. Sabra Warriner, two sons and two daughters, composed the family. Entering actively upon the occupations of a new country life, a pleasant and happy home seemed secure for this New England family; but the "sickly season" of 1838 came upon them, sickness entered their home, death darkened their door, and the loved forms of the mother and youngest daughter were soon laid away to rest in that now neglected mound on the bank of the lake. The others rose up from sickness, and with strong hearts entered anew upon the work of providing comforts for a home out of which so much light and joy had departed.

A mail route was opened this same year from Crown Point to West Creek, twelve miles, and Lewis Warriner was appointed post master, being the second or third one in the county. This office he held until 1849 when, in Gen. Taylor's administration, he was removed. When the administration changed, in 1852, he was again appointed, and held the office until he left the county in 1856.

In the State of Massachusetts he had been sent four times as representative to Boston, and filled other positions of honor and trust in his native State. In 1839 he was elected a member of the Indiana Legislature to represent Lake and Porter Counties, his competitors being, it is believed, L. Bradley, of City West, and B. McCarty, of Valparaiso.

So far as I can ascertain, he was the first citizen of

Lake County sent to the Legislature. In 1840 he took the first United States census in our bounds. He was again elected a member of the Legislature in 1848.

He was one of the constituent members of the Cedar Lake Baptist Church, organized in June, 1838, having been, with his wife, a member of the Agawam Baptist Church, in West Springfield, and remained true to his Christian profession until his death. He was an excellent neighbor, an exemplary church member, a useful, active citizen, and in public life, both in Massachusetts and in Indiana, discharged his official duties faithfully and to the satisfaction of his constituents.

His surviving children both having married and left the county, he, in 1856, went to reside with his son, Edwin B. Warriner, at Kankakee, Illinois, and afterwards with his daughter, Mrs. James A. Hunt. He died at his son-in-law's residence at Prairie Grove, Fayette County, Arkansas, May 14, 1869, being almost 77 years of age.

I quote the following: "As a man he always commanded the highest respect and confidence of his neighbors and acquaintances in all the walks of life, both public and private, and was always ready to give his influence and support for every object tending to benefit or improve his fellow man.

"As a Christian he was active and sincere, both in his church duties and in his every day life and examples, the influences of which were felt and acknowledged by his neighbors and associates as being consistent and earnest and of a character that quietly leads into the ways of truth and life."

Of his five children, one only is now living, Edwin B Warriner, of Kankakee.

JUDGE HERVEY BALL, A.M.

Hervey Ball was born in West Springfield, Massachusetts, October 16, 1794. His ancestors had lived in that region since 1640. He was educated for the bar, graduated at Middlebury College, Vermont, in 1818, and studied law for two years in that State. In 1820 he settled in Columbia County, Georgia, and was a member of the Augusta bar until 1834. Spending then a few years in New England, in 1837 he settled at Cedar Lake, being then forty-three years of age. He had been successful as a lawyer, was thoroughly educated and well read; he brought with him to Cedar Lake quite a large law and general library; but instead of devoting himself anew to his profession and becoming, as he easily might have become, a Circuit Judge, being then scarcely in the prime of life, he devoted himself to farming pursuits, except holding, for some years, the office of County Surveyor, and afterwards, for several years, that of Probate Judge, and in his later years administering justice among his neighbors as Justice of the Peace; giving his special attention to the training of his seven children and to general interests for the good of community. He was thoroughly identified for thirty years with the religious interests of the county, especially in forming and sustaining Sabbath Schools, and in originating and sustaining Baptist Churches. His interest extended outside of the county through the Northern Indiana Association, the meetings of which he usually attended, of which body he was sometimes Moderator; and he was also for a time Trustee of Franklin College. Ministers of any denomination were always hospitably welcomed and entertained at his house; and there both the Baptist and Presbyterian pioneers preached their first sermons. The Cedar Lake School House, on his place, has been already mentioned in this volume, and the literary, intellectual, and religious influences referred to of which it was the home. (See the article on Schools in Chapter X).

During his professional life, and even in college life, he had mingled much in the gay, the busy, and the polite world, and was familiar with the leading men of his State in political and religious life. Among his fellow students in college were Stephen Olin, and Rev. Mr. Bingham, an early missionary to the Sandwich Islands; he was familiar with Seymour and Governor Slade, of Vermont; his partner in the law was a member of Congress; his acquaintances and associates were the wealthy and the cultivated. He had traveled considerably and thus gained a large experience. The benefit of these associations and this experience were of great advantage to his children and the youth connected with them in their secluded home.

During his retired farmer life his associations were in part continued with the political and religious world, as he took a number of periodicals, agricultural, literary, political, and religious, and read extensively until the last year of his life. He wrote considerably for some agricultural papers, especially on the subject of bees. In keeping these he was for several years very successful. He was identified with the temperance, social, and agricultural interests of the county. The various positions in these which he filled have been elsewhere mentioned. He died at Cedar Lake, October, 13, 1868, wanting only three days of having reached the age of 74 years.

Thirty years of life thus spent, when a region is new, by one so active, so social, so thoroughly educated, furnished with so good a library, so solicitous for the moral and religious welfare of others, although producing no brilliant results in the great world, cannot have been spent in vain; but will leave their impress on society to future generations, and will show results more precious than fame or wealth in the great hereafter. He who writes on mind writes on that which will not die.

The four who have thus far been noticed in this Chapter were more or less intimate with each other and were all on very friendly and sociable terms. Religiously they were different. The former two have lived, it may be, more for this world. They have gained more or less of wealth, and are still living to enjoy it. The latter two, both active and prominent members of the Cedar Lake Church, very sociable and pleasant in the common walks of life, not shunning public or official duties, and discharging these faithfully, lived more, it may be, for the Great Future. They amassed not much of what the world calls wealth. They enjoyed a competency. And they have both gone where they know the realities of the unseen.

I have placed these four first as being, perhaps, representative men.

JUDGE SAMUEL TURNER.

In the spring of 1838 Samuel Turner and family, having removed from Pennsylvania to La Porte County, settled in Eagle Creek Township near the bank of Eagle Creek. Other, of the early settlers there, were D. Sargent, John Moore, A. D. McCord, and Mrs. Mary

Dilley, all of whom are now dead. Samuel Turner was one of the leading citizens of that part of the county, was soon elected Justice of the Peace, and about 1842 was elected Associate Judge, which office he held until his death.

For several years there was no cabinet shop nearer than Valparaiso, and, having learned to use carpenter tools, S. Turner was called on to make all the coffins used in the neighborhood, frequently taking lumber from the chamber floor of his cabin for that purpose, and always without any charge. Thus kind and obliging, respected and honored in the county, he died in 1847. His wife died in July, 1871, being 87 years of age; and the aged mother and grandmother, who lived with her daughter, Mrs. Dilley, died about January, 1855, having attained the age of 97 years.

One son, Samuel Turner, Jr., marrying a daughter of W. G. McGlashon, of Crown Point, died of a lingering disease in 1864; and another son, James B. Turner, Esq., of Crown Point, died August 14, 1866. One daughter, Miss S. P. Turner, still lives at Eagle Creek. One son, T. J. Turner, has been a prominent politician and lawyer, since leaving this county, in Freeport, Illinois, and now in the City of Chicago. The third of the survivors of this family is Judge Turner, of Crown Point.

JUDGE DAVID TURNER.

David Turner came into Eagle Creek Township in his youth, as a member of his father's family. His schoolboy days were spent in Pennsylvania. He entered while quite young into civil-official, and soon into political life, being elected Justice of the Peace in Eagle Creek when his father became Associate Judge, and in 1849 he was elected Probate Judge. This office he held until it was abolished in 1851. In 1854 he was elected as representative in the State Legislature, and in 1858 he was elected State Senator.

In 1862 he was appointed by President Lincoln United States Assessor, which office he still holds. In November, 1866, he was removed from office by President Johnson, but the Senate failing to confirm Johnson's appointee, in March, 1867, he was reinstated. Having had some experience in regard to financial difficulties, he is now acquiring affluence in the sunshine of popular favor and earthly prosperity.

A large and estimable family are gathered around him, and at his hospitable home the most distinguished visitors at Crown Point find a courteous welcome. He is an exemplary member of the United Presbyterian Church, a man of firm principle and undoubted piety. Such men in public life are ever blessings to community.

JUDGE H. D. PALMER, M. D.

Dr. Palmer, a graduate of Physicians' and Surgeons' College, at Fairfield, Herkimer County, State of New York, in 1834, entered Lake in the winter of 1836. He settled about two miles west of Centreville and commenced practice. He has continued in practice, also carrying on a farm, ever since. His rides extend from Dyer to Hobart and Lake. Had the most practice between 1850 and 1860. He built in 1841 the first frame house in that part of the county. He was elected Associate Judge to fill the vacancy occasioned by the removal of Judge Wm. B. Crooks, in 1838; having taken his seat in January of that year as County Commissioner.

This office of Associate Judge, he held with Judge Clark, and afterward with Judge S. Turner, for about thirteen years. Twice during that time he held court in the absence of the presiding judge. He has lately erected quite a fine residence, and is enjoying the comforts of a pleasant home.

J. W. DINWIDDIE.

The son of an early settler who made a claim near the edge of the county, J. W. Dinwiddie was a young man when our early settlements were made. He was born October 1, 1813. The family records date back for several generations. As early as 1835 or 1836, J. W. Dinwiddie was with his father and sister at Indian Town. He commenced farming. Found it unprofitable. He sold his farm and went to Illinois to work upon the canal. August 19, 1844, he was married, and returned to Lake County and bought in the fall of that year two hundred acres of land. He lived on it till July, 1845, and then resumed work on the canal. He again returned to this county in 1847 and went into business at Crown Point. In 1852 he returned to his farm, bought more land, and commenced farming operations on an extensive scale. He built, while Township Trustee, the school houses at Plum Grove, Eagle Creek, and on the prairie, then probably the three best in the county. He was County Commissioner; was recognized as one of the most energetic, and prudent, and thorough business men and farmers in the county, an excellent manager, firm in principle and successful in carrying out his plans; and was rapidly advancing in the accumulation of property, when sickness came unexpectedly upon him, and then death. He died

April 12, 1861, being 47 years of age. His death was deeply felt in the community. His wife, Mrs. M. J. Dinwiddie, a woman of rare executive ability, took the management of the large estate, which now contains about 3,500 acres of land,—the five children were then young—and she has succeeded admirably in her management. She has also carried on for some years a Sabbath School, is active in every good enterprise, and has exemplified how fully a true woman having wealth, position, intelligence, piety, and talent, can carry on business, do good, and be at the same time unobtrusive. retiring, refined, and womanly. Her children, three of them now grown up, have nobly aided her in her plans and efforts. In 1870 a new family residence was erected at a cost of some $2,500.

Among all the squatters of the years before the land sale, no one succeeded in securing such a choice selection of land, or of leaving for his family an estate so valuable as did the young sojourner at Indian Town. John W. Dinwiddie.

He has left three sons among us to bear his name, share the results of his efforts, and imitate his virtues.

DAVID BRYANT

Came to Pleasant Grove in 1835. His wife died in March, 1836, and was buried on Morgan Prairie, where also Agnew, who perished with cold, had been buried. no ground having then been set apart in that portion of the county for the repose of the dead. He married again December 2, 1837. This was the first marriage ceremony, so far as records show, in this county. The license was obtained in Valparaiso. The day was excessively cold.

In the spring of 1838 he went to Bureau County, Illinois, and spent some years. He then went to Missouri and staid a few years. He returned to Illinois. Went back to Ohio and staid five years; and in 1853 returned to this county. He settled at the "Fisher place." In 1854 he brought in one thousand and sixty-three sheep. He went again to Illinois, and again returned here. Has since visited back and forth. He now resides at Eagle Creek with his son-in-law, Wm. Fisher. He is well-off; a very sociable, friendly man, of religious principle; a church member; and is now 75 years of age. He is growing feeble, but retains the use of his mental faculties.

SIMEON BRYANT

Staid about a year in Pleasant Grove, then went to Indian Town. There he has ever since resided. The Indians had corn fields on his claim, or rather, he laid his claim on their fields. He however allowed them to plant corn on the land after he had fenced it. This gratified them. It had displeased them to have him settle on their fields, but he was so fearless, and kind, and obliging, that he gained their good will. (See Chapter III). He is now well advanced in life and quite feeble.

SAMUEL D. BRYANT

Settled first on what is now the Jones' place. He made his claim in the spring of 1835. He afterwards went to Ohio, from which State the Bryant families had emigrated, and spent a few years. He returned here and bought where he now resides, south of South East Grove, in 1854. He is now 82 years of age, and worked this summer binding oats in the harvest field.

There are several descendants of these Bryant families in Lake and Porter Counties, and in the West. They are enterprising, intelligent, and prosperous.

M. PEARCE

Made a claim in about 1838. He married in 1840 Miss Margaret Dinwiddie. In 1841 they commenced housekeeping in a double log-cabin. The present family mansion was erected in 1853. The chief attention of the owner was given to farming. He held in his township the offices of Justice of the Peace and School Trustee. He died April 4, 1861, of typhoid pneumonia. J. W. Dinwiddie staid with him and took constant care for a week, and went home and was taken sick with the same disease and died. Thus these two active men, in the prime of life, were taken from one neighborhood, when our country was plunging into the fearful scenes of the civil war. No two men have been missed more from any of our neighborhoods than were these.

M. Pearce also left three sons. The oldest, JOHN PEARCE, is now engaged in quite extensive farming operations, and is one of the very promising and enterprising young farmers of the county. In September, 1867, he married Miss Lizzie V. Foster, of Crown Point.

The other sons are yet young.

HON. B. WOODS.

May 25, 1836, Bartlett Woods left London, England. He landed at New York and came to Michigan City in August. In March, 1837, he made a claim in Lake County, on which he commenced improvements in the spring of 1838. He married a daughter of Samuel Sigler, also an early settler. With the exception of two years spent in Chicago, he has been a continuous resident on his farm. He holds for it, as a claim, one of the very few claim-entry certificates now to be found. For a number of years, being intelligent, talented, and a ready speaker, he has been a prominent man in the community. He held for two terms the office of County Commissioner. He was our representative at Indianapolis in the State Legislature in 1861 and again in 1865.

For the last three years he has been President of the Agricultural Society.

DR. J. A. WOOD

Has been already noticed as one of the earliest physicians practicing in this region. He went on horseback, according to the early custom when roads were scarcely known. He had a fine looking Indian or French pony, a thick set, heavy maned, sagacious, hardy animal, one to delight the eye of a boy; quite different in appearance from either of the two noted Indian ponies at Cedar Lake.

In one of his rides from Porter into Lake he was called into the vicinity of the Cady marsh. It lay in his route. The distance round was considerable. He was told white man had never crossed it. He thought if Indian could cross it on a pony he could. He ventured and succeeded; but he bore away some of the black mud of the morass. It was a dangerous ride. His was a nice pony for chasing wolves.

For several years he resided on the east side of Cedar Lake, and his house was one of the places for holding religious meetings.

He was appointed with J. V. Johns, Amsi L. Ball, and

John Sykes, a committee to report on Michigan Central Road, when at its opening a free ride was given to our citizens from Lake to Michigan City.

Having been familiar with the diseases of this region for more than thirty years, he has an experience of much benefit in his present practice.

CHARLES HAYWARD

Settled, in 1837, a little east of the place where now stands the Stone Church. Another Hayward family also settled near, both from England; and other English families, Jonas Rhodes, the brothers Bartlett and Charles Woods, the Muzzall families, and perhaps others from that same European island, settled in that part of the county. Prosperous representatives of these families are now living in the county.

Quite a number of English families have at different times made this region their adopted home.

H. YOUNG

Settled on the Miller place at Deep River, succeeding A. Hopkins, who had bought Miller's store. Of Miller himself little seems to be now known. I am told that his wife was part Indian, that he had sold property at Michigan City for $80,000 in gold and silver, and that he started his store and mill probably in 1836. His mill sawed one-half of a log. At his store much whisky, as well as other articles, is said to have been sold. H. Young sold the mill irons to Dunstan, opened himself a gun shop, and kept the place several years. The road to Hobart now crosses by the site of this old mill and early store and shop, and here in the spring-time, in high water, the river appears like a Southern stream that has overflowed the timbered "bottoms." Families are living near, but none are now living upon this spot, and one might fancy that it had always been a wild.

SAMUEL SIGLER

Made a claim near Turkey Creek. His log cabin is still standing on the first sand hill north of the Sykes place. His date of settlement is 1837. He had four sons and three daughters. One of the daughters married Hon. B. Woods, another married Joseph Mundell, and the third one,—not third as to age—married —— Walton, on Twenty Mile Prairie. Of the sons, Samuel is a merchant at Wheeler, Eli and Daniel are merchants at Hebron, and Wm. Sigler is a merchant at Lowell. The father, Samuel Sigler, died a few years ago at Hebron. The sons have been for several years prominent business men. Some of the grand-children are now in manhood and womanhood, and are scattered abroad and entering for themselves into active life.

A. L. BALL

Was one of the more mature men who was active and prominent in laying the foundations of our political and social institutions. He came from the State of New York with his son, John Ball, in 1836. I have elsewhere given his date of settlement 1837, but it can be inferred safely that he came in 1836. In March, 1837, an election was held at his house, as also at the houses of Samuel D. Bryant and R. Eddy, which was the first county election, and Amsi L. Ball receiving seventy-eight votes was elected County Commissioner for three years. This office he in the summer resigned to run at the August election for Representative. He received the vote of

Lake but not of Porter, and so failed to secure the position.

He was rather tall in person, a fluent speaker, a democrat of those days, probably aspiring, and capable of holding positions.

Solon Robinson was at that time a strong Whig — no wonder he did not like "Tylerism" — and he and A. L. Ball were politically unfriendly. Each has the credit of defeating, to some extent, the other's political aspirations. A. L. Ball continued, nevertheless, to be an influential, prominent man, but he did not remain a permanent citizen. It is said that domestic difficulties drove him away from his New York home, and he afterward, like a wise man, returned, between 1840 and 1850, the year I have not been able to ascertain, to his wife and his New York home.

DUDLEY MERRILL,

Who came with his brother William in 1837, bought the first claim made by A. L. or by John Ball, which was situated on the bank of Deep River south of "Miller's mill." He afterwards obtained land near and in Centreville, and his brother William erected a large frame dwelling-house on the edge of the grove opposite the Indian burial-ground. This brother died some years ago. Dudley Merrill is now living in the village of Centreville, or Merrillville, with three of his sons, and, with the exception of the care of his hotel, has mostly retired from active business life. Two of his sons carry on the store, one of them, John P. Merrill, being the Township Trustee and discharging very satisfactorily its duties, in his relations with the teachers very accommodating and pleasant.

The cheese factory and farm, west of the village, are now carried on by L. Merrill. It seems pleasant for a father to be able thus to retire from pressing business cares and have his sons around him to take up the laborious duties of life.

WM. N. SYKES.

A descendant of an ancient English family, the members of which have been Quakers, if of any religious profession, since the days of Fox, himself a native of New Jersey, as early as 1836. W. N. Sykes is found as a prominent name among the squatter records.

In person he was rather large, inclining to be portly, of fine appearance, neat in dress and person, gentlemanly in bearing, intelligent, and possessing a native refinement of mind.

He was the first County Surveyor, being appointed by the Commissioners in May, 1837. He also held the office of County Commissioner.

He never married, and sometimes boarded away from his own home.

He died in August, 1853, and his dust reposes in the Centreville Cemetery.

His brother, who has a large family, now resides upon the farm.

JOHN WOOD.

Another of the sons of Massachusetts, coming from the eastern part of the State, was John Wood, who made a claim and examined this region in 1835. Dr. Ames, of Michigan City, himself, and three or four others, spent a night in the cabin of Jesse Pierce on the bank of Turkey Creek during that tour in 1835. He settled in 1836, leaving Michigan City for his claim on Deep River July 4th, of that year. He found that, during his absence, Gen. Tipton, of Fort Wayne, United States Senator, had laid a float upon his claim in the name of an Indian, Quashma. The land, as a mill seat, was not properly subject to an Indian float; but he purchased the quarter section, paying for it, instead of $200, the sum of $1,000. He has now in his possession Quashma's deed and signature.

He erected a saw-mill in 1837, and about 1838 completed a grist-mill, the only one for some years in both Lake and Porter Counties. It was thronged with customers.

Living at first on the east side of the river, in a few years he erected more substantial buildings on the west side; his sons grew up and settled around him, the oldest now owning the mill, the second one a store, a third one farming, and a son-in-law the resident physician; a number of grand-children now nearly grown in their various homes; himself possessing ample means; he and the wife of his youth, who is a cousin of Mrs. Sarah B. Judson, and a noble New England woman, are now spending the evening of their days amid as much tranquility and happiness as one could well ask for in our earthly lot.

They have seen and experienced the changes of these past seven and thirty years, have been faithful toilers, and may now fittingly rest and enjoy.

JOHN HACK

Was the pioneer of the Germans, so many of whom from the densely populated districts of Prussia, from Hanover, Wurtemburg, and the late small principalities which now are united in the German Empire, have opened farms in the woodlands and have made their homes on our prairies.

Tall and dignified in person, patriarchal in manner, clear and keen in intellect, he was well fitted to be a leader and pioneer. He settled with quite a large family, in 1837, on the western part of Prairie West. There was then an abundance of room around them. In the summer evenings the family would gather around an out-of-doors fire, the smoke of which would keep off the musquitoes, and sing the songs of their native Rhine region, presenting a scene at once picturesque and impressive. Having shared their hospitalities one night in the summer of 1838, I had a fine opportunity to hear these beautiful evening songs of "the father-land." This family knew the privations of pioneer life. In common with others they shared the experiences of going to mill. One member of the family, M. Hack, was gone with horses to Gossett's mill, in Porter County, nine days. Other families soon settled near, and in a short time a chapel was erected, was consecrated, and regular religious services were held.

J. Hack was born in 1787, in one of those Rhine provinces that passed from the possession of France into the control of Prussia. He had enlarged views of government, and looked closely into the genius of our institutions. He lived to see a great change in Prairie West and over this whole region, and died in 1856.

Two of his sons became residents in Crown Point. The one, M. Hack, who kept the hotel, died a few years ago; the other, J. Hack, now carries on the blacksmith and wagon shops. He is now the oldest resident German, not in age, but in citizenship, in the county

H. SASSE, SEN.

In the summer or fall of 1838, Henry Sasse, Sen., the pioneer of the Lutheran Germans, coming from Michigan with a small family, bought the Cox claim at Cedar Lake, also a Chase claim. He came with some means, and like him who has just been mentioned, he was a man of more than ordinary intelligence and abilities. After improving his farm he sold to the Rasgen family and purchased a farm over West Creek, where he has ever since resided.

He has made three visits to his native region, the ancient kingdom of Hanover, crossing the Atlantic seven times.

He is now advanced in life, being some seventy years of age, and is well off in regard to property. Death has many times visited his household and he is left almost alone. His oldest son, Henry Sasse, Jun., has lived for many years on what was known as the Farlow farm, on the west side of Cedar Lake. He is a prosperous farmer, in the prime of life, and one of our truly intelligent teachers.

H. VON HOLLEN.

In the same year of 1838, and at about the same time, H. Von Hollen also came to Cedar Lake. He obtained the Taylor and Chase claim, about which an arbitration had formerly been held, and settled one-half mile north of H. Sasse. He was then a young housekeeper, and brought with him but little means. Being also intelligent and enterprising, he began to accumulate property. Like a number of others, he went into Illinois and worked on the canal for a short time. He bought the noted cranberry marsh not far from his claim. This proved to be an excellent investment. Industrious and economical he soon accumulated quite rapidly, and is now in the possession of ample means. He and his wife are still residing on the place where they first settled.

LEWIS HERLITZ,

The third Lutheran German, soon arrived and bought the Nordyke claim. He was a native of Pyrmont, a part of the principality of Waldeck, and was noted for his urbanity of manners. He built a nice residence on his woodland place, near the head of Cedar Lake, his sons and daughters grew up around him, and in September, 1869, being about sixty-four years of age, he died. Both L. Herlitz and H. Sasse were more advanced in life when they first settled than was H. Von Hollen, judging from the appearance. They were all probably born about 1802 or 1804.

JOSEPH SCHMAL,

One of the four Germans who settled on Prairie West in 1838 died many years ago.

JOSEPH SCHMAL,

One of his sons, is now a resident farmer at Brunswick.

ADAM SCHMAL,

Another son, farming on Prairie West for several years, having been elected County Treasurer, removed to Crown Point in 1866. He held the office for two terms, and still resides in town, holding for one year the office of Town Trustee.

WELLINGTON A. CLARK.

Among the enterprising young men attracted by the wild lands of the West was W. A. Clark, a native of Ontario County, New York, a clerk in a wholesale grocery store at Albany. His brother, S. D. Clark, was doing business in Ohio, and was a thriving merchant, possessing considerable capital. The Albany clerk made a visit to his merchant brother in 1838, and through him obtained a position as Supercargo on a schooner sent from Cleveland, Ohio, to Chicago, around the lakes. Few vessels at that time made regular lake trips. Disposing of his cargo at Chicago, W. A. Clark, then about twenty-three years of age, visited our county and arranged with Adin Sanger, a relative, to hold for him a claim. He returned to his brother in Ohio and reported his sales at Chicago. In the spring of 1839, before the land sale at La Porte, Sanford D. Clark came out on horseback, and found some of our settlers about starting for the land sale. He furnished Adin Sanger with money to enter for W. A. Clark three hundred and eighty-four acres, which was more than a squatter could preëmpt. He also, having a good supply of funds, loaned to J. H. Sanger, to E. Cleveland, and to A. McDonald, money for entering their claims; and thus saved them from the necessity of borrowing, as so many settlers did, at La Porte.

In the summer or fall of 1839 A. Sanger died, and W. A. Clark came out from Ohio with a buggy and commenced, in the fall of 1839, improving his West Creek farm. He was then beginning life for himself, with health, industry, perseverence, and energy, for his capital. Having ended his clerkship he begun to be a farmer.

A family from Michigan City, who had been on a claim near Deep River in 1835 or 1836, but who had returned to the civilization and privileges of that city, settled northwest of Cedar Lake on the Green place, in 1842. With this family, among the members of which were two young ladies who had just entered womanhood, W. A. Clark became acquainted. In December, 1843, he married one of these sisters, Miss Mary C. Hackley. The marriage ceremony was performed by Judge Wilkinson, who, uniting both pleasure and profit with business, took his trusty rifle along and on the way, and near the home of the bride, killed a fine deer. The Judge was a true pioneer.

In about 1846 W. A. Clark removed to Crown Point. He was now acting as an agent for Bragg in disposing of patent medicine, and soon became agent for Ayer, in the same line, and traveled over the State and made money. At Crown Point he built a good dwelling-house; returned to his farm and built an excellent farm-house; spent again a few years, including 1864 and 1865, at Crown Point; and once more returned to the West Creek home. In 1867 he erected and started the first cheese factory in the county; kept, some of the time, two hundred cows; became owner of a thousand acres north of Crown Point; and made improvements at the home place. In 1869 or 1870 he disposed of the thousand acres near Crown Point and now holds his West Creek lands, in amount thirteen hundred and twenty acres. Involved in business year by year, he has made money, and is now worth some

$50,000, being among the wealthiest of the citizens of the county. But few families hold property representing more than that amount. And this is the result of thirty-four years toil in farming, in other business, in dairying, and includes the rise in value of land. Such a result ought to satisfy a settler in the West. It is true, men in commercial life, and in speculations in the meantime, may have made their millions, and others have lost as much, and more rapidly. "Let the golden stream be quick and violent," said Ortugul; but when he looked again the mountain torrent was dry. Broad acres of rich lands are safer possessions than ships on the ocean with costly cargoes, or deposits in banks, or goods on the shelves, or " stocks " in the market.

W. A. Clark has two sons and one daughter. At his home his friends find a cordial welcome and an abundance of the comforts of life. As he is yet apparently in the prime of life, although some fifty-seven years of age, and so well known in the county, I need not mention his excellent traits of disposition nor analyze and record the qualities which have contributed so largely to his success. It is sufficient to say that his early capital, although well used, has not become exhausted. A business talent has doubtless controlled. Men, to quite an extent, can become what they will, if they pay the price.

D. R. MERRIS

First settled near the Lone Tree north of Plum Grove, in 1838, after traveling seventeen days with a team of oxen from Ohio.

He suffered severely with the rheumatism. For some five months scarcely slept. An Indian calling in one day, in broken English and by signs, inquired about his sufferings and prescribed a remedy. It was tried and proved very successful.

In 1840 he bought at Pleasant Grove; raised a hewed log house in 1841. A frame house was erected in this settlement in 1840 by A. Clark, and a frame barn by John S. Evans in about 1843. D. R. Merris was by trade a carpenter. He built the Methodist Church in the Grove in 1851; cost, $500.

A few years ago he sold his property in the Grove and removed to a farm on the old Indian-Town limits, a short distance south of Hebron, where he still resides, pleasantly situated, with abundant home comforts around him.

EPHRAIM CLEVELAND

Has been named among the early settlers at Pleasant Grove. He was one of the substantial citizens. He was Justice of the Peace, and Methodist Class Leader at the Grove for several years before his death. He died July 13, 1845, while yet in the midst of an active and useful life.

His son, T. Cleveland, is now a lawyer at Crown Point, and also proprietor and editor of the Crown Point Herald.

JUDGE R. WILKINSON.

As a member of that first party that came from the Wabash region and selected claims in 1834, R. Wilkinson's name and date of settlement in 1835 have been already given, and some of his experiences will be found recorded among the incidents. But little therefore need be mentioned here. In 1837, at the first August election, he was elected first Probate Judge in Lake county. This office he held for several years. In about 1849 he removed with his family to Missouri. One son, John B. Wilkinson, returned at the time of the civil war, and has since then resided in Lowell. He is in the service of the United States as mail-carrier between Lowell and Crown Point.

RUFUS HILL.

Became a resident in Pleasant Grove about the year 1839. He has one of the largest families in the county. Six sons are living who are men, Welcome, William, John, Charles, Martin, and Richard Hill, and several younger ones. He has had six daughters, not counting any among his young children. He is now about eighty years of age, attends to his affairs, and seems to be quite a hale and active man.

HENRY WELLS.

A native of Massachusetts, has been named as entering this county with Luman A. Fowler, on the day after Solon Robinson first pitched his tent on this soil. Sheriff of the county by commission at its organization, he served out the term of L. A. Fowler, the first elected Sheriff, and also the term of J. V. Johns, the second elected Sheriff, and was then himself elected and held the office eight years. He was appointed to the same office to complete the term of R. T. Tozier, who resigned. He was also elected County Treasurer and filled that office eight years. He was the third Swamp Land Commissioner. Probably no man in the county has passed more years here in official life.

For the past few years he has been somewhat feeble

and has retired from public and active life. He still retains the use of his mental faculties and is about seventy-two years of age. The best authority which I can obtain fixes his age as above, although it has been placed at eighty-two.

A large number of the early settlers were born about the year 1800. Very few much before that year.

Four sisters of H. Wells have resided among us, Mrs. R. Eddy, Mrs. Olive Eddy, Mrs. L. Gillingham, and Mrs. Sanford. The last one named is still living in Crown Point. His daughters are Mrs. A. Clark, Mrs. John Luther, and Mrs. S. R. Pratt. His two sons, R. H. and Homer Wells are now dealers in agricultural implements in Crown Point.

CAPT. JOSEPH P. SMITH.

Coming from the City of New York in 1836, being then about thirty years of age, J. P. Smith found a place for the exercise of his qualifications and tastes, even among the squatters. He and J. V. Johns, who came from the City of Philadelphia, perhaps in the same year, or earlier, have the credit of having possessed the best counting-house education of any who have ever settled in our county.

He held for many years the office of County Clerk. He also opened a store and did business a number of years. Among his clerks were some of our present prominent business men, Wm. Krimbill, H. S. Holton, and Alfred Fry. He commenced farming on the east side of School Grove and built the house now owned by J. Fisher, living on the farm some eleven years. His love for military drill and his Mexican campaign have been mentioned. For a New York City military captain and an officer in the army, his death was a singular and sad one. In September, 1861, he went to the western frontier and entered again upon a new settler's life on the Platte River. February 5, 1872, he was in the woods chopping with two boys and a hired man, when the Indians came upon them and shot them all dead with arrows. These were the first victims in the Indian massacres of 1862. Thus he who had trained men for dress parade and for civilized warfare, who had been exposed to the dangers of strife in Mexico, fell on his country's soil, while engaged in peaceful labor, like pioneer settlers one hundred years ago, by the noiseless weapons of American savages.

RUSSELL EDDY

Was born in Pittstown, Rensselaer County, New York, April 23, 1787. He was the son of Gen. Gilbert Eddy, who was in command of a part of the New York troops in the war of 1812, and was himself a paymaster at that time in the army. He was afterward a merchant in Troy, married Miss Ruth Ann Wells, of Massachusetts, removed to Michigan City in 1836, and in 1837 became a resident at Crown Point.

His two daughters, Eliza and Ruth Ann, married and died young. The former left a daughter, Juliet Townsend, who spent some time here on a visit during her girlhood, and who now resides with her husband in Washington City. His only son, Russell A. Eddy, is now a resident in Crown Point. His wife died in 1859. In 1861 he married Miss Abby M. Kimball, of New Jersey. He died on Sunday, July 1, 1871. being 84 years of age.

The obituary notice in the Register closes with these words: "Thus another of the old settlers of Lake County has passed away. His life work has ended. He has gone where earthly distinctions are nothing. Of him as of others, we may now say:

> 'No further seek his merits to disclose,
>   Or draw his frailties from their dread abode;
> There they alike in trembling hope repose,
>   The bosom of his Father and his God.'"

RICHARD FANSHER.

A member of the first exploring party who selected claims in 1834, as already recorded; losing a bundle of clothing, which the Indians found, and which they declined to restore, and, after meeting them in the West Creek woods, obtaining the value from them by selling them well watered whisky for furs: losing his claim afterward by an Indian float being laid on Section 17, and no opportunity offering to make its value out of Indian trapper or Indian trader; R. Fansher lived for a season on his first claim on the bank of the little lake which bears his name, and has since 1835 remained a citizen near or within the town of Crown Point.

In those early days, before temperance societies had reached the outskirts of civilization, a large portion of the first squatters thought it needful to have with them, for cases of emergency, a little whisky, or some other form of fire-water. On the east side of Cedar Lake, the families being engaged in fishing and mill-building, and being in the water considerable, it was thought needful to use some stimulating drink, and the more thoughtful descendants of those families are satisfied that too much was often used. At many of the trading points, as elsewhere stated, whisky, perhaps well diluted, was sold to the Indians for cranberries and fur. Some years afterwards, when the Lake County Temperance Society was organized, and prominent men of the county were members, a committee, it is said, was appointed to call on a certain dealer, now a prominent and well known citizen, whose name need not be recorded, and requested him to discontinue the traffic. "Oh," said he, "we are coming to the "cold water rapidly. What they drink now is *three-quarters water.*" That such a traffic was lucrative will not be questioned. I return from this digression into which the mention of the Indian incident has led.

R. Fansher is now about 73 years of age. He is quite active and vigorous, enjoying a good degree of health, doing considerable work in gardening. His son died in childhood. Three of his daughters, Mrs. Nicholson, Mrs. S. B. Clark, and Mrs. Clinghan, reside in Crown Point.

JUDGE WM. CLARK.

Judge Clark has been named as one of the earliest settlers at Crown Point, and in these records quite a full view has been given of the part he took in our first years of toil and privations. It is only needful to add here, that he was elected Associate Judge in 1837, which office he held for several years, that he spent one year between March, 1840, and March, 1841, at South East Grove, and then settled two miles east of town, where he spent the remainder of his life. He was a man of strong constitution and good mental powers. He lived to be 81 years of age. During the last year of his life he became feeble. He died July 6, 1869.

W. A. W. AND J. W. HOLTON

Were associated intimately with S. Robinson and Judge Clark in the settlements of 1835. Younger men by several years, one of them having a wife and young child, the other one not married, they have passed through the changes of these seven and thirty years and are not yet old. They are both now residing on farms about six miles north-east of Crown Point. W. A. W. Holton was the first Recorder of the county. He removed to Missouri and spent a few years, but again returned to Lake County. He is a man of much intelligence, and the family are connected with learned and cultivated men. J. W. Holton possesses quite fully some of the Holton eccentricities. One of these is, to wear a hat as little as possible. He has been a continuous resident since 1835. His aged mother resides with him. His family genealogy will be elsewhere given.

J. S. HOLTON,

A member of a different family, came to this county in 1844. Although not an early settler, as a business man, a merchant, and an office-holder, he has been for many years a prominent man in the county. He is one of the most wealthy citizens of Crown Point, and although now not in active business is yet in the prime of life.

PELEG S. MASON.

Like W. N. Sykes, Peleg S. Mason never married. Unlike him he led an almost hermit-like life. In his younger days he had passed through many adventures, had been among the islands of the South Sea, had caught seals, had spent years of life in wandering. Reaching this county, perhaps as early as 1835 or 1836, he was a candidate for Probate Judge, at the election in 1837. He was chosen as Register of Claims to succeed Solon Robinson, and held the office until the registering of claims ceased. He was in some respects eccentric. He was then in middle age, and it may be reasonably supposed had good cause for being the lone and sad-hearted man that he seemed. He was owner of some land in Georgia, and made trips on foot, across Kentucky and Tennessee, to look after his interest there. A trip occupied some six weeks. His residence was near the Outlet and not far from the present bridge. He often visited at Lewis Warriner's, at the post office. One winter, about 1847, he went over daily, as usual, to read the news. The weather was cold. One day he failed to come. The next day he failed, and L. Warriner went over to his house to see if anything had happened to the lone occupant. He found him out of fuel and down in his cellar, suffering with the cold, and trying in vain to find warmth. L. Warriner conveyed him to his own home, and gave him care and comfort, but in some two days he died. Thus a lonely man perished, one of whose inner life few knew anything.

Drawing near one morning, rather early, to a neighbor's dwelling, he heard the voice of singing and then the morning prayer, and it affected him deeply, recalling memories of a childhood and youth when he was neither care-worn nor lone.

He wrote once a touching reply to an invitation from the Cedar Lake Belles-Lettres to deliver an address.

The mystery of his life I am unable to solve, although aware of one its later dark passages, but I have recorded as one of the names that ought not to be forgotten in our history, the name of our last Register of Claims, Peleg S. Mason.

WM. ROCKWELL,

In October, 1837, settled on Prairie West. He was elected County Commissioner about 1840, and held the office a number of years. He was a faithful officer. He died in 1853 or 1854. His two sons, W. B. and T. Rockwell, are well known citizens at Crown Point.

RICHARD CHURCH

Settled on the same prairie, and near the same place, still earlier in 1837. His claim was made in 1836 and, on the authority of the Claim Register, the family settlement has been placed in 1836. But other evidence is in favor of 1837. R. Church was the father of seven sons, Darling, Austin, Alonzo, John, Charles, Munson, and Eli; and of four daughters. Most of these were men and women in 1837. A son-in-law, Leonard Cutler, made a claim also in this same neighborhood, and broke up that season one hundred acres of prairie, the largest breaking then in the county. The work was done by G. Parkinson, of South East Grove. The Church and Cutler families were among the constituent members of the Cedar Lake Church. Richard Church died many years ago.

Darling Church's wife was a daughter of W. Rockwell. The wife of C. L. Templeton, of Cedar Creek, is another daughter. These families came from the State of New York. Nearly all of the large Church and Cutler families are yet living, but no member is remaining in this county. Some are in Michigan, some in Illinois, some in the far West, some in Wisconsin. All are intelligent, enterprising, and virtuous; and many are active and excellent church members in their own communities. They have been sadly missed here. Mrs. Alonzo Cutler, the third daughter of R. Church, resides in La Porte County. Her husband is wealthy and her sons enterprising.

Other members of this large family are referred to in this volume.

JUDGE BENJAMIN MCCARTY.

Succeeding Dr. Lilly on the east side of Cedar Lake, having given a county seat to Porter County, he was an active competitor for the location of the county seat in Lake County with Solon Robinson and George Earle. A village had been commenced by Dr. Lilly on the northeast declivity of the lake bank by a hotel and a store. This, for a few years, was a central point where neighbors gathered, where religious meetings were held, and out from which influences of some kind reached the surrounding settlers.

B. McCarty had a large family, consisting of his wife, two daughters, and six sons. These sons were Enoch Smiley, Wm. Pleasant, Franklin, F. Asbury, Morgan, and Jonathan. E. S. McCarty, probably in 1840, erected a brick kiln, and thus supplied the settlers with material for chimneys. The family kept some of the best horses then in the county, and the sons, two of whom were young men, gave more attention to dress and looks than most of the settlers' sons. They had enjoyed more advantages than some others, and were naturally aspiring. In a few years the family moved to the prairie and opened a farm in what is now called Tinkerville, where the Hill family have resided for many past years. The two older sons soon commenced teaching and married. The oldest one, E. S. McCarty, married a lady from White Post; the second, W. P. McCarty, married a daughter of Rev. G. Taylor, in Pleasant Grove. The older daughter married Israel Taylor, son of Adonijah Taylor, who lived at the Outlet; the younger daughter married George Belshaw. For several years the family remained on the farm; the father, B. McCarty, had the title of Judge, but I am unable to learn its origin.

He was not on the strong side politically, in this county, and so was not elected to the highest offices of honor or trust. He had, however, represented the two counties of Porter and Lake before becoming a citizen of Lake.

Selling his prairie farm, at length, he removed to Iowa with some of his sons. The others and one daughter, Mrs. George Belshaw, went to the Pacific coast. Franklin McCarty alone remained at Tinkerville on a farm.

EBENEZER SAXTON,

In whose door yard is the old Indian dancing-ground, and in whose garden is the Pottowatomie burial place of the McGwinn village, is another of the early settlers yet remaining, one whose life has been marked by many struggles, and one who has had more than an ordinary share of trials and conflicts.

Originally a native of Vermont, he came to this county from Canada, at the time of the Patriot War in 1837. (The Sherman family and M. M. Mills came from the same region at about the same time.) Having sold his Canadian farm on a credit, he started with his family in a wagon drawn by oxen, and traveled four hundred miles to Detroit. He at length entered Lake County, crossed Deep River at Liverpool on a ferry boat. Eight families, it appears, were on board, with ox teams and loading. The boat sunk. The families were taken over. The boat was relieved of some of the weight, raised, caulked, and the oxen brought over. E. Saxton had now five dollars in gold. Coming to Turkey Creek, the team for the first time on the route, stuck fast in the mud. He gave two dollars to a man near by for helping them out. He reached Wiggins' cabin and entered, and rested, and finally located.

A few of his early experiences are illustrative of new settlement ways and trials.

He bought on Door Prairie ten bushels of corn for twenty days' work. Corn was two dollars a bushel, and work was one dollar a day. He gave a man one half of this to take it to mill, and obtained therefore for the work of twenty days the meal of five bushels of corn. He went to Door Prairie and rented some land of one Dr. Wilkinson, for which he was to pay two dollars an acre. The doctor delayed to write out the contract, the wheat grew and promised a large yield. The doctor denied the contract, and as it was only verbal and no witness to it was at hand, it could not be proved. E. Saxton consulted a lawyer. The advice given was to take two-thirds of the crop and leave one-third for the owner of the land, according to the established custom. This he did, and locked up ninety bushels in a barn, and took twenty bushels to mill. When near the mill his load upset into the water. The miller furnished him with one hundred pounds of flour. He left the wheat to dry and returned home. The doctor, the owner of the land, during his absence, not satisfied with the landlord's third, obtained a landlord's warrant, opened the barn and had the ninety bushels sold at ten cents a bushel. All therefore that E. Saxton obtained for his labor, and for more than a hundred bushels of wheat rightfully his own, was the hundred pounds of flour. The result had been too disheartening for him to return to the mill. The landlord had the power and there was no redress.

One other effort in obtaining provisions met with a different result. In March, 1838, he bought, of a man from Michigan City going to Crown Point, fifteen hundred pounds of flour. He was to pay in team work at two dollars a day. The work was to be done at Michigan City. He went with his team; did one-half of the amount of work, and was ready to do the other half; then the man discharged him, as he wanted no more work. Some time afterward the Michigan City man entered suit at Liverpool for the remainder that was due to be paid in money. A capias came for E. Saxton to appear at Liverpool. He took Wiggins along behind him on his horse. Passing out of Turkey Creek, Wiggins unfortunately slipped off into the water. He did not drown, and remounting, proceeded. The trial came on, the bargain was proved, and the Justice decided fifty cents in favor of the plaintiff. So the other half of the work for the fifteen hundred pounds of flour was never done. The suit disposed of the contract.

E. Saxton lost his wheat stacks one year by fire. This involved him and others in a lengthy law case.

He is now quite advanced in years, has passed through

many vicissitudes, has evidently possessed a strong constitution, and enjoys a vigorous old age.

He once crossed the prairie between his home and Crown Point, to bring Solon Robinson across to Lake C. H., in the short time of twenty minutes. It was in the winter, the prairie was crusted over with ice, no fences were in the way, and his horses were fleet.

JAMES ADAMS.

In the year 1835 James Adams passed through Liverpool on his way to Chicago or Fort Dearborn. He returned in the winter to Michigan. In January, 1837, during the Patriot's War in Canada, he was sent by Gov. Mason and Gen. Brady, from Detroit to Chicago, as messenger extraordinary to obtain soldiers from Fort Dearborn to aid in the defense of Detroit. There was, it may be remembered, a stage route then between these two places. The sleighing was at this time good. Warmly clad, furnished by Gen. Brady with a pair of good fur gloves, receiving instructions to make the distance in twenty-four hours if possible, he left Detroit at four P. M. in a sleigh drawn by a good stage horse. At each stopping place, the distance between being about twelve or fifteen miles, he gave the attending hostler a few moments for changing his horse, requiring the best horse in the stable, and dashed on. At eight P. M. of the next day he entered Chicago; thus making the distance in twenty-eight hours, probably the shortest time in which a man ever passed over that route drawn by horse power. He delivered his instructions to Captain Jamison, who chartered the stage coaches and sent the soldiers immediately to Detroit. J. Adams was allowed to remain off duty for four weeks.

In 1840 he was on the stage route from Michigan City to Chicago. In 1842 he bought in Lake County. In October he became a resident, and continues to reside on his well cultivated farm between Merrillville and Hobart. He has an excellent well of water. There is a strip running across that neighborhood, about three miles long and eighty rods wide, where good water can be obtained at a depth of from sixteen to eighteen feet. On each side of this narrow strip it is needful to go about forty feet to obtain water.

J. Adams is very sociable and hospitable, and the friend who finds himself there at night-fall is sure of a cordial reception, and will find well furnished rooms and abundance of home comforts.

MAJOR C. FARWELL,

The son of an early settler on West Creek, himself a member of that party who spent July 4, 1833, in the unbroken solitude of what is now the county seat of Lake, from whom I learn that several families were in that company, that they duly celebrated that anniversary day, and remained in the locality about a week,— left his father's place on West Creek, settled at School Grove, erected a blacksmith's shop, and made plows. In 1841 he removed to Crown Point, built a hewed log shop, in 1842 put up a frame building, stocked plows, and made wagons. He also made a few buggies and some cutters. He sold out about 1851 to Dr. Farrington, went to Hickory Creek, remained some three years, went to Iowa City, rambled for some five years over Colorado, Idaho, and Montana, and is now residing at Carthage, Missouri. He probably should be called our first plow, wagon, and buggy manufacturer.

DON CARLOS FARWELL,

Another member of the same family, who went westward many years ago, now resides in Virginia City, Montana Territory.

JOHN BROWN

Came to South East Grove in 1840. His brother, who has been elsewhere mentioned, came in the same year; and another brother, Wm. Brown, still later. John Brown is one of the few men in Lake County who has lived unmarried. For some twenty years his home has been with the Crawford family. He owns a rich farm, is well-off, is open-hearted, sociable, and intelligent. He has passed the meridian of life.

CYRUS M. MASON

Became a resident here in 1840. The Farmer family, into which he afterward married, became residents in 1838. Mrs. Mason is therefore one of our early inhabitants. C. M. Mason was chosen as one of the two first elders of the Presbyterian Church at its organization in 1843 or 1844, and has ever since been identified with its interests. He resides a short distance east of town, has a good farm, and seems to be in a situation for spending a pleasant evening of life, as he, like the others, who "have borne the burden and heat of the day" in building foundations, looks forward to an enduring home.

AMOS HORNOR,

A young man when the members of his father's family, in 1834 and 1835, made choice selections of wild land and laid claim to woodland and prairie west of Cedar Lake, is the only one left in the county as representative of those first claimants. He came to Crown Point about

1844, married Miss Mary White, who died April 17, 1845, at the age of eighteen years. He married again in 1857, made his home at Ross, and is one of the principal citizens of that village.

His brother, Henry Hornor, died May 8, 1847, being twenty-seven years of age.

The other members of that large family returned to the Wabash region.

DR. H. PETTIBONE

Is the oldest resident physician in Crown Point. He located here in 1847. (In that year, not in 1846, as given in the table of physicians, Dr. A. Stone left Crown Point). Dr. Pettibone has acquired an extensive practice. He married Mrs. H. S. Pelton, formerly Miss Eliza Hackley, and has built a nice residence on the place once occupied by H. S. Pelton and by Milo Robinson. The grove near his house is supposed to be the spot where the United States surveyors camped in the summer of 1834.

Although not himself one of the earliest settlers, his family connection places him among them. His father is a retired physician, from the East, who has been living for several years in town with his sons, the doctor and D. K. Pettibone, and his own son Henry Pettibone, having spent some time at Hanover College, is now at home, a promising medical student. His older daughter is a member of the Seminary at Oxford. The younger daughter attends the home schools. Dr. Pettibone approves of educating children. His means are ample, his real estate interests being considerable and his practice still large.

In 1869 thirteen physicians of the county formed an agreement to establish uniform rates, adopting a "Fee-bill

of the practicing physicians of Lake County, Indiana."
Into this agreement Dr. Pettibone declined to enter, adhering to his own more moderate charges.

LUMAN A. FOWLER

Was one of the earliest settlers. His name has been several times recorded. He seems to have been the most popular man in the county for sheriff, having been elected for five terms of that office. He spent, after his first settlement here, some time in California. He returned here, again held office, and died in April, 1870.

MILO ROBINSON,

A brother of Solon Robinson, who engaged with him in merchandising and who kept the first public house, died, as elsewhere mentioned, in 1839.

H. S. PELTON,

A successor in location and business to those above named, was a successful merchant and rapidly accumulating, when he suddenly died in 1847.

W. G. MCGLASHON,

Whose date among us is 1846, has been connected with the mercantile interests of Crown Point during some twenty years. He was first a clerk for Wm. Allton, on the east side of the square, in 1850; then for Turner & Bissel, successors to J. W. Dinwiddie, on the west side, for six months; then for D. Turner, Turner & Cramer, and for Strait, during the next four years. He was then clerk in the store of A. H. Merton, successor to Turner & Cramer, for one year and a half; and leaving Merton was clerk for John G. Hoffman, on the south side, during the next year and a half. He now, in 1858, went into business for himself on the east side, in the building now occupied by Goulding and Son, and soon removed to the south side. In 1860 he purchased a stock of goods in Boston and occupied the building now occupied by H. P. Swartz's drug store. He here received as a partner M. L. Barber. He removed to the south side once more, kept the post office and did the express business, after the completion of the railroad; bought out M. L. Barber, and finally closed business and retired to a farm some four miles south of town in 1867. In 1871 he returned to Crown Point and resumed the occupation of trade. This he is still continuing, in the building formerly occupied by H. Farmer on the south side of the public square. His twenty years' experience has given him a large acquaintance with those who buy and sell in Crown Point.

HON. MARTIN WOOD,

Although not an early settler, has furnished materials which will readily work in here.

April 4, 1848, he came among us. He commenced the practice of the law. He also taught in the public school. He married Miss S. Taylor, of Pleasant Grove, August 26, 1849. He settled on a suburban farm of fifty-five acres in 1855. Ten acres are now enclosed with ornamental trees. He has a large orchard, containing besides apples, pears, quinces, and peaches. He has a variety of small fruit and much ornamental shrubbery. He has some twenty varieties or more of ornamental trees, rare varieties and a large amount of evergreens, and has devoted time and expense to adorning his place. His evergreens number about eight hundred. They include arbor vitæ, red cedar, Norway spruce, Scotch pine, white and yellow pine, silver spruce, Austrian pine, Weymouth pine, Siberian arbor vitæ, balsam fir, and juniper. He has just erected a new dwelling-house, is having a large law practice, and this fall, for the second term, has been elected a member of the State Legislature.

MAJOR E. GRIFFIN

Is our next oldest resident lawyer. His date of settlement is 1857. He was gaining position rapidly in his profession, and at the time of the Civil War he entered the army. He received the position of pay-master, which gave him the title of Major. Returning to Crown Point he soon obtained a very lucrative position in locating and managing the Vincennes, Danville, and Chicago railroad. He was now afflicted with disease, and returned to his home, where he spent many weary months, and for some time was not expected to mingle again in the business affairs of life. He did at length recover some degree of health, and although not able as formerly to engage in forensic arguments, is now resuming, to some extent, the practice of the law. He has, associated with him in business, a young and promising lawyer, a late graduate of Michigan University, J. W. Youche.

He has commenced the erection of a large and costly dwelling house. He has been a large owner in Railroad Addition, and has laid out himself an addition to Crown Point.

TEACHERS.

O. H. SPENCER

Came to Lake County in 1848. He has lived ever since near or in Hobart. He taught his first school in 1852, when near sixteen years of age, and has taught in this and in Porter County, near the line, forty-seven terms. His wife has taught in the same region, twenty-seven terms. Surely a good teacher's record.

REV. H. WASON,

A native of Massachusetts, for many years a resident pastor at Vevay, Indiana, became the first pastor of the Lake Prairie Church in 1856. He has ever since resided on Lake Prairie, is the owner of an excellent farm, has been President of the Sabbath School Convention and Agricultural Society, and in 1867 represented the county in the State Legislature. Both he and his wife, (who is a woman of sterling qualities, an excellent pastor's wife, a good singer), have been successful teachers. Their elder daughter graduated at Oxford recently, and the younger is now a student at that seminary. Their son, attending the Wabash' College for a season, is now devoting his energies to the cultivation of the farm. Such families are very valuable in a community. Such peaceful, loving, Christian homes, of comfort and abundance, make us think what earth and home might be.

Some one once wrote.

"Holy and fervent love! had earth but rest
For thee and thine, this world were all too fair."

MELVIN A. HALSTED.

I come again to a business man, to one whose name is written in large characters at Lowell. So near as I can ascertain, in 1845 he settled on a farm at the south end of Lake Prairie. He went to California when the gold discoveries were made known. He returned with means, and commenced a mill and improvements at Lowell. He laid out a town. A business centre was formed and grew quite rapidly. He drew the Pleasant Grove village prospect and interests to his mill seat and its surroundings. He laid out money faster than it came in. Thus he became financially somewhat involved.

In 1857 he sold the Lowell mill property to Sigler, Haskins, and Scritchfield, and went to Southern Illinois and then to California. Returning with quite ample means in 1864, he bought back the Lowell mill, bought the McCarty mill, and was also the owner of the Foley mill, thus having the exclusive control of all the mill property south of Crown Point. He began to improve Cedar Lake, to make use of it as a reservoir of water for summer and autumn drought. As by keeping the water up in the spring some of the low lands, meadow and marsh, south of Cedar Lake would be flooded longer than usual, the owners of these lands raised objections to his improvements. Quite a lengthy and expensive law suit was the result, terminated at length by the rights of the landholders being defined and secured.

Continuing to spend money rapidly, after erecting as trustee, the Lowell School House, and building with others, the brick factory, he disposed once more of all his Lowell interests, and returned to the Pacific coast to resume the business of accumulation. The order of his life seems to have been to accumulate there and to expend here. One more ready and lavish in expending has not dwelt among us, and no one therefore, in proportion to his means,— and these have been quite ample — has done more in aiding useful material, and also moral and religious interests, than M. A. Halsted.

JOHN KROST

Is one of our citizens who, by means of talent, and intelligence, and effort, has become prominent in the county. In April, 1853, he became a resident, first as clerk in the store of Sanders, at Hobart, for a year, then as clerk in the store of Hale and Kenney, at Merrillville, for about six years, and then, for the next two years, a farmer. In 1862 he was elected County Treasurer, and held the office till 1867. In 1868 he was elected auditor, and is now, 1872, in the second term of that office. He is accommodating, courteous, and gentlemanly; and has a pleasant home on Main Street, enjoying with his family the advantages of position, comforts, and refinement. His three sons, Frederick, Joseph, and John, are distinguished among the boys at Crown Point for their *politeness;* and if they continue to practice their present qualities they will be quite sure to unfold into a noble type of manhood.

ZERAH F. SUMMERS,

A son of Benjamin Summers, of Ohio, came to Crown Point in November, 1854. He became County Surveyor about 1856. In 1859 he was elected County Clerk, and held that office until 1867. He married a daughter of Ambrose S. Thomas, of New York. In 1865 he erected a warehouse at the depot and commenced buying grain. He purchased the warehouse occupied by M. L. Barber, erected a grain building at Cassville, and has shipped from the three houses during these five years, a large quantity of grain.

He was engaged several months as civil engineer in laying out the Vincennes, Danville and Chicago railroad.

He is a good engineer, an excellent business man, sharing largely in the confidence of his fellow citizens throughout the county.

JAMES H. LUTHER,

Who in 1833 settled in La Porte County, and married a Lake County girl, Miss P. A. Flint, in 1840, became a resident here in 1849. He kept the hotel, now the Rockwell House, from 1852 to 1854, having married, as a second wife, Mrs. M. M. Mills. In 1852 he was elected Justice of the Peace. In 1860 he was elected County Auditor and held the office for two terms. He discharged the duties of that office with great fidelity. He has also held the offices of Township Assessor and of School Director. He is one of the Crown Point capitalists. Whether a lineal descendant or not of Martin Luther the Reformer, he has not been able yet fully to establish; but he is strongly in favor of social reforms, and is liberal in his views in regard to religious teachings. He possesses excellent qualities as a citizen, a neighbor, and a friend, and is deservedly held in high esteem by those who share his friendship and confidence.

MRS. MARIAH ROBINSON.

I make room for the names of a few representative women in this Chapter of Sketches, but have records concerning only a few. The following extracts are taken from the Crown Point *Register* of March 7, 1872:

"Mrs. Robinson was born November 16, 1799, near Philadelphia, in which city her early life was spent. She was married to Solon Robinson in Cincinnati on the 12th of May, 1828, and after a few years removed with him to Madison, Indiana, subsequently to Rock Creek, in Jennings County, and in 1834 she came with her husband, an assistant, and two small children, beyond the then borders of civilization, to this extreme northwest corner of Indiana. They journeyed hence by the slow and measured tread of oxen, camping out nights, and cooking their own meals each day. They found here nothing but the rude wigwams of the red man;" and Mrs. Robinson saw their log cabin rise, "watching its progress with peculiar interest, as the little kingdom which she was soon to enter as queen. Ah! those happy days of privation, and struggles, and hardships, when the woman of such indomitable energy and perseverance is permitted to work side by side, hand in hand, with her co-worker, to lay the foundation of a future home of plenty and comfort, where, surrounded by her family, she expects to glide softly down the decline of life, enjoying the reward of her faithful labors! But alas! in this case, a hope so cruelly blighted. All the hardships of pioneer life were hers to encounter, and all the privations as well as all the indescribable terrors one experiences when settling among only savages." Often, when she was alone with her children, the Indians would call into her cabin, and at first she was quite startled by some of their actions. They never, however, offered to do any real harm.

"Thus commenced Mrs. Robinson's life in this place — a life of toil and hardship, which has continued such until within the past few years. * * * *

"In 1852 her desertion by her husband, leaving her with the care of her four children, at an age when a father's influence was most needed, left her worse than widowed. Yet through the twenty remaining years of her life, in which griefs have multiplied, having buried both her sons in early manhood, she has nevertheless maintained her characteristic cheerfulness, ever closing her heart upon her own sorrows but opening it always to the wants and griefs of others. The poor have always blessed her for her charities. The sick have been cheered and comforted by her care and sympathy. Sabbath Schools and benevolent societies have never had their solicitations refused, and churches have shared alike in her generosity.

"She was truly a remarkable woman; possessed of a remarkable degree of efficiency and executive ability; companionable alike to old and young; always cheerful and vivacious, she was always welcomed into any circle; and never at enmity with any person in the place during all these forty years."

She died February 28, 1872, at the residence of her son-in-law, Frank S. Bedell. Her two daughters, Mrs. J. S. Strait, of Minnesota, and Mrs. L. G. Bedell, were with her during her last days.

"She welcomed death, and her life went out sweetly, peacefully, with a sustaining faith in God."

MRS. H. HOLTON

Has been mentioned as the first teacher whose name is on record here. She also was one of the pioneer women in the country, coming in February, 1835. She is still living near Crown Point with her son, J. A. W. Holton, being almost four-score and ten years old.

MRS. JUDGE CLARK,

Settling at the same time, died many years ago.

MRS. L. A. FOWLER,

Whose husband was for many years so prominent in official life, is yet living in a pleasant residence in the northwest part of town.

MRS. J. P. SMITH,

Is also yet living, and spends part of her time in the West and a part with her daughter, Mrs. Keily, in Crown Point.

MRS. R. FANCHER AND MRS. HENRY WELLS,

Also both died several years ago.

MRS. RUSSELL EDDY,

Still another of the first settlers in Crown Point, a woman of great industry, energy, and hospitality, a very active member of the Presbyterian Church, also died a number of years ago. She was, so far as is known, the first Sunday School teacher in Lake County, and as such her name is here recorded for honorable remembrance. She was a member of a large Massachusetts family, and at that time, before any Presbyterian or Baptist Church had been organized, she was holding a letter of dismission from the Baptist Church at Troy, New York. The first annual report of the Secretary of the Lake County Sunday School Convention, contains this record: " Hers is the first name in the Sabbath Schools of our county. Her school was commenced probably in 1837, four years after the first school held in Chicago. It was not called a Sunday School on account of the opposition to religion all around her, but was a gathering of the children to study the Scriptures."

MRS. LUCY TAYLOR,

Wife of Adonijah Taylor, of East Cedar Lake, and

mother of a large family of children, an estimable woman, an affectionate wife and mother, making home pleasant by her cheerfulness and life, was born in Vermont, August 12, 1792. She was one of the first four or five women making homes for their husbands and children on the east side of the lake. She was baptized by Elder Thomas Hunt in 1850, and became a member of the Cedar Lake Church. She was the last but one of all the early matrons in that part of the county, and died December 10, 1869, being seventy-seven years of age.

MRS. J. A. H. BALL

Has been already mentioned as one of the first teachers. She is the last survivor, in this region, of the early settlers around Cedar Lake, who were then in or near the prime of life. The daughter and grand-daughter of physicians who attained considerable success in their profession, and who had practiced for long years in the same town and resided on the same spot, she either inherited or had acquired skill and inclination for the practice of medicine. Bringing from her father's home a well filled medicine chest, lancets, tooth-pulling instruments, apothecaries' scales and weights, with the knowledge of their uses, she found these all extremely useful to her own family and to her neighbors amid the prevailing sickness of 1838 and the wants and accidents of many later years. Her education in the best schools of the city of Hartford just when Mrs. Sigourney retired from the position of a teacher, when Prof. Sumner and Mrs. Lincoln were giving instructions in natural science, and Prof. Patton was conducting a school in which both the solid and ornamental branches were taught, and her acquaintance with those who were the leaders in literary and social life in that city between the years 1819 and 1824, fitted her peculiarly for teaching. Botany until about this time had been taught in Latin, but it was now introduced in an English garb into Hartford by Dr. Sumner, a distinguished botanical author, whose lectures she attended; having also for a teacher a grand daughter of Gen. Putnam. The botanical knowledge here gained, having a teacher so enthusiastic, was very accurate and practical. She had also, a rare acquirement even now, given attention to Hebrew, and wrote those old characters with facility and beauty. But her training in her father's home fitted her for a very different and highly needful service. She dispensed medicine not only to her own family but to her neighbors, in what is now the township of Hanover. She was often called for to visit the sick, and to go for miles in the still hours of night where there was human suffering. If she considered the patient quite dangerous she would recommend the calling of a physician. If not very dangerous she would treat the case herself.

Small in person, but of dauntless courage and great nerve power, she extracted teeth for stout men and women who wondered that she had so much strength. She bled when necessary.

One day Thomas Farlow, of Michigan City, was brought into her home quite seriously hurt by having been thrown from his wagon. To prevent inflammation or congestion it was needful for him to be bled. She took her lancet and bled him with the coolness and success of an army surgeon. Had she given attention to surgery, so far as entire control of her nerves was concerned, she would have taken off a limb from her own child or a stranger, if necessity required it, with entire calmness. But needlessly she would never inflict pain. For medicines and for extracting teeth I think she generally received pay, for her time she received no remuneration. Thus, for many years, she performed to quite an extent the duties of a female physician, besides attending to her household duties, having the care, as a very faithful mother, of seven children, and performing a teacher's work. She had in those days very keen eyesight, and although her health remained firm, her eyes, probably from excessive night-work, before the days of sewing machines, gave way. She suffered with them for years and nearly lost the sight of one.

Although in the decline of life she has as yet firm health, a descendant of a long-lived family, and still attends to the wants of the suffering where duty calls. Had she commenced life some years later, and so shared the opportunities now granted to women, she would quite surely have become a distinguished female physician. As it is she has in this department served her generation well.

A member in her young days of the Baptist Church at Agawam, Massachusetts, she was a member of the Cedar Lake Church, and afterward of the Baptist Church at Crown Point, and now is a member of the North Street Church. She is quite generally known in the central and southern parts of the county.

There are many others, no longer among us, of whom it would be pleasant to have some memorials preserved.

but I find little material for making any records concerning them. Among these I name H. Nordyke, Solomon Russell, Jonathan Gray, Lyman Mann, Calvin Lilley, Adonijah Taylor, Horace Taylor, Horace Egerton, S. P. Stringham, John Foley, and Washington Dille around Cedar Lake. And there were, it may be remembered, more than four hundred others; but few of whose names, perhaps, can be snatched from oblivion. Some have written their names, as it were, in a bold hand across the county, and they will not soon fade out; others only made an entry in some corner, in dim characters, and already these are illegible. The legibility of the name will not prove the worth of the man.

There are also a number yet remaining among us, whom if I begin to name, I shall not know where to stop, who may justly feel that they are entitled to a record upon these pages. And no doubt they are; but which one of them has furnished me any material for such a record? Perhaps when a revised edition is published the material will be readily obtained. I have made records where I found material; but do not claim to have made records concerning all who were meritorious.

I claim, however, for all who endured the privations, hardships, and exposures, which were the lot of those planting our social and civil institutions upon this then virgin soil, and who murmured not nor repined, a part of that meed of praise recognized as due to the founders of States. Some of them were encouraged, I trust, by what President Elliott says animated the founders of Harvard University, "The beautiful hope of doing good." He whose soul is glowing with this hope is nerved for no little endurance.

I hope that over the resting-place of none of them might truthfully be written the old, severe epitaph :

> "Here lies a man who did no good,
> And if he'd lived he never would :
> Where he's gone and how he fares,
> Nobody knows and nobody cares."

There is authoritative teaching somewhere, that we should do good to all men as we have opportunity.

Young men of Lake have gone out into other counties and States, and have been succeeding well. Eli Church, from Western Prairie, member of the Cedar Lake Lyceum, went to the Pacific coast and accumulated, in the staging business, some forty thousand dollars.

Edwin Church and brothers, sons of Darling Church, are now doing a business in one of the towns of Michigan, amounting, it is said, to one hundred thousand dollars a year.

Darius G. Farwell has been carrying on a drug store in Brooklyn, New York. Dr. E. J. Farwell is now practicing medicine in Chicago, and also carrying on a drug store.

E. B. Warriner is engaged in one of the large furniture stores of Kankakee City.

William Hill is engaged in large farming operations near the Pacific coast.

Ross Bryant went, years ago, to Valparaiso, made money, and has lately opened a commission house in Chicago.

There are now growing up in the county a number of promising boys, whose strong arms and active minds will be needed ere long in life's duties and conflicts. For what posts of duty, or for what walks in life, they are fitting, no human foresight can tell. We have no richer treasures than our truly obedient, polite, modest, truthful, and therefore noble boys. May they not share in that experience which N. P. Willis has vividly portrayed in his poem on "Ambition," and find they have gained at last

"All things but *love* — when *love* is all we want."

And there are also in our homes many fair and lovely girls, as frail perhaps as fair, — " rose-like in beauty,"— who, if properly nurtured and trained, may yet reach a vigorous, glorious womanhood. And they too will be needed. Earth has many paths for them to tread. As teachers, or physicians, or missionaries, or writers, or artists, open pathways are before them. They are our jewels, and they need to be carefully polished and faithfully guarded.

"There is light in the cabin of Long Bow, for the Red Fawn is there." Said of Indian father and Indian maiden. These make much of the light in our homes now, and all too soon will they try for themselves life's realities. A generous culture for body and mind is what they need to fit them for toil; for earth's daughters should toil as well as earth's sons. They should toil, but not drudge; should be cherished and loved, not petted and spoiled. As the daughters now are trained so will the future mothers be. Well will it be if these learn what

SKETCHES OF EARLY SETTLERS.

Monod has said of woman, "Her vocation by birth is a vocation of charity."

PRINCIPAL OFFICERS OF LAKE COUNTY.

I have made these lists from a comparison of different county records, correcting from other sources where they were incomplete.

SHERIFFS.

Henry Wells, appointed by the Governor March 8, 1837; Luman A. Fowler, 1837; J. V. Johns, 1839; Rollin T. Tozier, 1841; Henry Wells, 1843; Henry Wells, 1845; Luman A. Fowler, 1847; Luman A. Fowler, 1849; Janna S. Holton, 1851; S. B. Strait, 1853; Job D. Bonnell, 1855; Jesse E. Pierce, 1857; L. A. Fowler, 1859; L. A. Fowler, 1861; Andrew Krimbill, 1863; Andrew Krimbill, 1865; H. G. Bliss, 1867; H. G. Bliss, 1870; John Donche, 1872.

COUNTY COMMISSIONERS.

A. L. Ball, S. P. Stringham, and Thomas Wiles, first board, elected 1837. In January, 1838, H. D. Palmer, appointed by the Circuit Court, took the place of A. L. Ball, who had resigned to run for representative. In May, Benaiah Barney, appointed by the Associate Judges, took the place of H. D. Palmer, appointed Associate Judge; Derastus Torrey, 1838; Henry Wells, 1839; W. Rockwell, 1840. (Some uncertainty here, as members of the first board were probably reëlected, and that fact I do not find recorded). W. N. Sykes, 1843. (Again uncertainty). S. T. Greene, 1846; S. Parrish, 1847; Augustine Humphrey, 1847; Robert Wilkinson, 1848. (Some omission here). A. D. Foster, 1854; A. Humphrey, 1856; G. W. Lawrence, 1857; John Underwood, 1858;

Adam Schmal, 1857; G. L. Foster, 1861; Daniel F. Sawyer, 1861; A. Schmal, 1862; Aaron Konkright, 1862; G. L. Foster, 1863; A. Konkright, 1864; Wm. Brown, 1866; Alvin Green, 1867; H. C. Beckman, 1867; K. M. Burnham, 1870; J. Burge, 1870.

PROBATE JUDGES.

Robert Wilkinson, elected in 1837; Hervey Ball, 1844; David Turner, 1849. Office abolished in 1851.

CLERKS.

Solon Robinson, 1837–'43; Joseph P. Smith, 1843–'47; D. K. Pettibone, 1847–'59; Z. F. Summers, 1859–'67; W. W. Cheshire, 1867 ——.

RECORDERS.

W. A. W. Holton, 1837; J. P. Smith, August 1838. The office was probably held by him until he was elected Clerk, and then the two offices were united in one person till 1845. Major Allman, 1845–'56; Amos Allman, 1856–'64; Sanford D. Clark, 1864–'72.

TREASURERS.

J. W. Holton, 1837; Milo Robinson, 1838, (died in 1839), and who succeeded is uncertain. As near as can be ascertained, the next Treasurer was A. McDonald, probably from 1840 to 1845; the fourth was W. C. Farrington, 1845 to 1848. Then followed H. Wells, 1848 to 1855; J. S. Holton, 1855 to 1859; E. M. Cramer, 1859 to 1863; John Knost, 1863 to 1867; Adam Schmal, 1867 to 1871; John Brown, 1871 to ——.

ASSOCIATE JUDGES.

Of these there have been but few, as the term of office was seven years and the office itself ceased in 1851. The following by appointment or election held this office in the county:

W. B. Crooks, W. Clark, H. D. Palmer, Samuel Turner, A. F. Brown, W. Rockwell, and Michael Pearce. A. F. Brown was elected in October, 1849, but died before entering upon the duties of the office. W. Rockwell and M. Pearce were elected shortly before the office was abolished.

AUDITORS.

The duties of Auditor were at first divided between School Commissioner,— H. S. Pelton being elected to this office in 1837, and giving $10,000 bonds, while at the same time the bonds of the Sheriff were $5,000, and of the Treasurer only $2,000,— and the County Clerk, who also acted as Recorder.

The first who seems to have occupied this as a distinct office was Joseph Jackson, elected in 1847 or 1848. He seems to have held the office until 1852. The second was D. Crumbacker, from 1852 to 1861. The third was James H. Luther, 1861 to 1869. The fourth was John Knost, 1869 to 1873. Auditor elect this fall, who will be the fifth, is H. G. Bliss.

COUNTY SURVEYOR.

W. N. Sykes was appointed by the Commissioners in 1837. He did not serve. Chancellor Graves was next appointed in May 1838. He also never accepted the office, and died in August. No other appointment appears on the Officer's Record Book in the clerk's office, till 1852. The duties of the office, however, were discharged, during many of those years, by Hervey Ball; the field notes came first into his hands, and he unquestionably held the office. In 1852 W. N. Sykes was again appointed. He died in 1853. Then succeeded, John Wheeler, 1853 to 1856; Matthias Schmit, 1856 to 1858; John Fisher, 1858 to 1866; Walter de Courcey, 1866 to 1868; A. Vander Naillen, 1868 to 1870; John Wheeler, 1870 to ———.

REPRESENTATIVES.

The counties of Lake and Porter formed one representative district until 1850.

At the first election in 1837, J. Hammel, of Porter County, was elected by the two counties representative. Lewis Warriner, of Cedar Lake, was elected in 1839. Cline and S. Campbell, of Porter County, were also our representatives, the latter elected probably in 1842.

Of the citizens of our own county, A. McDonald was the next representative, and continued to be reëlected, with one interval of rest, until 1855. This interval was filled by Lewis Warriner, who was elected representative in 1848.

The following is the order of the succeeding representatives: D. Turner, 1855; A. McDonald, 1857; Elihu Griffin, 1859; Bartlett Woods, 1861; D. K. Pettibone, 1863; Bartlett Woods, 1865; H. Wason, 1867; E C. Field, 1869; Martin Wood, 1871, and reëlected in 1872 for the session of 1873.

———

Lake County has furnished as Senators, for our senatorial district, D. Turner, elected in 1856 for four years, and R. C. Wedge, elected in 1870.

———

Our county records have furnished no data for determining the individuals sent to the General Assembly. The above is believed to be accurate. A Porter County record proves that A. McDonald was candidate for the legislature in 1847, and it states that he had twice before that year represented the two counties. Whether elected in the years 1843 and 1845, or in consecutive years, is uncertain. This however remains as the fact, the above records being accurate, that for eighteen years, from 1837 to 1855, two counties forming our district, Lake County sent but two men to the Indiana Legislature; a fact not very flattering to our political leaders, but a fact, it may be, very creditable as showing our freedom from political intrigue and ambition.

CHAPTER XII.

THE PRESENT. 1870–1872.

The events of the three years of this present decade are yet fresh in the memory of us all, and a record need only be made of the leading events which we wish to preserve for the interest of others.

Improvements have been going on quite rapidly, both in the towns and among the farming community. Those in the villages have been already noticed.

The two following *Castalian* records, for the month of February, 1870, will preserve the remembrance of a beautiful phenomenon and of one business or commercial operation:

"On Saturday afternoon, February 5th, a remarkable natural phenomenon was witnessed in the south part of the county. It was that appearance known as *sun-dogs*, a term which Webster thus defines: 'A luminous spot occasionally seen a few degrees from the sun, supposed to be formed by the intersection of two or more halos, or in a manner similar to that of halos.' Halo he defines thus: 'A luminous circle, usually prismatically colored, round the sun or moon, and supposed to be caused by the refraction of light through crystals of ice in the atmosphere.' The appearance of February 5th, was remarkable for its brilliancy, its appearance when the sun was so far from the horizon, and appearing on an afternoon so warm and pleasant. At four o'clock it was first seen by our observer, but it had been noticed by some on the marsh long before. At four, bright appearances, almost equal to suns, were seen on each side, several degrees distant from the real sun, which was then also very bright. These were prismatically colored. From each a well defined curve extended upward, meeting over the sun, where a third, less brilliant but singular glow of light, and color, and curve, appeared. A line extended from each also, downward, nearly to the horizon, forming an almost entire circle round the sun, some fifty or sixty degrees in width, with three bright appearances in the line of the curve. A small bank of cloud lay, apparently, under the sun; but who would suppose that on that day it could have contained crystals of ice? This bank seemed to dissolve away before sunset, and the sun-dogs disappeared. No storm, no cold, in this region, followed. Different observers have remarked that they never saw such an appearance on so warm a day, nor ever saw such brilliant sun-dogs."

"The White Water Ice Company, Cincinnati, have been doing quite a business at Crown Point this month. At this writing their men are busily engaged taking the ice from Fancher's Lake, loading cars, and building ice stacks. Some eighty men are employed daily, and thirty teams. These may be seen on East Street and Main Street every hour, wending their way from the Lake to the depot. Some are building, in the meantime, a 'stack' at the Lake, and others erecting one near the depot.

"These stacks are one hundred feet in length and sixty in width, estimated to contain, each, when completed, twenty-five hundred tons. The ice is cut in blocks of the same size, by means of ice plows and saws, twenty of which blocks make a load, weighing more than a ton. If the weather continues favorable for the business, these stacks will probably remain till summer, and then our crystal water, in its solid form, will go southward, for cooling purposes, to be used by the inhabitants of far-off cities, who know nothing of the lake in the woods from whence it came. This business, picturesque and *cool* as it looks, is a part of the commerce of civilization, a part of the great work of exchange. It puts money into Crown Point, and takes what was and will be water away. Six acres of ice, in blocks twenty-two inches square, will make for the markets of the South, how many tons? A visit to the lake, while the cutting and packing are going on, is interesting. The ice is first carefully laid off into squares by an instrument called a marker. Seams are next cut several inches in depth along the marked lines in one direction by an ice plow. Hand saws are then used to cut across these seams at proper distances, and another tool is employed to complete the breaking in the plowed seam. These strips, twenty-two inches in width, and some eight feet in length, are floated in, by means of spikes, to the foot of a slide. One man then attaches a grapnel to the outer end of the floating ice slab, and it is drawn by horse power up the slide. As it leaves the water another man with a fitting tool separates it into squares along the marked, unplowed seams. These cakes are then delivered on a platform for loading, and at the stack are taken up a number of feet, from whence they slide rapidly down to the ice floor. From twelve to sixteen squares make this slide at once, and it is a lively sight. A number of men are there ready, with appropriate tools, to pack the cakes. Two of these slides are used at the stack now being built at the lake. From seeing a slide of a few feet, one might imagine a little, yet very faintly, how that slide worked constructed once among the Alps, which was several miles in length. The rapidity of motion there must have been fearful. This is simply pretty. The plows used here are worth one hundred dollars a piece; the markers some eighty dollars. The company must pay out at least one thousand dollars a week. A nice thing for Crown Point in these close times."

The great excitement of the year 1871 was the action of the Kankakee Valley Draining Company. A bill passed the State Legislature in the winter of 1869 and 1870, known as the Kankakee Drainage Law. A company was formed under this law, consisting of George W. Cass, of Pittsburgh; George N. McConnell, of Indiana; W. D. Wright, of Cincinnati; and eight other persons, who proceeded to issue some $2,000,000 in bonds, running twenty years, and to make assessments upon lands amounting in all to more than four millions of dollars. In this county it was claimed that 61,438 acres would be affected by the ditches which the company proposed to dig, and benefit assessments were laid on these lands to the amount of $597,794. When the map of their proposed work and amount of assessments were filed in the recorder's office a strong spirit of opposition to the movement was manifested in this and the adjoining counties. There were grave objections to the bill itself, to the provisions of the law, and serious doubts as to any real good resulting from such outlays of money as that company might make. I quote from a publication in 1871 the following:

"This company cannot drain the Kankakee without destroying a great natural dam of stone, some sixteen miles in extent, at Momence, Illinois, eight miles from the Indiana line, and as it is a valuable water-power, whose proprietors have a perpetual charter from the State of Illinois, and a paid-up capital of $1,250,000, it is not likely that the waters of the Kankakee will be reduced one inch by this company. The whole thing is a stupendous fraud upon the public * * * * * ."

Meetings of the citizens were held at different places; a strong, wide current of popular sentiment set full against the operations of the Kankakee Valley Draining Company; and the probability seems to be that the benefit assessment will never be collected.

Some more large ditches, judiciously cut, might be a benefit to the dry marsh, but this is gradually becoming sufficiently dry not only for pasturage and grass but for cultivation.

The Kankakee region in our bounds may well be called wild, strange, and magnificent. A river is its southern limit, a singular, lonely river, yet a river abounding with wild life. Between the river and the prairie are about seventy-five square miles of wet and dry marsh and of wooded islands. Beginning on the east these islands are named thus: Little Beech Ridge, Walnut Knob, Honey Locust, Big Beech Ridge, Warner's Island, Fuller's Island, Red Oak Island, Brownell's Island, and White Oak Island. These are in Township 32, Range 7, and Township 32, Range 8. The last named grove or island is one of the largest in the region, extending for some three miles, from Section 30 in Range 8, eastward. In Township 32, Range 9, beginning on the west side, these islands of timber are thus named: Sugar Grove on Sections 29 and 30; Ash Swamp north of Sugar, in 20; River Ridge from 33 to 36; Stave Shanty, north of River Ridge on 34 and 35. In this are two dwellings and several Indian mounds. Also, Wheeler's Island on the east side of 26, extending into Section 25, in which is one dwelling house; South Island, on 24, containing two dwelling houses; Bolivar Island, Long Willow or Crab Apple Grove, and School Grove Island.

These ridges and islands are all sandy. The timber is white and black oak, ash, cotton-wood, soft maple, sycamore, and swamp burr oak. The last is said to be the best timber in the region for fencing purposes. Some of these varieties, especially the ash, will grow in the water, and thus they make a regular swamp. Getting this timber out in the winter is called "swamping."

On the western side of the county G. W. Cass and W. F. Singleton hold a large tract of this marsh land. A turnpike road has been constructed near the river, extending eastward for several miles, and thus opening the way for additional settlements on the islands and the sandy ridges. A saw mill still further east, nearly south of Orchard Grove has been put in successful operation.

CUMBERLAND LODGE.

To this year, of 1872, may be accredited the beginning of Cumberland Lodge Farm, on School Grove Island, in the Kankakee Region.

The first settler on this island was John Hunter, by occupation a hunter and trapper. He spent a number of years along the Kankakee, following his favorite occupation, and camping on different islands. After moving from island to island for ten years he bought six acres on School Grove Island, and made that his headquarters.

Heath and Milligan, of Chicago, afterward bought land on the island. They, with eight other Chicago gentlemen, built in the grove in the fall of 1869, and established a hunter's home, which was called Camp Milligan. The house is evidently constructed for hunters' headquarters. It is kept by G. M. Shaver and family. Hunting parties come from Chicago and other cities, spend a few days, register their success, and enjoy the exercise. No game is allowed to be sold. From September to November are the months for hunting, or more properly for fowling. The game is mostly ducks, geese, and brants. Some of the entries in the Hunters' Record Book kept at Camp Milligan, may be of interest. Eight gentlemen, in a few days, shot sixty-six snipes and five hundred and thirteen ducks. Another says, four gentlemen shot fifty snipes and five hundred and fifteen ducks. "September 11th, Sunday, no shooting." Another entry mentions shooting from September 1st to 17th, "except Sundays." G. M. Shaver alone killed four years ago eleven hundred ducks, besides other water fowls.

In one of these hunting parties, that visited the island

in 1871, were two enterprising English gentlemen, William Parker and Captain Blake, who were on a hunting tour in the West, and who were so much pleased with the location, that having made since then a trip to Europe, they have this year returned and have invested quite a sum of money in lands on the island and in the adjoining marsh, and in buildings, and in stock. They have erected a dwelling house, barns, and kennels; have imported from England some sixteen of the choicest blooded dogs known to sportsmen; also some choice Alderney cows, and horses; and have imported or purchased other choice stock. They have a black bear and some foxes. Both of these gentlemen are excellent sportsmen, and, in the words of Captain Blake, they "expect to combine business with pleasure."

Camp Milligan still remains and is visited as usual.

The improvements near by, made by these English gentlemen, bear the name of Cumberland Lodge, and bid fair to be, in the importation and improvement of stock, very beneficial to the farming interests of Lake. The results may show that this new style of farming and this commencement of importation, from the island of Great Britain direct to a little island in the Kankakee Region, were among the important events in our county for the present year.

These gentlemen seem to be abundantly supplied with the means needful for accomplishing large enterprises.

The great excitement of 1872 has been

"THE BURGLAR."

THE EXPLOSION, THE PURSUIT, THE ARREST, AND THE TRIAL.

THE EXPLOSION.

On Sunday morning of June 9th, a crowd assembled in front of the Treasurer's Office, in Crown Point, amid very unusual circumstances. Some $46,000 were known to have been in the safe within the vault the night before, together with a tin box of supposed valuables of unknown value deposited the day before by a stranger; and now, as the anxious citizens gathered round, they saw a broken wall, ruined vaults, an open safe, and abundant evidences of a fearful explosion. They learned that a stranger, of singular appearance and marked individualities, who entered the town the Friday before and had been observed by many of the citizens during Friday and Saturday, had deposited with the County Treasurer for *safe keeping* a box represented to contain valuables. This box, made of tin, some eight inches in length and five in width, was deposited on Friday and taken out on Saturday morning. It was again deposited on Saturday afternoon, to be called for on Monday morning. The treasurer had no suspicion, and retired at evening, in entire confidence, to his home. The stranger also retired, pretended to take the evening train, but was seen lurking around town at a late hour Saturday night. It was also ascertained that about one o'clock the tall, singular looking stranger, commenced work upon the outer door of the office and bored above and below the lock fourteen holes through the door. Soon an explosion was heard by the night watchman and three other citizens who were near the Rockwell House at that hour, and these hastened to the office from whence the sound proceeded. The stranger fled at their approach, the treasurer was aroused, the ruined vault was examined, the money was found within the building, and the anxiety of those most deeply interested was relieved. The little box which came so near placing $46,000 in the hands of an artful, designing man, was found to have contained a strip of tin, a gun lock, a watch, a percussion cap, and, it is supposed, some gunpowder and nitro-glycerine. The whole was ingeniously arranged to produce an explosion at an hour indicated by the watch, and caused by the motion of the watch. But for the wakefulness of a few citizens the money and the stranger would have departed to unknown regions in that eventful night of June 8th.

THE PURSUIT.

The baffled, inchoate burglar, amid the exchange of pistol shots, eluded the grasp of his discoverers, made good his retreat to the woods, and, doubtless in a sullen, disappointed, vexed mood, having missed a prize almost within his reach, retired southward toward the Kankakee wilds.

The County Commissioners met on Tuesday, June 11th, ordered repairs, offered a reward of $1,000 for the apprehension of the fugitive, and James H. Ball, J. W. Hughes, and J. Kain, started in pursuit. It was found that the tall and disguised stranger had been seen about sunrise north of Lowell, and soon after sunrise had passed through the Lowell Cemetery, and had been hailed near noon above Oak Grove, had passed southward through the Kankakee Marsh, and at four o'clock P. M. was at Beaver Ditch, where he sold a watch and continued southward. At dark he had stopped near Beaver Lake and spent the night at the house of Newton Nichols. The next day he was seen by herdsmen passing southward along the east side of Beaver Lake, and was last seen a mile and a half south of Morocco. These facts the pursuing party ascertained; but after a diligent search through that region and from Rensselaer to Kentland, learning from the citizens of Morocco "that burglars, horse thieves, and desperadoes, are often tracked to that vicinity, where they seem to disappear," they returned without a prisoner to Crown Point.

THE ARREST.

Weeks passed, and months passed, and no discoveries were made tending to secure the person of the fugitive. But in September a message came to Crown Point from Warsaw, Indiana; it was speedily answered; and on Tuesday, September 24th, the Sheriff of Lake, H. G. Bliss, accompanied by John Kain, E. C. Field, Esq., and the Treasurer, John Brown, arrested a supposed criminal in Warsaw, and on the evening of the same day he was securely lodged in the county jail at Crown Point, amid considerable excitement among the citizens. The question now was whether this tall and singular looking prisoner was the tall stranger seen on our streets last June. The public were deeply interested in the solution of the question, and strong and conflicting opinions were at once expressed by various citizens.

THE TRIAL.

After the usual law preliminaries and some delays, the second day of October was set for the examination of the prisoner before Justice Fry. The morning came, and the Court House was thronged as it had never been before at a justice's examination or trial. The ladies of Crown Point crowded the galleries as they had never done at any court during our existence as a county, while from day to day the trial progressed; manifesting a strange interest which had never been exhibited till now for or against any prisoner. And yet not so strange, for a remarkable prisoner appeared before them. He was tall, strongly built, swarthy and pale, just recovering from sickness, marked in his individualities, a man whom one would expect to recognize among ten thousand. He was called Col. Battles, was said to have been an officer in the Southern Rebel Army, and was a man of acknowledged immoral character. He was claimed to be the same stranger who so nearly succeeded in carrying away from our county $46,000, and several of the ladies were to appear among the witnesses in behalf of the State and for the defense. The question under examination was, the identity of this tall, dark looking prisoner, and that tall, disguised stranger who was held responsible to civil law for an attempted but unsuccessful burglary. The counsel for the State were E. C. Field and T. J. Wood: for the prisoner were Barnard and Barnard, T. S. Fancher, and Griffin and Youche. The examination continued with increasing interest during Wednesday, Thursday, and Friday; excellent order prevailing in the court room; many citizens giving strong testimony for and against the prisoner; and on Friday evening and Saturday long and able speeches were made by the attorneys. The progress of the trial, as numerous witnesses were examined who had seen the stranger and now saw the prisoner, brought distinctly to notice the great difference which exists in the observing power of different individuals. Some were confident that the stranger and the prisoner were one, others as confident that they were two; and some were quite uncertain. After hearing patiently the evidence and the arguments the justice decided that the prisoner should be held for trial at the Circuit Court, placing his recognizance at $2,000.

The counsel for the prisoner made out, a few weeks afterwards, a writ of *habeas corpus*, and another examination was held before Judge Gillett, of the Common Pleas Court. This resulted in the release of Col. Battles, and the great burglar excitement was ended. The thousand dollar reward remained in the treasury of the county.

Hoping to perform the part of an impartial historian, I add; that, while, it may be, no jury would have convicted the prisoner under the strongly conflicting testimony, the conviction is strong on many minds that Justice Fry rendered a perfectly correct decision; and that there are those, who heard the first examination, and who noticed particularly the different manners in which the two classes of witnesses proposed to identify, in whose minds no reasonable doubt remains that Col. Battles was in reality the inchoate burglar.

In closing this chapter a few reflections and remarks are added.

For the first fifteen years of our history the only communication with the Chicago market was by the regular team route, the three and four days' wagon trip. For the next fifteen years much business was done, by means of railroad transportation, at Lake and Hobart, at Dyer and Ross. Thus thirty years passed. What complete facilities the third fifteen years will furnish cannot now be told; but the Great Eastern Road, the Danville Road, the road along the Kankakee marsh, and the projected Continental, are almost bringing a market to every man's door. Fifty years will doubtless show the possession of the facilities of an old country. The children will almost forget the ways in which their fathers went to market. Hardships are soon forgotten by those who enjoy their benefits.

The following, as one illustration out of many, may seem, years hence, almost incredible:

George Parkinson, of South East Grove, in the winter of 1839 and 1840, sold pork at Michigan City for one dollar and fifty cents a hundred weight, hauling it some forty miles. He sent a load of grain. The proceeds were returned, the man who did the hauling received his pay, and about fifty cents were left. Those now enjoying and yet to enjoy the benefits purchased by persistent effort, may do well to remember some of their fathers' early struggles.

Comparatively few families preserve records, either of their ancestry or of the more important events in their own history. Many families have not preserved the date of their settlement in Lake. As examples of family dates preserved from one generation to another, I place on record here the following:

I.—THE HOLTON FAMILY.

Wm. Holton came over from England in the ship Francis in 1634; he died 1691; John Holton died 1712; William Holton died 1757; John Holton died 1797; Joel

Holton born 1738; Alexander Holton born 1779; J. W. Holton born 1807. And this makes one line from the ship Francis, fourteen years after the landing of the May Flower, to an old settler of Lake County, now a resident on a Deep River farm.

II.—THE DINWIDDIE FAMILY.

In this family line David has been a favorite name. Records have been burnt or lost containing the dates of David Dinwiddie, 1st; David Dinwiddie, 2d; David Dinwiddie, 3d; David Dinwiddie, 4th. Then follow David Dinwiddie, 5th, born 1724; David Dinwiddie, 6th, 1755; Thomas Dinwiddie, 1787; a brother of Thomas, David Dinwiddie, 7th, 1792; J. W. Dinwiddie, 1813; a brother David Dinwiddie, 8th, 1816; Oscar Dinwiddie, 1845. This family name is known in United States history, one member of the family, in the time of Washington, having been Governor of Virginia.

III.—THE BALL FAMILY.

Francis Ball came from England in 1640; Jonathan Ball, born 1645; Benjamin Ball, born 1689; Charles Ball, 1st, born 1725; Charles Ball, 2d, born 1760; Hervey Ball, born 1794; T. H. Ball, born 1826; Herbert S. Ball, born 1856. Thus six generations in this line come between the English ancestor of 1640 and a Lake County youth born at Cedar Lake.

Another family in this county possess heirlooms which have been handed down from father to son, which are said to have been brought over in the May Flower. The records however are not in this county. This is the family of Ebenezer Saxton.

Still another resident of the county, Augustine Humphrey, settting here in 1840. whose family have nearly all passed away, has records in the possession of his brother which are said to give a connected line back to the Norman Conquest or the Battle of Hastings, 1066.

The value of such records as the above may seem slight to some, — and they are placed here simply as samples of what family records mean — yet families possessing such would not willingly part with them, and where slight records are handed down from generation to generation, and especially where diaries are kept of important or interesting events, it is easy for an annalist to find material for his work. Of such choice material, carefully collected, the foundation for standard histories is made.

For want of well-kept records there are disagreeing dates even in United States history. Much more is this the case as we go back toward the dark shadows of a remote antiquity.

Thirty-eight years have now passed away since the first settlement in this region. Only twelve more years, or eight years after the centennial celebration of our national existence, will bring us to the *semi-centennial* celebration of the settlement of our county. If good records are kept by those now acting, a fair fifty years' view may then be taken of the growth of Lake: and then I am sure there will be some appreciation of the work accomplished by this unpretending volume, in treasuring up many facts that would otherwise have been buried in oblivion. While not done as it would have been done had more time and more means been at my disposal, I cheerfully and hopefully commend it to the consideration of my fellow citizens. And if in the land of the living when the rich autumn comes of the year 1884, although perchance a distant wanderer, I shall hope to find a place then in the great gathering of the sons and daughters of Lake. And with the loved ones among them I shall hope at last to *dwell*, in the *great*, the *fadeless*, the *beautiful* HOME.

MONROE'S
SERIES OF SCHOOL READERS.

The Publishers have the pleasure of announcing that they have recently completed a Series of School Readers, by Prof. LEWIS B. MONROE, Professor of Vocal Culture and Elocution in the Massachusetts Institute of Technology.

The thorough and enthusiastic study which the author has given to this subject, and his long and successful experience as PRACTICAL INSTRUCTOR of Schools, Teachers, Clergymen, Public Speakers and Readers, have eminently qualified him for the task he has undertaken. These Books are PROFUSELY ILLUSTRATED BY THE BEST ARTISTS, and in mechanical execution are superior to any school books now published.

The Series is so arranged that the FIRST, SECOND, THIRD AND FIFTH READERS FORM AN ABRIDGED COURSE, peculiarly adapted to the wants of ungraded schools in the smaller towns.

"The lower books contain the '*Word Method*,' '*Phonic Analysis*,' the old '*A. B. C.' Method, and 'Object Teaching*,' thus enabling the teacher to choose the course with which he is the most familiar, or the one he can teach most successfully.

In the Fourth Reader is a feature never before presented in any school book—that of representing by illustrations and diagrams, the manner of forming every sound in the language.

By this means the pupil can see at a glance the position of the tongue, lips and jaws, necessary to produce the correct English sound.

In the introduction to the Fifth Reader are the most essential portions of the system of physical and vocal training, taught with success by Prof. L. B. MONROE, in the public schools of Boston."

PRICES OF MONROE'S READERS.

	Retail.	Introduction.	Exchange.
FIRST READER	$0.30	$0.20	$0.15
SECOND READER	.50	.34	.25
THIRD READER	.75	.50	.38
FOURTH READER	1.00	.67	.50
FIFTH READER	1.25	.84	.63
SIXTH READER	1.50	1.00	.75

F. S. BELDEN,

COWPERTHWAIT & CO.,

PUBLISHERS.

Agent for Introduction,

335 Wabash Avenue, Chicago.

MONROE'S VOCAL GYMNASTICS.

A new work on Physical and Vocal Training for the use of Schools and for Private Instruction. No teacher, pupil, or public speaker can afford to be without this little manual. Retail price, $1.00.

Established 1856.   *Incorporated* 1873.

F. T. JUNE, Pres.   H. B. HORTON, Secy.
J. G. COLEMAN, Treas.

CAPITAL, $100,000.

SHERWOOD SCHOOL FURNITURE CO.,

(SUCCESSORS TO H. M. SHERWOOD,)

Manufacturers of the most approved styles of

SCHOOL AND CHURCH FURNITURE,

Hall Seats and Railroad Settees.

Also, Dealers in SCHOOL APPARATUS OF ALL KINDS.

Office & Warerooms, Nos. 103-109 South Canal Street, Chicago.

JOB BARNARD.   M. C. BARNARD.

BARNARD & BARNARD,

Attorneys and Counsellors at Law and Notaries Public,

OFFICE OVER BAKERY,   CROWN POINT, IND.

ELIHU GRIFFIN.   J. W. YOUCHE.

GRIFFIN & YOUCHE,

ATTORNEYS AT LAW.

Will practice in all the courts, and attend to any kind of legal business. Counsel and correspondence in English or German. Office in brick block, under the REGISTER printing office, CROWN POINT, IND.

THE CROWN POINT REGISTER.

PUBLISHED EVERY THURSDAY BY F. S. BEDELL.

TERMS:

One year, (in advance)..$2 00
Six months,   " 1 00

THE CROWN POINT HERALD.

PUBLISHED EVERY WEDNESDAY BY T. CLEVELAND.

TERMS OF SUBSCRIPTION:

Single copy, one year..$2 00
Single copy, six months.. 1 00
In advance.

THE LOWELL STAR is published every Saturday by E. R. BEEBE.

TERMS:

One year, in advance............. $2 00 | Three Months, in advance....... 50 cents.
Six Months   "   .... 1 00 | One Month,   "   ......25 cents.

MARTIN WOOD. THOMAS J. WOOD.

WOOD & WOOD,
Attorneys and Counsellors at Law,

Crown Point, Ind.

OFFICE TWO DOORS NORTH OF PRINTING OFFICE.

Will attend to business in all the Courts of the State and United States, District and Circuit Courts, and all business relating to Real Estate.

T. CLEVELAND,
ATTORNEY AT LAW,

OFFICE IN HERALD BUILDING, East Side Public Square,

CROWN POINT, Ind.

H. P. SWARTZ,
CROWN POINT, Ind.,

DEALER IN

Pure Drugs, Medicines, Chemicals,

DYE STUFFS, PERFUMERY AND TOILET SOAPS, COMBS, BRUSHES AND FANCY GOODS, TRUSSES, SHOULDER BRACES AND SUPPORTERS,

SCHOOL BOOKS, PAPER, PENS, PENCILS, &c.,

POCKET KNIVES AND CUTLERY.

TUFT'S CELEBRATED ARCTIC SODA WATER in its Season.

GEO. W. WATERS,
LOWELL, Indiana,

DEALER IN DRUGS & MEDICINES,

Chemicals, Paints, Oils, Varnishes, Glass, Putty, Fine Soaps, Sponges, Brushes, Perfumery, Dye Woods and Dye Stuffs generally, Pure Wines and Liquors for medicinal use,

and other articles kept by druggists generally.

PHYSICIANS' PRESCRIPTIONS CAREFULLY COMPOUNDED.

AMOS ALLMAN,
Real Estate Agent & Conveyancer
CROWN POINT, LAKE COUNTY, INDIANA.

Having an abstract of Lake County from the Recorder's Records, am prepared to furnish Abstracts on short notice. Also, attend to the payment of Taxes, etc.

OFFICE IN THE TREASURER'S OFFICE.

WILLIAM WOODS,
PRODUCE
Commission Merchant,
No. 161 E. KINZIE STREET, CHICAGO.

Choice Dairy Butter received daily.

GEO. G. ROBINSON.   GEO. L. VOICE.

GEO. G. ROBINSON & CO.,
MANUFACTURERS OF
SASH, DOORS, BLINDS, & MOULDINGS,
DEALERS IN
LUMBER, LATH, & SHINGLES.

Office and Factory, 367, 369 & 371 *Sedgwick Street, Near Gas Works Yard, Hawthorne Ave.*

CHICAGO.

INTER-OCEAN.

The leading republican paper in the Northwest.

THE INTER-OCEAN will continue to be the Organ of the People in the larges sense of the word ; insisting upon the preservation of the rights of the many as against the few. To this end it will maintain an unceasing warfare against the *abuses and extortions of* ALL CHARTERED MONOPOLIES ; not attempting to destroy the just rights of any, but determined to bring every special privilege granted by legislative act under control of the power that conferred it ; believing that the public conscience is the true court of final resort in all questions affecting the relations of corporations and the people.

In Literature, General News, Foreign and Domestic Correspondence, Local Matters, and all that goes to make a FIRST-CLASS

Commercial & Family Newspaper,

It does not intend to be excelled by any publication in the country.

THE COMMERCIAL DEPARTMENT

will be conducted with great care, and everything possible will be done to make

THE MARKET REPORTS

such as the FARMERS and BUSINESS MEN of the Northwest can RELY UPON.

THE AGRICULTURAL DEPARTMENT

will be carefully edited by a gentleman of ability and experience.

The Religious and Moral Character will be guarded with especial care, and nothing will be admitted into its columns, either as advertisement or reading matter, improper for the family circle.

While the INTER-OCEAN will especially represent the great interests of the Northwest, it is the intention to make it a

NATIONAL NEWSPAPER,

One that will be found interesting and useful to Americans in every part of the globe.

TERMS OF SUBSCRIPTION :

Daily, by mail, (payable in advance) per year...............................$12 00
Daily, by mail, (payable in advance) per quarter............................ 3 00
Daily every other day, (three times per week) per year..................... 6 00
Paper for Sunday..$2 00 extra.
Weekly, single copy, one year.. $1 50
Four copies, one year..   5 00

Sample Copies Free. Money can be sent by draft, money order, express or registered letter, at our risk. Address

INTER-OCEAN,
119 Lake St., Chicago.

MASON & HAMLIN
CABINET ORGANS

THE ONLY American Musical Instruments of such extraordinary and recognized excellence as to command a wide sale in Europe, notwithstanding competition there with products of cheap labor.

ALWAYS awarded highest premiums, including the Medal at the Paris Exposition. Of hundreds of Industrial Exhibitions, there have not been six in all where any other organs have been preferred to these.

UNIVERSALLY recommended by eminent musicians as possessing excellencies not attained in any others. See opinions of ONE THOUSAND, in Testimonial Circular.

EXCLUSIVELY employing several important inventions and embracing every real improvement.

THE MOST EXTENSIVE and complete factories in the world, producing better work at less cost than otherwise possible.

PRICES FIXED, and as low as consistent with scrupulous employment of only best material and workmanship.

NEW STYLES. Five Octave Double Reed Organs now ready at very low prices, $110 and $125 each.

ORGANS FOR RENT with privilege of purchase, for quarterly or monthly payments. First payment, $12 and upwards.

Illustrated Catalogue and Testimonial Circular, with important information about Organs, which may save purchasers from dissapointment in purchase of inferior or worthless instruments, or payment of high prices, sent free.

Mason & Hamlin Organ Co.,
80 & 82 Adams St., Chicago, Ill.

CARSON, PIRIE, & CO.

RETAIL DEPARTMENT,

MADISON AND PEORIA STREETS,

CHICAGO,

Make Interesting Prices on all classes of

DRY GOODS,

And have as fine an Assortment as any House in the West.

JAMES H. BIGGS,
(LATE HART & BIGGS),

Real Estate & Note Broker

No. 190 DEARBORN-ST., HONORE BLOCK,
CHICAGO.

Real Estate purchased, managed and sold; Taxes paid. Special attention given to acre property in Cook Co., Ill., and Farms and unimproved lands in Lake Co., Ind. Correspondence solicited.

Jos. E. Young, Pres't. J. S. Holton, Cashier.

THE SAVINGS BANK
— OF THE —

MARKET SAVINGS AND EXCHANGE BANK,

277 SOUTH CANAL ST., COR. VAN BUREN.

☞ On money deposited AFTER THE FIRST and BEFORE THE TENTH day of any month, interest will be allowed for the whole month, provided the money so DEPOSITED remains at least three months.

Office Hours from 10 a. m. to 3 p. m.

FOR THE ACCOMMODATION OF WORKING PEOPLE, the Bank will be kept open Saturday and Monday Evenings, from 6 to 8 o'clock.

Interest at the rate of six per cent. per annum.

OFFICERS AND DIRECTORS.

JOS. E. YOUNG,	PRESIDENT.
H. S. OSBORNE,	COUNSEL.
J. S. HOLTON,	CASHIER.

JOHN LEHMAN,

DEALER IN

Watches, Clocks, and Jewelry

STORE ONE DOOR SOUTH OF HACK'S EXCHANGE,

CROWN POINT, INDIANA.

JAMES H. BALL,

ATTORNEY-AT-LAW & NOTARY PUBLIC

CROWN POINT, INDIANA.

HACK'S EXCHANGE, CROWN POINT, IND.

This popular Hotel is still prepared to entertain the Travelling Public in the best manner. Accommodations First Class. A good Stable is attached. Free 'Bus to and from all trains.

MRS. A. HACK. Proprietress.

A. D. PALMER,
CEDAR LAKE, LAKE COUNTY, INDIANA,

DEALER IN

DRY GOODS, GROCERIES,

Hardware, Queensware, Boots and Shoes, Hats and Caps,

READY-MADE CLOTHING,

DRUGS AND MEDICINES, PAINTS AND OILS, SCHOOL BOOKS, STATIONERY, &c.

Country Produce taken in exchange for goods.

H. C. BECKMANN,

DEALER IN

Dry Goods, Groceries,

HARDWARE,

CROCKERY, PAINTS, OILS, ETC.

BRUNSWICK, Lake County, Indiana.

JOHN M. FOSTER,

(Successor to SCOTT & FOSTER,)

DEALER IN

AGRICULTURAL IMPLEMENTS,

HEAVY HARDWARE, COAL AND LIME,

CROWN POINT,   INDIANA.

H. PETTIBONE,

PHYSICIAN & SURGEON,

CROWN POINT, Ind.

Office on the West side of the public square.

E. C. FIELD,
ATTORNEY AT LAW,

CROWN POINT, Ind.

OFFICE OVER SAUERMAN'S HARNESS SHOP.

J. A. WOOD, M. D.,
PHYSICIAN & SURGEON,

OFFICE AT HIS RESIDENCE, ONE MILE EAST OF LOWELL,

LAKE COUNTY, Ind.

T. S. FANCHER,
Attorney and Counsellor at Law,

Collections a specialty.   *CROWN POINT, Ind.*

SUMMERS & FOSTER,

DEALERS IN GRAIN,

CROWN POINT, IND.

LAKE COUNTY
NORMAL SCHOOL,
AT
CROWN POINT, IND.

For terms, inquire of   **T. H. BALL.**

www.ingramcontent.com/pod-product-compliance
Lightning Source LLC
Chambersburg PA
CBHW031420230426
43668CB00007B/369